Antler, Bone, Horn & Hide

Projects You Can Make at Home

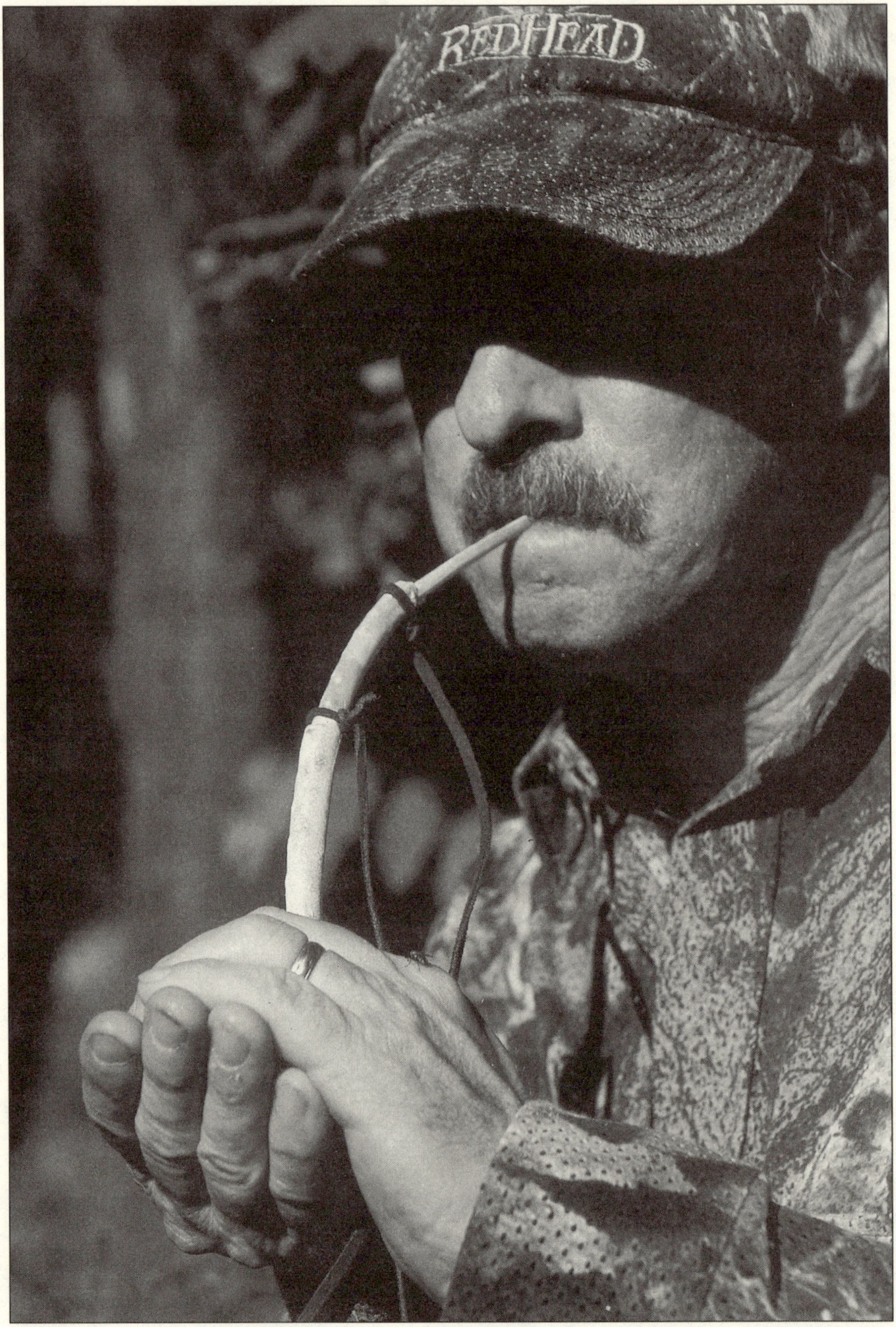
REDHEAD

OUTDOORSMAN'S EDGE®

Antler, Bone Horn & Hide

Projects You Can Make at Home

Monte Burch

Copyright © 2004 Woods N' Water, Inc. and Bookspan
All Rights Reserved

Brief quotations may be used in article reviews. For any other reproduction of the book including electronic, mechanical, photographic, recording, CD-ROM, videotaping, laser or computer disc, or other means, written permission must first be obtained from the publisher Woods N' Water, Inc.

All photos by author unless noted otherwise.
Cover photos by author.

Published by: Woods N' Water, Inc.
Peter and Kate Fiduccia
P.O. Box 65
Bellvale, NY 10912

Printed in the United States of America
10 9 8 7 6 5 4 3 2 1
ISBN: 0-9722804-4-8

TABLE OF CONTENTS

Preface vi
Introduction: What You Need vii

Part 1: Antler, Bone, and Horn Projects

Basic Tools for Working with Antlers 1
        Chapter 1: Antler Projects 5
Tools Needed for Bone Projects 27
        Chapter 2: Bone Projects 29
Tools Needed for Horn Projects 41
        Chapter 3: Horn Projects 43

Part 2: Leather Projects

Tools and Materials for Leather Clothing Projects 51
        Chapter 4: Leather Clothing 53
Tools and Materials for Leather Footwear Projects 79
        Chapter 5: Leather Footwear 81
Tools and Materials for Leather Accessory Projects 99
        Chapter 6: Leather Accessories 101
Tools and Materials for Decorating Leather Projects 127
        Chapter 7: Decorating Leather 129

Part 3: Furs, Feathers, Jewelry, and More

Tools and Materials Needed for Fur & Pelt Projects 137
        Chapter 8: Furs and Pelts 139
Tools and Materials Needed for Feather Projects 155
        Chapter 9: Feathers 157
Tools and Materials Needed for Jewelry & Miscellaneous Projects 167
        Chapter 10: Jewelry & Miscellaneous Projects 169

Epilogue 177
Directory of Resources 179
Glossary of Terms 181

Preface

In addition to meat, the skins, furs, bones, horns, antlers, and feathers of animals, reptiles, and birds have been invaluable to mankind throughout the ages. Early man learned to turn these valuable materials into clothing, weapons, and tools. Early products were primarily utilitarian, but eventually became decorated, or decorative, for a variety of reasons. Many of the early decorations were added for ceremonial reasons. Some decorations denoted the owner. Later, many items were simply decorated for beauty.

Native Americans were and still are some of the best artisans in the use of these natural materials. Pilgrims, settlers, and then mountain men borrowed ideas from the Native Americans to create their own antler, bone, leather, and feather clothing, weapons, and tools.

Many of today's buckskinners learn the ancient skills to create these same products. And many hunters simply like to display their trophies and use as much of their game as possible. Others enjoy creating useful and decorative items from natural materials collected from wild game.

Growing up on a farm, we utilized everything as much as possible. We butchered several pigs each year, and as my grandad explained, "We used everything but the squeal." As I became older and took up hunting, I also learned to utilize other products from my hunts in addition to the meat. As a youngster, I was lucky to have an uncle knowledgeable about creating a number of pioneer-type projects. Then, and now, part of my desire in making many of these projects has been to learn about some of my Native American ancestry.

A wide range of projects are included in this book. Some are ancient designs, such as moccasins and buckskin clothing. Others are more modern ideas, such as using shed antlers for home decoration, including lamps.

For many years, I've had a great deal of fun creating projects from these natural materials. I hope you enjoy creating your own antler, bone, leather, and feather projects as well.

Introduction

What You Need

Creating the projects in this book can require lots of tools or just a few. Many designs are simple craft projects that can be done on the kitchen table. Others require a work surface or area set aside just for the task. A solid work table with a smooth top is a prerequisite. This can be a simple handmade workbench, a purchased bench, or a sturdy tabletop. A bench with a height convenient for working while standing is best. You'll also want some sort of cabinet or closet to store the materials, tools, and good lighting, because many of the projects in this book are delicate or require close work.

Following are some of the tools needed for the various project materials. You may wish to add to the list or get started with fewer tools. Traditionalists may, in fact, choose the more primitive methods and tools to create many of the old-time projects.

More modern projects require more modern tools and techniques. In addition, a number of specialty tools are needed for some of the techniques and projects. Most of these can be handmade and are shown in their respective chapters–for instance the bow or box bead loom.

Antler, Bone, and Horn

A hacksaw can be used to cut these materials, while a variety of hand rasps, files, and sandpaper can be used to shape them. A hand drill can be used for drilling chores. A bandsaw also does a great job of cutting these hard materials to shape. While a disc or belt sander makes quick work of shaping, a polishing wheel is needed to polish the finished items. A metal grinder is needed to shape some knife handles.

A number of woodworking tools are needed for making plaques, threading electrical wire, and attaching items. You'll need a saber saw or bandsaw for cutting out plaques, a router to finish off the edges, and a sander and sandpaper. Of course, you'll need a hammer, handsaw, tape measure, and square. A cordless electric drill is extremely versatile and can be used for any number of chores. You'll need drill bits, rotary rasps or sanders, even polishing wheels for the drill. If you're carving antler, bone, or horn, a rotary grinder is invaluable. Defleshing bones and horn requires a pot, an outside heat source, and a cage to hold items to "age."

Leather and Feather

Leatherworking requires, above all, a sharp knife. The best tactic is to have several, including a good skinning or all-around short-bladed knife. A hobby knife with a variety of blades and a utility knife with extra blades is also a good idea. A pair of game or other heavy-duty shears can also be used to cut some light leathers.

A revolving punch, with six tubes, allows you to punch different-sized holes for different kinds of stitching and lacing. An awl can also be used for these chores, as well as for lining up the holes for lacing. A lacing awl has rows of spaced teeth so you can punch several holes at the same time. Spacing is kept even by always putting the first tooth into the last of the previous set of holes.

A variety of needles, for stitching thread and lacing are required. A glover's needle is best for heavy-duty leather. An automatic awl makes stitching many projects quick and easy. Waxed thread is carried in the awl. The awl is pushed through the leather and the thread stitched. A lacing cutter can also be made to cut lacings to the desired width.

You'll need a wooden mallet and stamps for stamping and embossing leather and an edge creaser and edge beveler to round off edges of thicker leather projects and smooth the edges. A modeling tool with a tracer on the opposite end is handy for tooled leather projects. You'll also need paints, paint brushes, and waxed linen thread, along with a rubber-based cement.

Working with Squared Drawings

Many of the patterns for projects in the book are shown as "squared drawings." The squares in the drawing each represent one inch. To create a full-size pattern, you can draw one-inch squares on a sheet of paper or you can purchase graph paper, with one-inch squares already marked, at craft and art supply stores. Then count the squares to the point where each pattern line in the drawing crosses a squared line. Count the same number of squares on your paper and place dots at these intersections. Then connect the dots to create your own full-sized pattern. You will probably have to round out and smooth the lines somewhat, but you will now have a pattern that is full-sized and ready to use.

Transferring Bead, Quill, or Paint Patterns

Transferring beadwork, quill, or paint patterns onto a leather garment or accessory can be done in several ways. First lay a piece of tracing paper over the pattern and trace around the design. Then place the tracing paper on the garment, arranging the design to suit, and tape it in place. Slip a piece of carbon paper under the tracing paper and trace around the design to transfer it to the garment.

Another method is to rub the back of the tracing paper with pencil lead or chalk. Lightly wipe off the excess with a clean cloth or tissue. Again, trace around the design to transfer it to the garment.

A dressmakers tracing wheel and carbon paper can also be used to transfer straight lines, grid patterns, or to mark for fringe cuts.

Cutting Lacing

Lacing is used for many of the projects in this book. Lacing is normally cut from midweight leather and should range from 1/8 to 3/16 inches in width for most projects. Lacing cut from leather dyed a different color from that of the project can provide a pleasant contrasting color.

Lacing can be cut in several ways. Mark short pieces on the back of the leather with a pencil and a straightedge then cut with scissors or with a sharp craft knife and metal straightedge. For longer pieces, drive a nail into a large piece of wood or work surface. Then push a sharp craft knife into the wood. The distance between the nail and the knife is the width of the lacing. Create a starting cut, then simply pull the edge of the leather between the nail and knife. You can create a long piece of lacing in this manner as it will cut in a continuing inward spiral. Use lacing cutters that are available at leather craft supply stores.

PART ONE

ANTLER, BONE, AND HORN PROJECTS

The hard portions of game animals and birds–the antlers, bones, and horns–can be made into a wide variety of items. Their uses range from handles on knives and other tools to ornaments for home and body. Working with these materials is usually fairly easy and the projects in this section range from buttons and toothpick holders to more complicated projects such as powder horns and lamp bases made from shed antlers. Incidentally, collecting shed antlers for the various projects is in itself a fun and interesting hobby.

BASIC TOOLS FOR WORKING WITH
Antlers

- 3/8-inch drill bit (lamps, wall sconces)
- Baking soda (European mount)
- Belt grinder
- Brass rod (games)
- Countersink bit (stang handle knife)
- Clamps (lamps, wall sconces)
- Clear plastic bag (European mount)
- Decorative screws and bolts (pulls and handles)
- Drill bit
- Drill press
- Drill press vise
- Electric drill (portable or hand)
- Electrical fixtures (lamps, wall sconces)
- Electricians drill bit (lamps, wall sconces)
- Epoxy
- Felt (antler mounts)

- Goggles (European mount)
- Gripper pliers (buckles, buttons, and bolos)
- Hairdressers whitener (European mount)
- Hydrogen peroxide (forty percent solution)
- Jewelers compound (stag handle knife)
- Lag screws (pulls and handles)
- Linseed oil (staining and finishing antlers)
- Metalworking files (stag handle knife)
- Picture frame hanger (European mount)
- Rivet and rivet set (stag handle knife)
- Rubber gloves (European mount)
- Sandpaper (stag handle knife)
- Screws
- Shanked buttons (buckles, buttons, and bolos)
- Spiral-cut wood dowels (lamps, wall sconces)
- Stain (antler carving and finishing antlers)
- Vinegar (European mount)
- Vise
- Wood clamp
- Wood screws (lamps, wall sconces)
- Wooden base (antler carving)

Most of the projects in this book are considered craft projects. Many of the projects can be done on the kitchen table, but a separate work place with a sturdy bench makes many jobs easier.

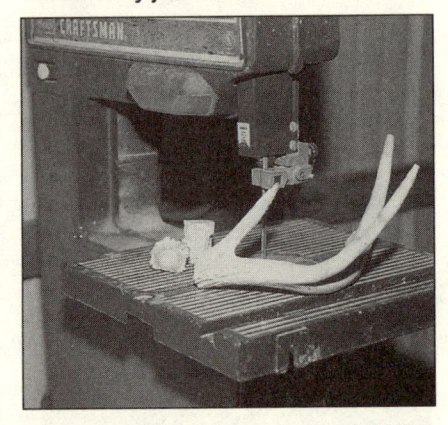

A bandsaw makes quick work of cutting materials such as antler, bone, and horn.

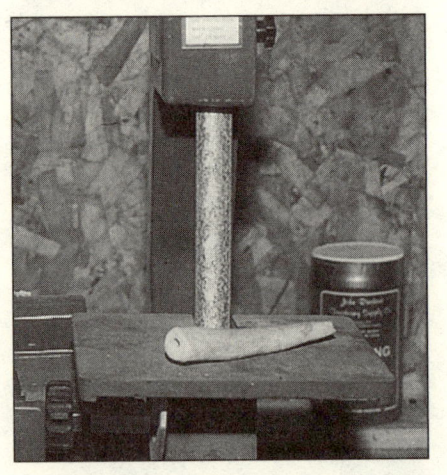

A hot glue gun is used for glueing many projects together.

A belt and disc grinder is used for sanding and shaping

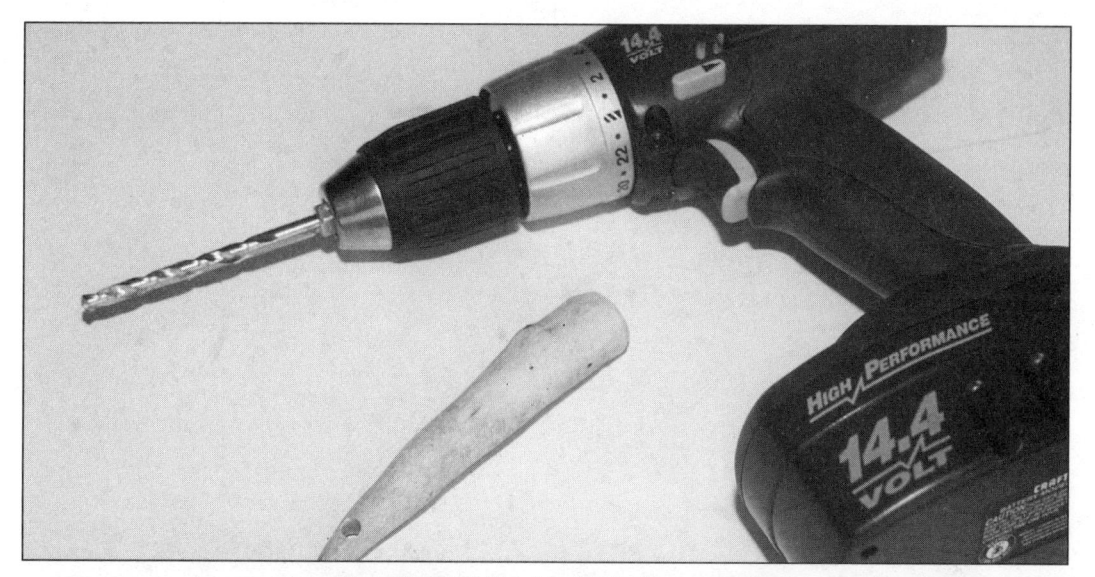

A cordless electric drill is invaluable for many chores.

A good, sturdy vise is necessary for many antler, bone, and horn projects.

For many leather and feather projects, a sharp knife is necessary. A hobby knife set with a variety of blades is a good idea.

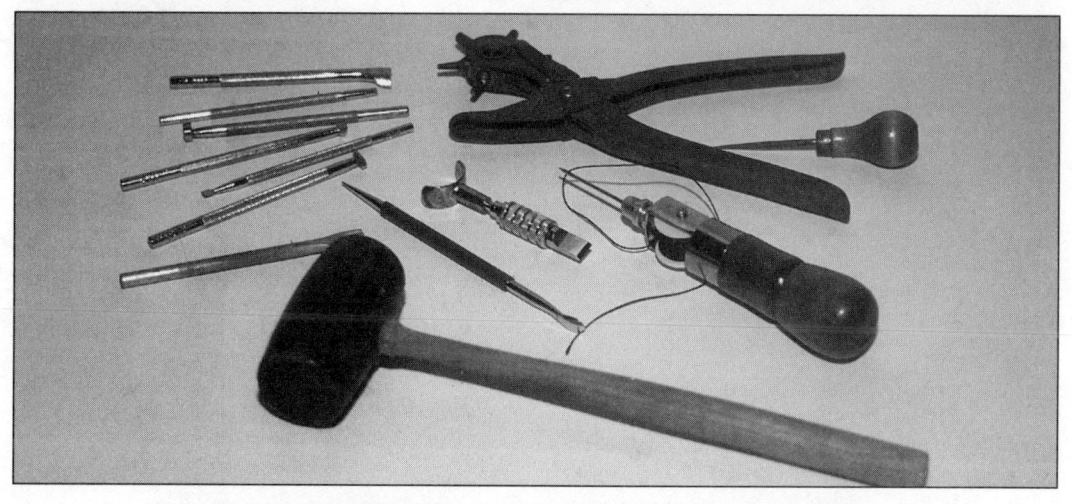

A wide variety of specialty tools is also required for leather projects.

1

ANTLER PROJECTS

Antlers from deer, elk, moose, and caribou have been some of the most often utilized animal by-products throughout the ages. Easier to work than bone, antlers offer a very versatile material. Native Americans used antlers for tools such as "billets" or hammers and pressure tools for chipping stone arrowheads and spear tips. They also made handles for metal knives and stone or metal hide scrapers, spear and harpoon points, clubs, wedges for a variety of chores, and even spoons. They also made decorative pieces including bracelets, roach spreaders (made from leather or horn and used to hold horsehair and/or a feather upright for a roach headdress), combs, hairpins, and figurines (fig. 1-1).

Antlers and imported stag are extremely popular for a variety of projects in modern days as well. Deer and elk antlers can be used as handles for knives, fireplace tools, doors, gates, and cabinets. Fastened together in elaborate shapes, antlers can be made into lamps and chandeliers. They are still

1-1. Antlers are some of the most popular project materials. *(Photo Peter Fiduccia)*

Antler, Bone, Horn & Hide

popular for buttons, belt buckles, and other decorative items.

Antler is durable and easy to care for. Antlers taken from animal heads (as opposed to those sheds found on the ground) are usually well-preserved and require little care. Merely wipe them clean with a soft rag dampened with a little furniture oil. Shed antlers that show a bit of deterioration, can be maintained by wiping them with vegetable oil until they stop soaking up the oil.

Ancient Tools

A billet, or striking tool, for breaking off pieces of flint for arrowheads can be made from the heavier sections of the butt end of an elk or moose antler. Simply cut a section about a foot long using a handsaw or meat saw. Then round and smooth the cut edge with a file (fig. 1-2).

The tip of an antler makes a flint knapper or pressure tool. To use, hold the flint on a piece of leather in the palm of your hand and apply pressure with the antler tip to break off chips.

1-2. Antlers were used for some of the most common ancient tools. Sections of antler were often used as billets or flint knappers for creating stone weapons.

You can make a hide scraper from the curved section of a large elk antler by fastening a piece of metal or a sharpened flint scraper in place with rawhide lacing. Wet the rawhide and wind it around a portion of the blade and handle and tie it off. When the rawhide dries, it will shrink and securely hold the parts together.

You can also use antlers to create spoons, decorative combs, and other items. The possibilities are limited only by your imagination.

Knife and Tool Handles

Knife and tool handles can easily be made from sections of antler and have been a traditional material for many years. Early knife and tool handles were either bone or antler.

Antler Tip Letter Opener

This unusual letter opener utilizes a whole, but small, deer antler. To make the blade, grind down a small file on a belt grinder. Shape the file end to form a narrow protrusion or tang to fit into the handle (fig. 1-3).

Shape a brass hand guard on a belt grinder and cut a slit in the center to fit over the blade tang. This can be done by drilling a

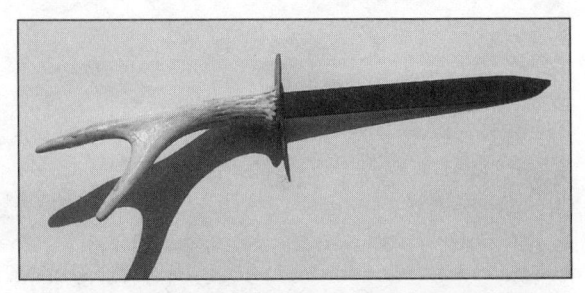

1-3. The letter opener shown is made from a piece of antler and a small file ground into a blade.

ANTLER PROJECTS

series of holes on a drill press, then using a small file to smooth the slot opening.

Position the antler handle in a drill press vise and make sure it is at the proper angle. Then bore a hole for the blade tang. Dry fit all parts. Then mix two-part epoxy and place it in the handle hole. Insert the blade guard over the blade and insert the tang into the handle hole. Wipe away any excess epoxy that may have been squeezed out.

SHED-ANTLER-BASE KNIFE

The bases of both large and small shed antlers make very attractive knife handles (fig. 1-4). Large antler bases can be used on hunting knives. Smaller antler bases work well on kitchen knives or on the tiny patch knife shown (fig. 1-5). The knife and guard are available from Dixie Gun Works. See the resource list for additional information.

As with the letter opener, the first step is to select an antler base that is appropriate for and fits the knife blade's shape and design. Lay the blade on the full antler to make sure it will fit and that the blade tang will go into the base properly. Since most antler bases curve somewhat, make sure there is enough straight length for the tang. You may have to trim the tang to fit. Once you have determined the proper length needed, cut off the antler using a hacksaw or band saw. Make sure the cut is angled properly to match the guard and blade.

To drill a hole in the antler for the tang, position the antler in a vise and use a hand or portable electric drill. Make sure you keep the drill bit at the proper angle. An easier method is to clamp the antler base in a wood clamp, making sure it is at the proper angle. Then bore the hole using a drill bit in a drill press (fig. 1-6). dry fit the tang with the guard in place and redrill the hole or grind off portions of the tang to make a smooth but snug fit. Once you are satisfied with the fit of all the pieces, mix epoxy and place it in the

1-4. Antler bases make extremely attractive hunting knife handles. *(Photo courtesy Davis Custom Knives)*

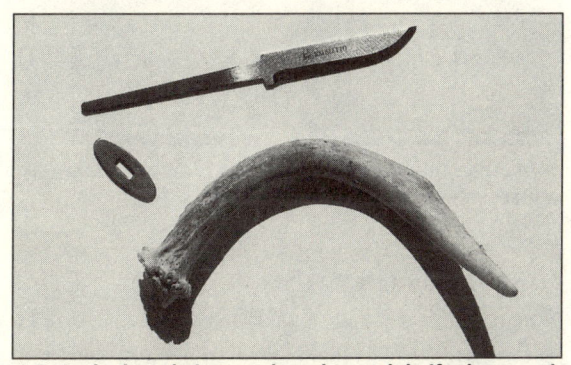

1-5. Antler base knives, such as the patch knife shown, utilize a narrow tang blade, antler base, and a brass guard.

1-6. The antler base is held firmly in a vise or clamp, the hole drilled, the blade inserted over the tang, and the tang epoxied into the antler base.

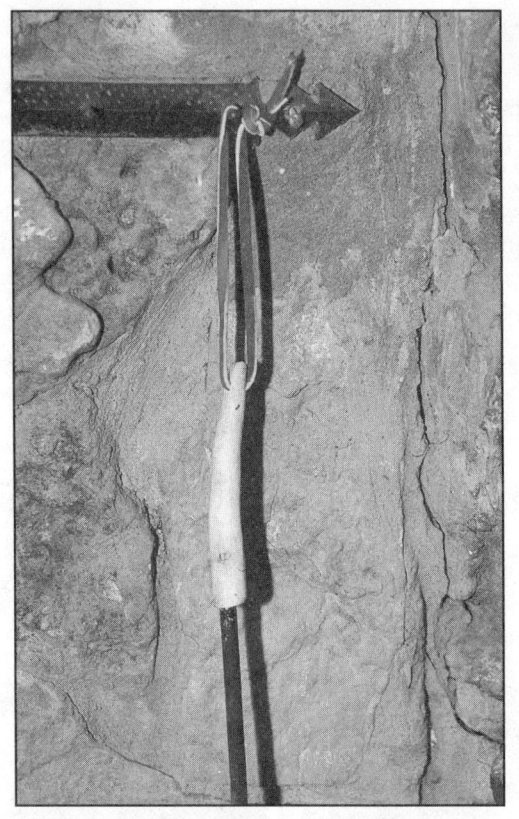

Antler, Bone, Horn & Hide

1-7B. Antlers can also be used to make attractive kitchen knives, forks, spoons, nutcracker sets as well as any number of other items. *(Photo Peter Fiduccia)*

hole. Push the blade guard over the blade and the tang into the hole. Make sure everything fits properly, then wipe away any excess epoxy and allow the piece to cure.

Fireplace Tools and Other Utensils

The same method can be used for fastening antler tips, antler bases, or even cut sections of antler to items such as fireplace tools, axes, saws, barbeque tools, kitchen knives, forks and spoons, nutcracker sets, and other items (figs. 1-7A and 1-7B).

1-7A. The same method can be used for fastening antler tips to fireplace, barbecue, and other tools.

Stag Handle Knife

Stag or antler is a traditional material for full-tang knives as well. The material is excellent for butcher knives, as well as hunting, skinning, and even pocket knives. These types of handles consist of two separate pieces of stag or antler fastened over the full, flat tang of the blade (fig. 1-8). This type of flat tang is called a "scales tang." The handles may simply be glued in place with epoxy. More commonly they are fastened with rivets. A combination of the two methods can also be used.

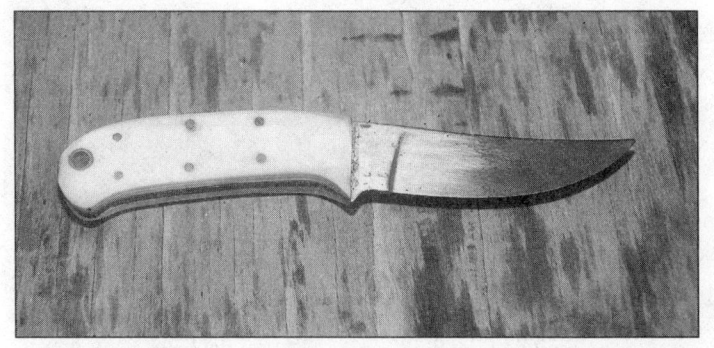

The first step is to select a section of antler or stag that will totally cover the wide, flat tang and provide a comfortable rounded handle. Once you are satisfied with the section needed, cut it to length (fig. 1-9). Then

1-8. Stag or antler sections are often used to cover both sides of a full-tang knife blade.

ANTLER PROJECTS

1-9. The first step is to cut the antler in half lengthwise and rough-shape the handle blanks.

1-10. The next step is to locate and mark the blade pin holes in the antler sections, then bore the holes through the handle blanks.

place the section in a vise and cut it lengthwise through the center. Cut from one direction down to the vise, turn the antler section 180 degrees and continue the cut until the two pieces separate.

This will produce a somewhat rough cut. You can flatten and smooth the cut with a block of wood and coarse sandpaper or you can use a power disc sander to make sure the cut is smooth and flat. Dry fit the pieces on the blade tang to make sure they fit flat and smooth against the tang. Once you are satisfied with the fit, clamp one piece to the tang and use a drill bit and hand or portable electric drill, or a drill press, to drill through the existing holes in the blade tang and through the antler piece. Then position the opposite antler piece in place and drill the rivet holes for it as well (fig. 1-10).

Some rivets consist of two pieces, one fitting into the end of the other. These also usually have a larger flat end. To make the recessed holes for these larger end pieces, use a countersink bit of the

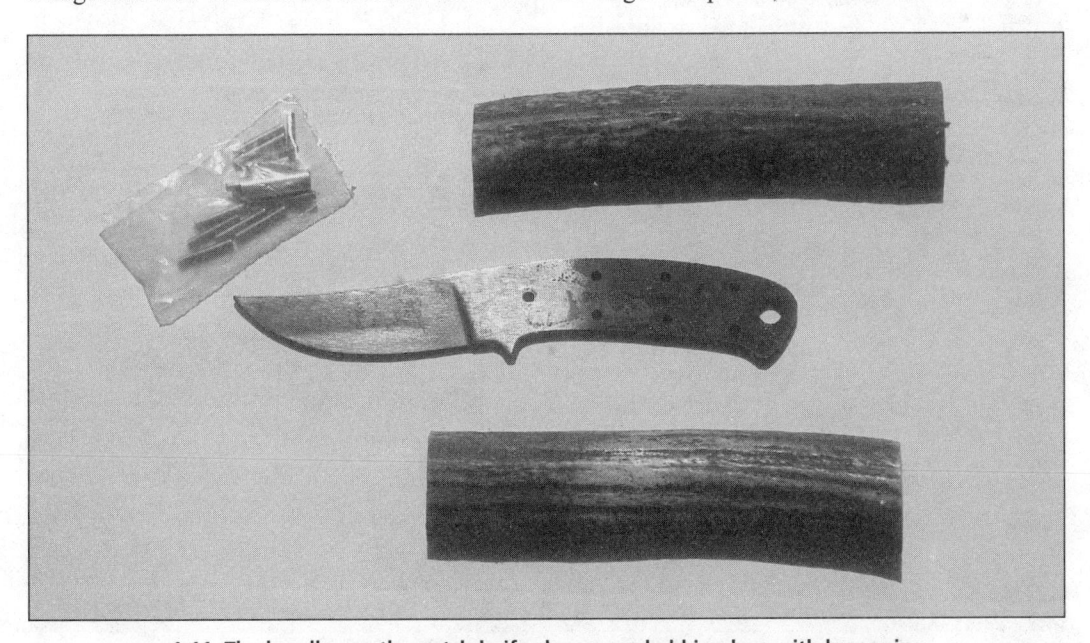

1-11. The handles on the patch knife shown are held in place with brass pins.

Antler, Bone, Horn & Hide

1-12. Epoxy can be placed on the blanks, the blanks positioned over the blade tang, and the brass pins driven in place.

1-13. If the antler sections are thicker than the pin length, a small punch must be used to drive the pins in place.

proper size. These types of rivets must also be set using a rivet set, which you can make yourself (fig. 1-11). A rivet set consists of a bolt or piece of steel rod the size of the rivets, or slightly smaller, which is then clamped in a vise with the top edge slightly protruding. The rivets and pieces are pushed in place and positioned over the rod end. Then a similar piece of rod is used to tap the rivets together. In most instances you will not need to use epoxy, as the rivets drive tightly together, holding both handle pieces securely on either side of the tang (figs. 1-12 and 1-13).

The next step is to file or grind down the edges of the stag or antler pieces to fit the outside shape of the tang. This can be done with any number of tools, including metalworking files, rotary tools such as a Dremel, or with a belt or disc sander. The latter make the chore quick and easy. With this type of construction, the outer sides of the handle are left in the round, or smoothed down slightly, just to the tops of the rivet heads. Once the handle has been shaped to suit, polish it using a polishing wheel and jewelers compound.

1-14. Antler knobs and handles can really set off rustic furniture.

ANTLER PROJECTS

Another type of rivet is the one-piece style such as shown on the small boot knife. In this case, drill the holes, check the rivets for fit, then use epoxy to hold the handles and tap the rivets in place. Then grind down the edges to fit the shape of the tang and grind down the sides even with the rivet ends to produce a smooth, flat surface. Finally, smoothly round and polish all surfaces.

PULLS AND HANDLES

Antler knobs and handles can really set off rustic furniture and cabinetry (fig. 1-14). Either the antler bases or sections cut from the antlers can be used. For drawer and door knobs, cut off the antler bases at the length or "depth" needed. Make sure these cut ends are smooth and flat. Bore a pilot hole in the center of the cut. To fasten the knobs in place, bore a hole in the door or drawer. Place a screw through the hole in the door or drawer from the inside and position the end of the antler base over the screw on the outside. Turn the antler piece to anchor it in place. Woodworkers glue can be used to hold the screws tighter in the antler pieces (fig. 1-15).

Because of the great variety of antler shapes, they can be cut in sections and used in many ways as handles for cabinets and furniture. One method for using curved sections is to simply cut a section, sand it flat on the back of each end, and fasten it in place with screws through the back of the door or drawer (fig. 1-16).

Large antler sections can be flattened on the ends and portions removed from the back to create finger space. Or you can use three pieces of antler to create a handle that extends from the piece of the furniture. In this case, use two short sections of antler as spacers between the handle section and the door. Place long screws through the door, through the spacers, and into the handle section. Sand and shape the ends of the spacers to fit the general curvature of the antler handles where they meet (fig. 1-17).

1-15. The simplest method is to use an antler base as a knob. Bore a hole from the back of the door or drawer and drive a screw through the hole into the sawn-off antler base.

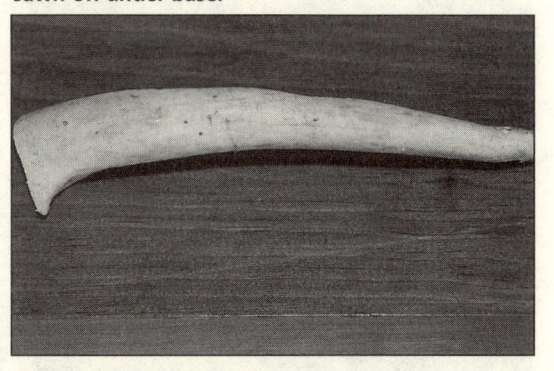

1-16. Sections of antler can also be used as handles. Fasten both ends with screws from the back through the door or drawer.

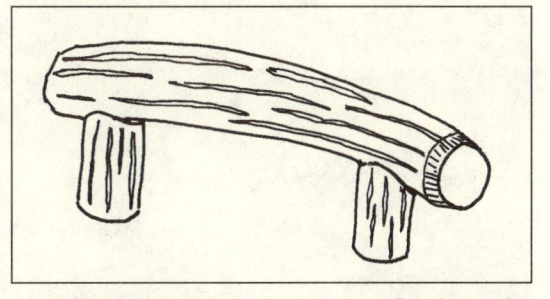

1-17. Short sections and a long section of antler can be shaped and fastened in a U-shape to create a deeper door or drawer handle. The short sections are epoxied to each end of the longer section.

1-18. Large antler sections make great entry door handles as well as barn and gate handles.

ANTLER PROJECTS

Antler bases as well as sections and tips can also be used as decorative knobs on kitchen and bath faucets. In most instances, however, the materials must be glued in place with epoxy, making them permanent. If antler bases are glued in place on an upright stem and the faucet must be repaired or removed, the antlers will have to be cut off. Faucets utilizing horizontal levers are much easier to add the antler handles to, and the antlers do not cause problems if the faucet must be repaired. Installation is fairly easy in both cases. Simply bore holes in the antlers to fit the faucet stems or lever handles and glue the antlers in place with epoxy. Large antler sections make impressive entry door handles (fig. 1-18). They can be fastened in place with lag screws recessed from the rear or inside of the doors. Alternatively, use decorative bolts through the door and antlers.

Antler sections make great gate and barn door handles as well. Antler door handles definitely add a special touch to all entrances at hunting lodges.

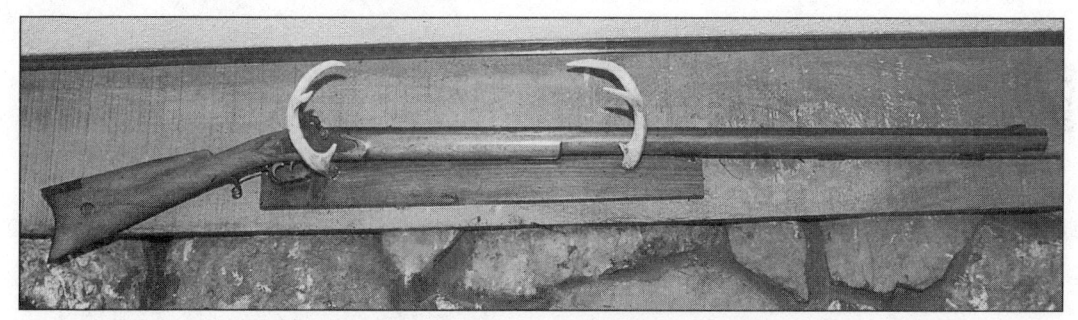

1-19. Antler sections, fastened to wooden boards, create racks for guns, bows, coats and hats. It's a good idea to select matching antler tips.

RACKS AND HOOKS

Curved antler sections and tips make great coatracks, gun racks, and hooks for towels and other items (fig. 1-19). Cut the sections to the desired length, angling the cut to hold items. The easiest method to attach the hooks is to fasten them to a wooden plaque or rack from the back with screws and epoxy (fig. 1-20). Then anchor the rack to the wall.

1-20. Locate the position of the antlers, bore holes through the board, bore starting holes in the antlers, then fasten in place with epoxy and wood screws countersunk from the back of the board.

Antler, Bone, Horn & Hide

Candle, Toothpick, and Match Holders

Sections of antler can be cut, smoothed, and positioned to hold candles. Short sections can be bored with a large-diameter bit and used to hold toothpicks or matches (fig. 1-21).

Frames for Pictures and Mirrors

Antlers can be arranged around a wooden frame to add a hunting motif to large mirror and picture frames. Attach the antlers with screws placed through the back of the frame and into the antlers. Epoxy glue can also be used for additional strength (fig. 1-22).

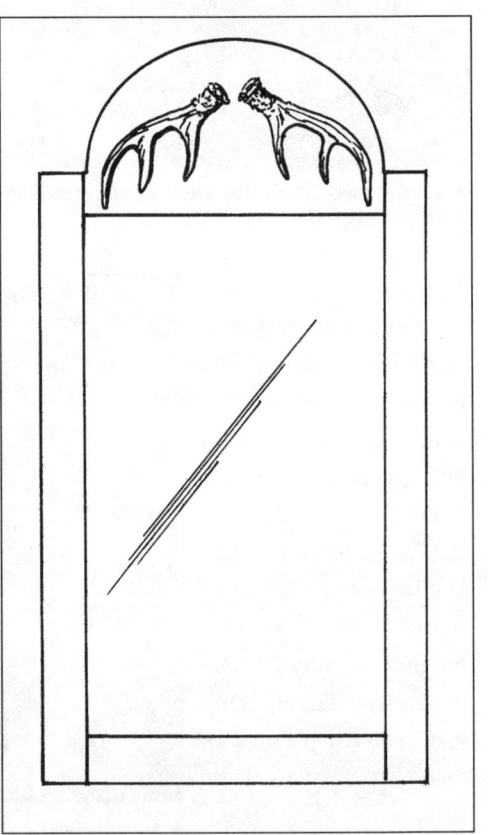

Furniture

Large antlers can be joined together to create furniture such as tables and chairs. Bolts and epoxy are often used for this type of construction. What you can build is limited only by your imagination and the number of antlers available.

Lamps, Wall Sconces, and Chandeliers

One of the most popular uses of antlers these days is for lamps, wall sconces, and chandeliers (figs. 1-23, 1-24 and 1-25). A number of companies make and

1-21. Sawn-off sections of large antlers are bored to create toothpick and match holders.

1-23. One of the most popular uses of antlers is for lamps, wall sconces, and chandeliers. Most of these are now being made from synthetic antlers.

1-22. Antlers, arranged around a wooden frame, add a rustic touch to a mirror or picture.

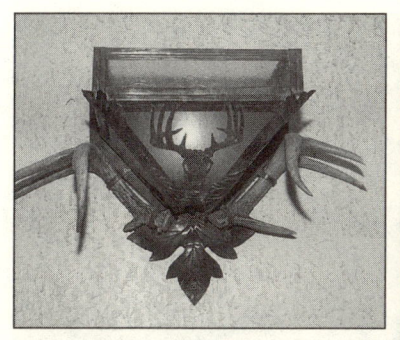

ANTLER PROJECTS

1-24. Elegant wall sconces from Big Cedar Lodge in Branson, Missouri, utilize metal, antlers, and glass.

1-25. Iron wheels and large antlers are used to create spectacular chandeliers such as the one shown at Big Cedar Lodge, Branson, Missouri.

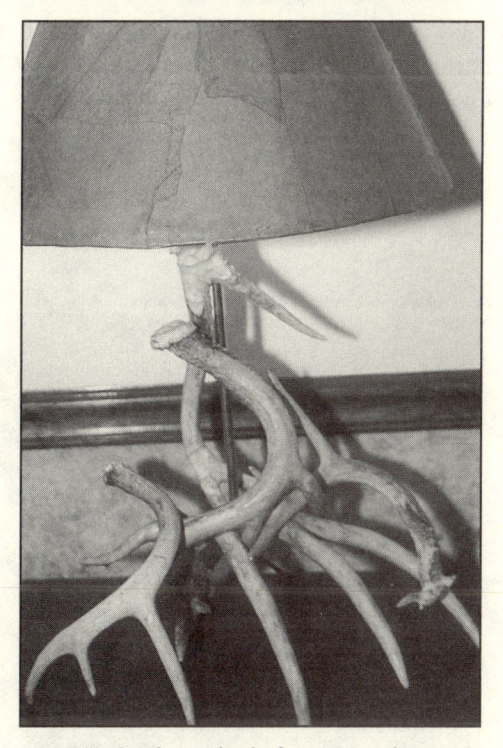

1-26A. A simple method of creating a lamp utilizes a lamp tube, lamp parts, and antlers.

sell these items. For the most part, however, they are manufactured from synthetic antlers. You can make your own if you have a fairly large supply of antlers. Dropped or shed antlers are the best choice for these projects. Deer, elk, or moose antlers can all be used.

The biggest problem is threading the electrical wiring through the antlers so the wiring is concealed. (Synthetic antlers are molded with a hollow area for the wiring.) In making up your own, you will have to use a long electricians drill bit to bore concealment holes, then cleverly thread the wire through the joined antlers.

The first step is to lay out the shape you desire. Then use a pencil to mark the joining areas of the antlers. If the project is small, such as a wall sconce, epoxy may be all that is required to join the antlers together. On larger pieces, you can use wood screws in areas where they will not show. A better method is to use wooden dowels. Mark the location of the joints and, using a 3/8-inch bit, bore matching holes in each antler. Make sure the holes are deep enough for the dowels selected. Spiral-cut wood dowels with glue grooves are best. Thread the electrical wires through before joining the pieces. Place epoxy glue in the holes in the antlers, insert the wood dowel, and use clamps to squeeze the parts together and hold them

15

Antler, Bone, Horn & Hide

until the epoxy sets thoroughly (figs. 1-26A through 1-26F).

Finally, add the electrical fixtures, such as bulb holders, and chain to suspend the light. Electrical components are available from several sources for wiring your own lighting.

BUCKLES, BUTTONS, AND BOLOS

Buttons are easily made with modern tools (fig. 1-27). Merely saw the antler into thin slices with a bandsaw or hacksaw and then drill holes in the center of each button with a drill press or electric drill (figs. 1-28 and 1-29). Hold the buttons with gripper pliers and use a polishing wheel and jewelers compound to polish them smooth. For even easier buttons, use epoxy to attach polished button slices to flat, shanked buttons.

Thong fasteners for pouches and gear bags can be made from short pieces of thin antler sections. Cut a groove around the middle of the fastener using a small round file. Cut a slot in the outer flap through which the antler section

1-26B. The antlers are held or clamped in position, holes bored to route or accept the lamp tube.

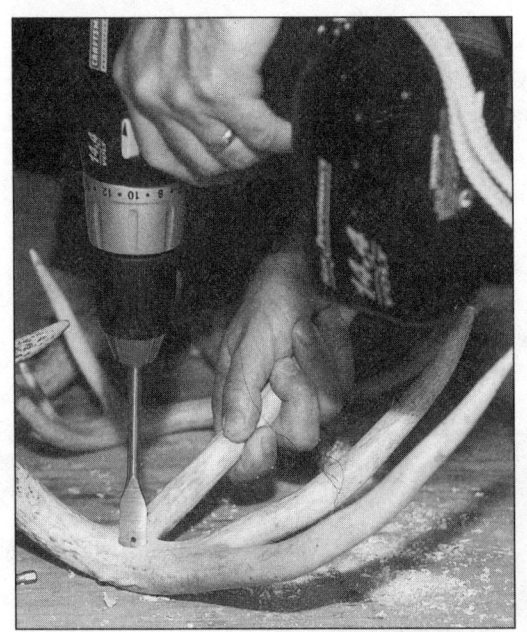

1-26C. The bottom of the antler base must be recessed to accept the tube nut.

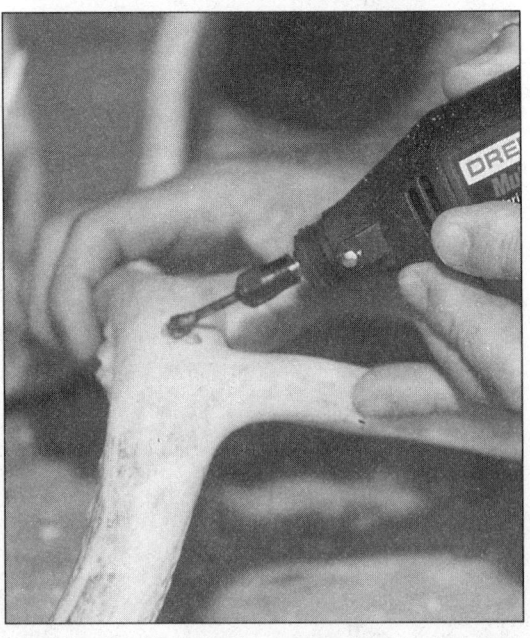

1-26D. If the antler is not flat on top, an area must also be routed for the upper tube nut.

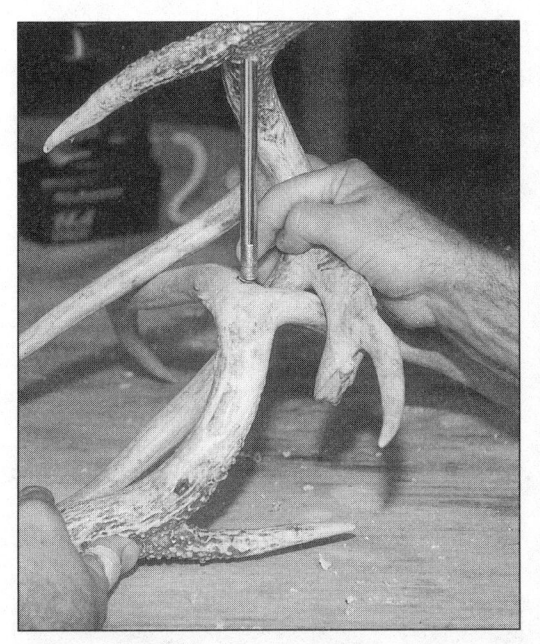

Antler Projects

1-26E. The lamp tube is then threaded through the antlers and fastened in place with holding nuts to the bottom antler.

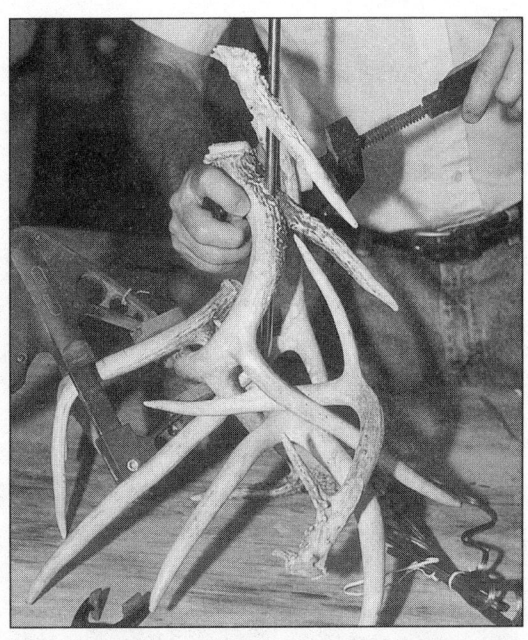

1-26F. Additional antlers are epoxied in place and held with clamps until the epoxy dries thoroughly

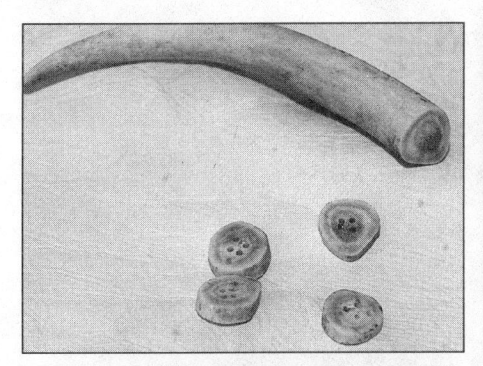

1-27. Antlers can easily be made into buttons.

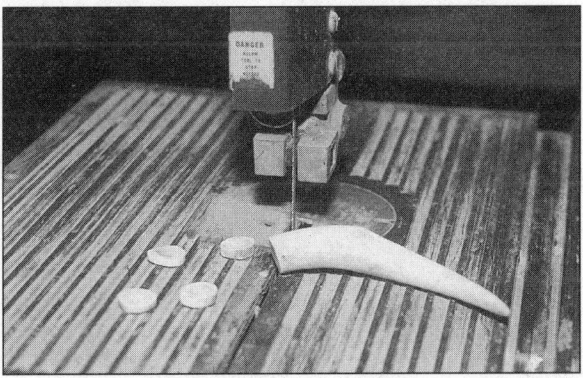

1-28. Thin sections are sawn from the antlers.

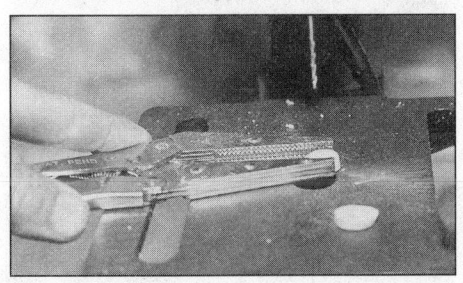

1-29. Holes are bored in the thin sections. The buttons must be held tightly with a pair of gripping pliers while drilling.

will fit. Tie a thong around the groove in the antler section and punch two holes in the inner pouch piece. Lace the thong through the holes in the pouch inner piece and tie it in place. Leave enough thong for the antler section to easily slip through the outer flap.

Belt buckles can be made from slices of large antler section or from the pedicel end of shed antlers. These can be left natural, stained, or carved and painted.

Antler, Bone, Horn & Hide

You can also sand them smooth and paint designs on them. Glue the finished antler pieces to a metal buckle blank, available at leather craft supply stores.

Bolo ties can be made using antler pedicel bases as the fastener. Merely bore holes through the sides of the base to hold the tie material. The ends of the ties can be decorated with small antler tips. Drill a hole in the larger end of the antler tipslightly larger than the tie. Insert the tie into the antler tip and fasten it in place with epoxy.

Games

A single, shed antler makes a great-looking cribbage board and a fun piece for your hunting cabin. Polish the antler

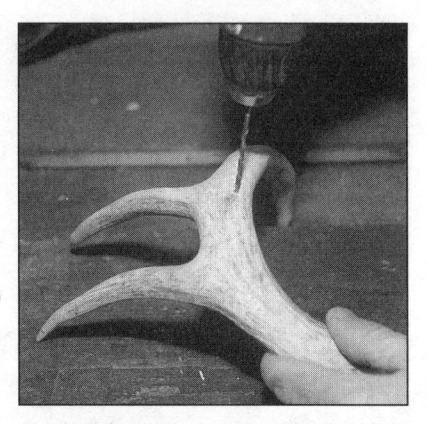

1-30. A single large antler makes a very interesting cribbage board.

1-31. Antlers can be used in many other household decorations including setting them in fireplaces or decorative pots. *(Photo Peter Fiduccia)*

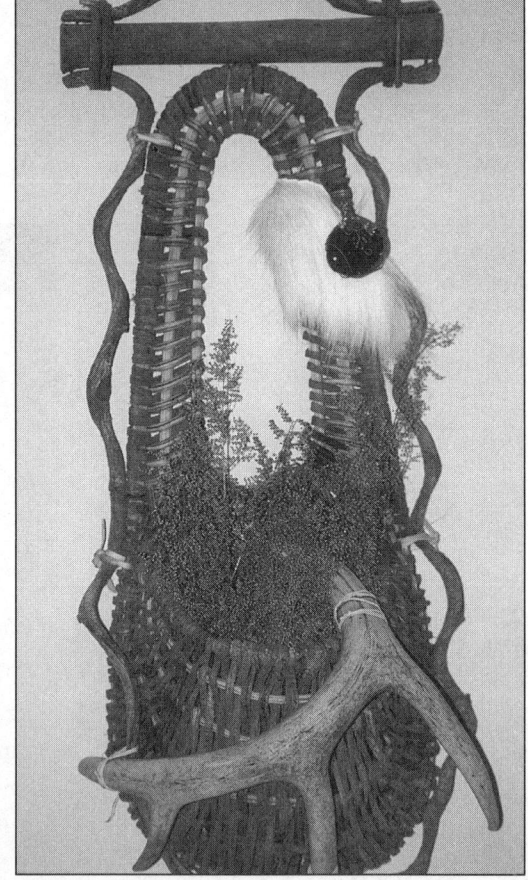

1-32. Antlers can also be used in creative wall hangings. *(Photo Peter Fiduccia)*

ANTLER PROJECTS

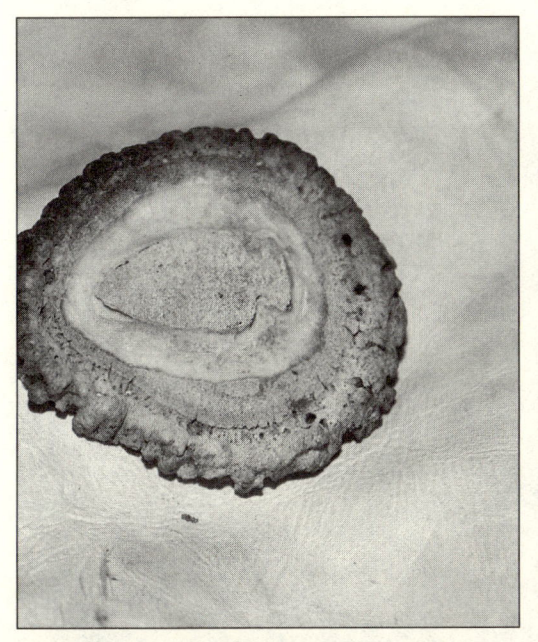

1-33A. Antler carving is an ancient art. Shown is a simple design from an elk antler base.

1-33B. A Dremel tool makes carving easy.

fully, then bore tiny holes in the underside of the antler (fig. 1-30). Make the pegs from a piece of brass rod, cutting it into short lengths to fit into the holes, then smoothing the ends. Bore a large hole in the butt end of the antler and carve a wooden plug to fit. This hole can be used to store the pins.

ANTLER CARVING

Antler carving is an ancient art (figs. 1-33A and 1-33B). Almost any type of antler can be used, but moose, caribou, and fallow deer antlers are the best choices because of their palmations. Small carvings can be made on the juncture (where the tines meet the main beam) of deer and elk antlers.

Draw the design on the antler, then cut the material away using a rotary tool such as a Dremel. To set off the carving, stain the uncarved parts of the antlers dark, but leave the carved section unstained. Placing the carved section on a wooden base also adds to the design.

ANTLER MOUNTS

A very popular method of displaying trophy antlers is cutting the skullcap flat across the top of the skull on a line from the middle of the eyes to the back of the head. Clean the skullcap of all hair, brain matter, and flesh. Fasten the antlers and

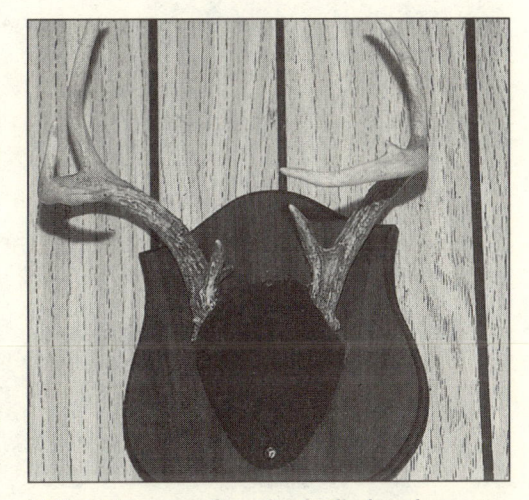

1-34. Antlers are often simply displayed on a trophy board. The skull plate is covered with velvet.

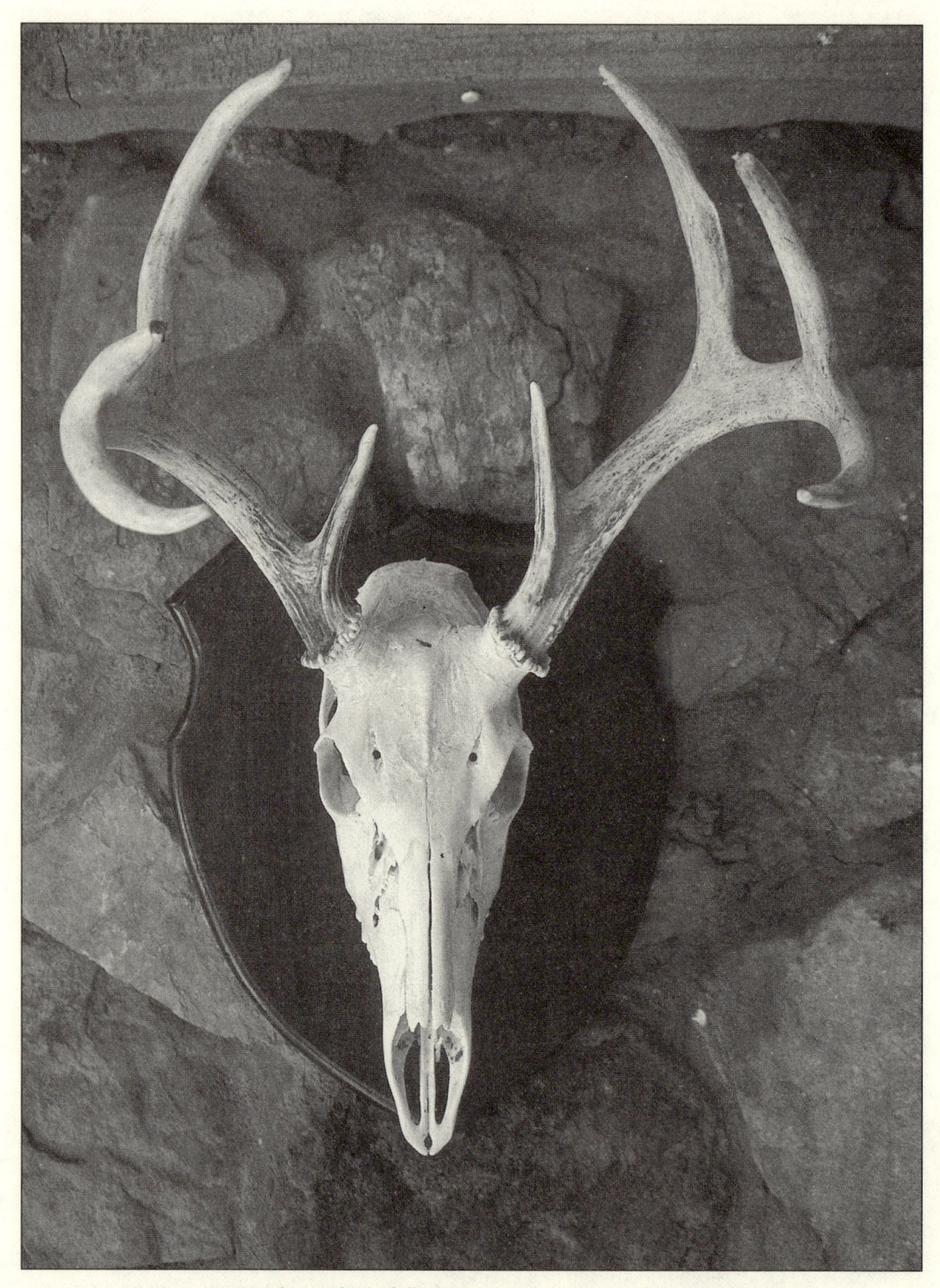

1-36. A very popular method of displaying trophy antlers is the European mount.

ANTLER PROJECTS

skullcap to a wooden plaque with screws through the skull plate into the plaque. Cover the skull plate with a piece of felt glued in place (figs. 1-34 and 1-35).

EUROPEAN MOUNT

An extremely popular alternative to a full head mount of trophy antlered animals is a European mount. Much less expensive than a full taxidermy mount, European mounts are beautiful and easy to do at home. And they take up less wall space and height than a full head mount (fig. 1-36).

The first step is to remove the head from the carcass at the top of the spinal column, then skin the skull completely. Once the head has been completely skinned, remove the eyes and detach the lower jaw by cutting through the muscles on both sides of the jaw. Remove the lower jaw and cut away the tongue. Scrape and remove as much meat, muscle, and fat as possible from all portions of the head.

Place a large pot of water over a fire outside, using a campfire, fish fryer, or Coleman camp stove. The biggest problem is finding a pot big enough to hold a large head and antlers (fig. 1-37). In addition, it is almost impossible to clean the pot thoroughly after use. You definitely do not want to use your best stockpot. An old, discarded, or inexpensive water-bath canner makes a great choice. I use the same pot for boiling traps, melting wax for de-feathering waterfowl, and other messy, outdoor chores. Note: This is an outside-only job. Do not attempt this on the kitchen stove.

1-35. Antler display kits include all the parts necessary and make mounting the antlers easy to do.

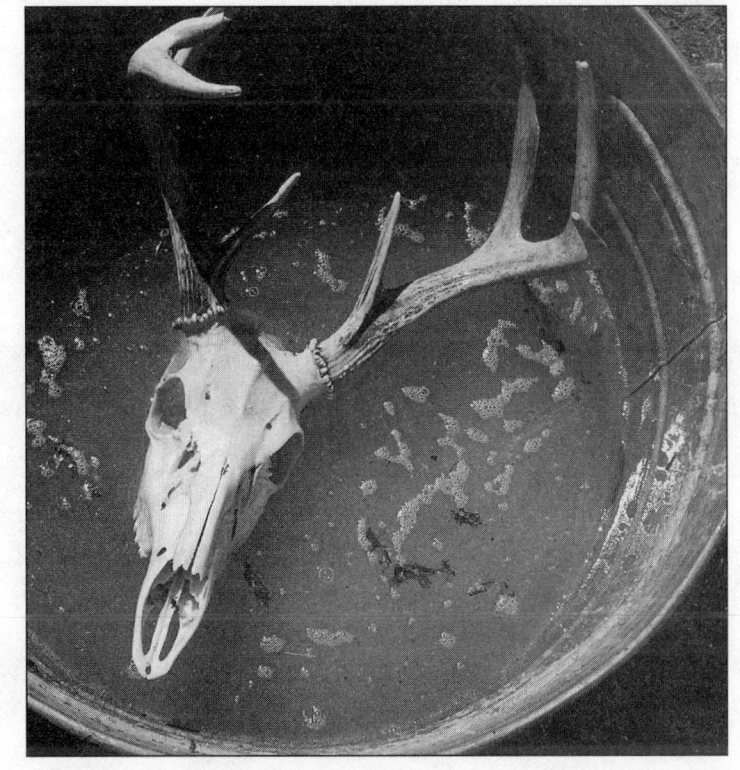

1-37. The head is first boiled and cleaned of all meat and brains.

Antler, Bone, Horn & Hide

Simmer the head several hours to soften the tissue remaining on the skull as well as the brains inside. Make sure the entire skull is covered with water up to, but not above, the antler bases. Throw in a handful of baking soda to help cut the grease created from it cooking.

It is important to have the water at a rolling boil before you place the head in the water. Then turn down the heat or move the pot around on the campfire to reduce the rolling boil to a simmer. Simmer for a couple of hours, adding hot water to maintain the correct water level as needed.

Remove the head from the pot, allow it to cool, and then cut or peel off any meat, fat, muscle, or membrane. Pour off the water and check for pieces of bone or teeth that may have become loosened and fallen out in the process.

After you have removed all loosened meat and membranes, place the head back in the pot, add fresh hot water, and simmer for another couple of hours. Again, it is important the water be at a full rolling boil when the head is added. Then immediately reduce the heat to a simmer. After a couple of hours, remove and cut or pick off any remaining meat, fat, muscle, and membrane. Use a wire to pick meat out of the tiny holes in the skull. You can pause overnight between steps, but make sure the head is protected from pets and wild animals. In addition, it is best to remove the meat while the head is still warm.

The hardest part of the entire operation is removing the brains from inside the skull. After being softened by boiling, the brains have to be picked and pulled out through the brainstem opening in the base of the skull. Commercial taxidermists use special beetles for this process. (A home version of this process is described on page 23). Otherwise, use a stiff wire, such as a coat hanger, to break up and pull out most of the brain matter. It is not an impossible chore but is messy and takes time. Once you are sure the majority of the brain matter has been removed, flush the inside of the skull with hot water several times to remove any pieces that might remain.

After a thorough cleaning of all meat, muscle, fat, brain, and membrane, the skull is then bleached to

1-38. The skull is coated with a beautician's bleach mix.

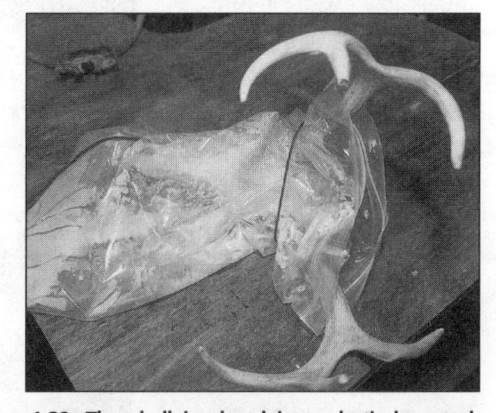

1-39. The skull is placed in a plastic bag and allowed to sit in the hot sun for several hours, then washed and varnished.

Antler Projects

produce the popular bleached-white skull. Laundry bleach should not be used because it tends to soften the bones of the skull. Household hydrogen peroxide is also not strong enough to do the chore. Use a solution of half hairdressers whitener and half forty percent hydrogen peroxide. Both items can be found at your local beauty shop or beauty supply house. Mix the ingredients in a plastic or glass (not metal) container.

Wearing rubber gloves and goggles, brush the mixture onto the skull (fig. 1-38). Seal the skull in a clear plastic bag and place the bag, skull, and antlers on a white surface in the direct sunlight (fig. 1-39). Make sure the skull is protected from pets and children. Allow the solution to sit and work for several days. Then remove the skull from the bag and wash it off using a solution of one part vinegar to four parts water. This will stop the bleaching action. Then wash the skull thoroughly with clean, cold water.

1-40. An antelope makes a great European mount.

1-41. The outer sheaths must be removed, then the head cleaned and bleached.

A European mount can be fastened to a plaque with screws from the back of the plaque. Or you can drill a hole below the brainstem opening and fasten the mount on a hook or picture frame hanger.

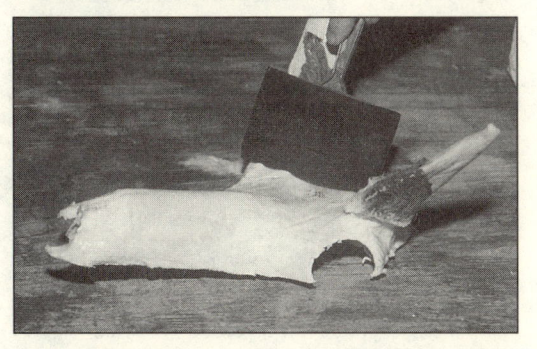

Antelope Mount

This technique can also be for animals with horns such as the American antelope (fig. 1-40). However, special care must be taken to preserve the horny sheaths covering the bones of the skull. The first step is to cook the skull to clean it using the same method described earlier in this chapter. The horn sheaths will slip off the bony sheath (fig. 1-41). It is important to clean all the soft tissue from the sheaths. Then use white craft glue or thin plaster of Paris to "glue" the horns back in place (fig. 1-42).

1-42. The head is varnished and the sheaths glued back in place.

Antler, Bone, Horn & Hide

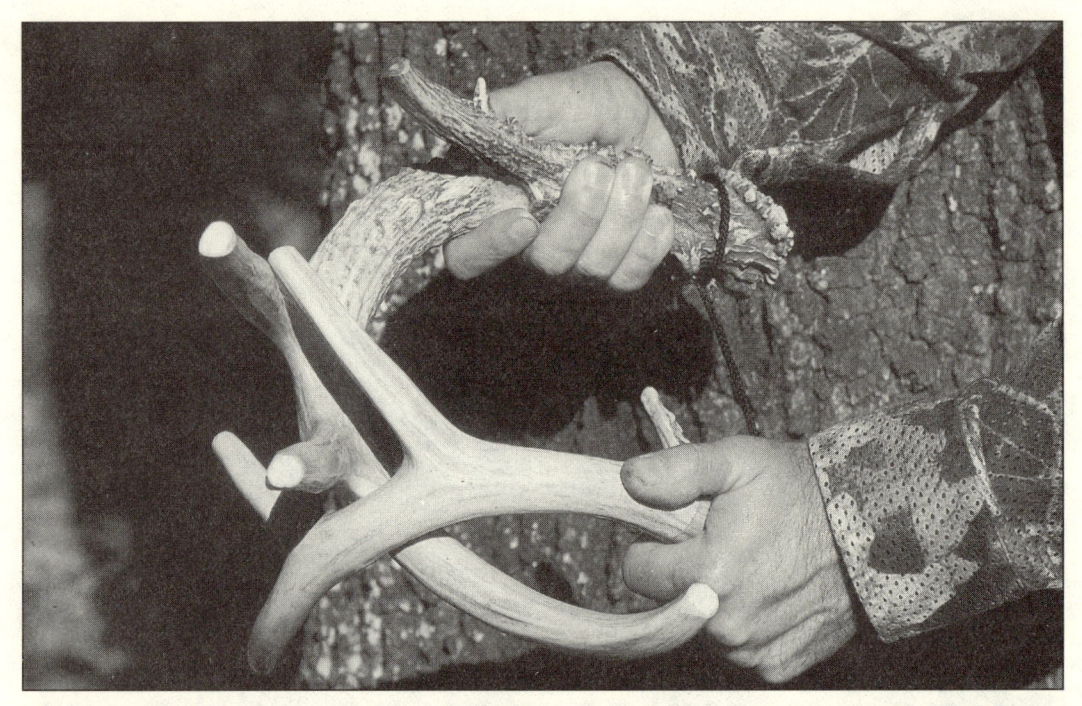

1-43. One of the most popular uses for antlers for hunters is a set of rattling antlers. The tips should be cut off for safety and a thong used to tie them together.

Shed Antlers

Shed hunting is a popular way of locating antlers for projects. Male deer shed their antlers each year, usually between the months of January and April. Antlers form in early summer as living tissue under a protective covering called velvet. Growing antlers are supported by a rich blood and nerve supply and are the fastest form of bone growth known. Each year they grow into fantastic shapes, harden for use as weapons, and are finally cast in late winter. The cycle is repeated annually until the animal dies.

The antler casting process is amazing in itself. Antlers are joined to a deer skull at special junctures called pedicels. During the time of the year when antlers are prime for fighting, these bony connections are

1-44. Shed antlers, if found early enough, are great for all antler projects. If the shed antlers are left in the woods, they will eventually be chewed by rodents.

ANTLER PROJECTS

extremely strong. Under tremendous impact, an antler may break off, but it almost never breaks at the pedicel. As the deer mating season wanes and a buck's blood testosterone level drops, mineral resorption from the antler bases occurs. In a few day's time, antlers that once couldn't be knocked off simply fall off. In some cases, both antlers may drop together. In other cases, days or weeks may pass before the second antler is shed (fig. 1-43).

1-45. Antler can be stained with wood stain and finished with varnish, then buffed with steel wool for a finished appearance.

Looking for shed antlers is a springtime hobby that grows in popularity each year. Hunters use late winter as a prime time to scout deer movements and look for the antlers of "the buck that got away." But with the growing popularity of antlers for decorative uses, nonhunters may also be interested (fig. 1-44). Items ranging from furniture to knife handles may incorporate antlers as a way of bringing the outdoors in. Shed hunting combines exercise and adventure for all ages, and the payoff yields some of nature's finest and most durable artwork.

No special tricks are used to find antlers. It is largely a matter of legwork. By the time antlers are shed, bucks are in a routine that involves finding the best winter food available. Start by looking near unharvested grainfields, food plots, and other places with choice food. Trails will be well defined between bedding and feeding areas, and antlers are often dropped along these trails. Windbreaks and timbered creeks are also likely shedding areas. Walk the fence lines. Antlers often fall off when a buck jumps the fence.

Be prepared to do a lot of walking. A pair of binoculars is helpful for checking distant objects that may be antler parts obscured by vegetation.

STAINING AND FINISHING ANTLERS

Usually antlers have their own distinct coloration. In some instances, however, shed antlers may be bleached from being out in the sun. In this case, wood stain can usually be rubbed in to provide coloration (fig. 1-45). By the same token, healthy antlers, and even fresh sheds, usually have a sheen to them. Dull antlers can be freshened by rubbing them with linseed oil. ■

TOOLS NEEDED FOR
Bone Projects

- .22 rifle bore brush
- Anvil
- Awl
- Bandsaw or hacksaw
- Beads, glass or wooden
- Belt grinder or disc sander
- Electric drill and bits
- Fly-rod line guide
- Hairdressers whitener
- Hammer
- Hardware cloth
- Hydrogen peroxide (forty percent solution)
- Ink, Indian or drawing
- Laundry bleach
- Leather gloves
- Leather lanyard
- Medium grit sandpaper
- Pencil
- Polyurethane
- Safety glasses
- Sandstone rock
- Wire, stiff

2

BONE PROJECTS

Native Americans and early settlers used bones from various birds and other game in many ways. They made a wide variety of tools, weapons, ornaments, and musical instruments from the bones available. Although bone is somewhat hard to work, Native Americans learned to utilize simple tools to create different bone objects. In many instances, the bones were simply broken with a large rock or hammer stone to achieve the rough shape of the tool needed (fig. 2-1). When long pieces were to be split off the bone, the bone was first scored with a sharp piece of flint. Then the pieces were broken off on the scored line. Larger pieces were worked into larger tools, such as axes and scrapers, tiny splinters into needles, awls, and other small objects. A piece of sandstone was then used to shape and smooth the bones. A sandstone with a groove cut in it was used to sharpen very fine points.

2-1. Bones from various animals and birds were common materials used by Native Americans. The first step was to shatter the bones into sharp pieces.

You can use these same ancient methods to shape bone or substitute modern tools such as a hacksaw or bandsaw for cutting and a belt grinder or disc sander for smoothing.

Before making any bone projects, the first step is to clean the bones. This can be done by cooking the bones to loosen the meat, sinew, and ligaments. Don't overboil or you'll soften the bones. Once the water comes to a boil, place the bones in the water and turn the heat down. Simmer the bones for approximately one hour. The bones can then be cleaned by pulling and scraping the meat and other matter away.

Antler, Bone, Horn & Hide

Awls, Needles, and Pins

To make awls, needles, or pins from bone, first break the bones using a large hammer and anvil to splinter them. Make sure you wear leather gloves and safety glasses when doing this chore. Then choose from the small pieces to make the different items. Rough shaping can be done on a belt or disc sander. Or tack a piece of medium-grit sandpaper to a work surface and move the bone pieces against the sandpaper to shape and smooth them (fig. 2-2). In most instances ancient needles didn't have perforations in their tops, except for some produced by the Iroquois and by some tribes in California. Perforations, however, can be made with a drill bit and portable electric drill.

2-2. The pieces were then shaped on sandstone. Shown is the making of a bone awl.

Raccoon and Otter Penis Bones

Some of the more unusual pins, and later black powder picks and even toothpicks, were made from the unique penis bones of raccoons and otter. These bones have natural indentations for holding sinew or thread and a natural curve so they made great primitive needles (fig. 2-3).

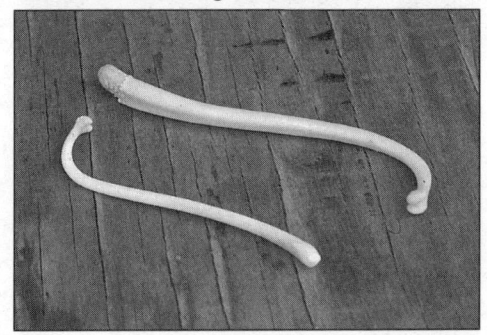

2-3. Some of the more unusual bones include the penis bone of raccoon and otter. They were used for many decorative items.

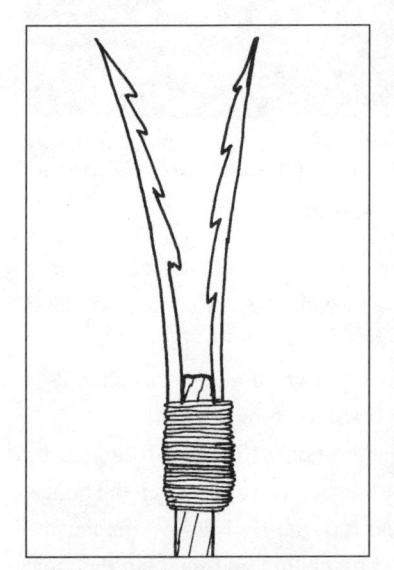

2-4. Bones were shaped into a number of spears and other weapons by Native Americans.

Weapons

The long bones of animals such as elk, bison, and deer were traditionally used for projectile points on arrows, spears, daggers, fish spears, and harpoons (fig. 2-4). Frog gigs and fish spears utilized three separate barbed pieces. Ingenious shaft straighteners were also created for straightening arrow shafts. The jawbones of horses and bison were made into clubs by grinding down the teeth and sharpening the jaw section (fig. 2-5). If you're interested in primitive weapons, making your own projectile points is fun and easy. The first step is to crack the long bones to break them into long sharp splinters. Then use a piece of coarse sandpaper or sandstone to shape the pieces as desired. Fasten arrow points in place with sinew, spear points with rawhide.

BONE PROJECTS

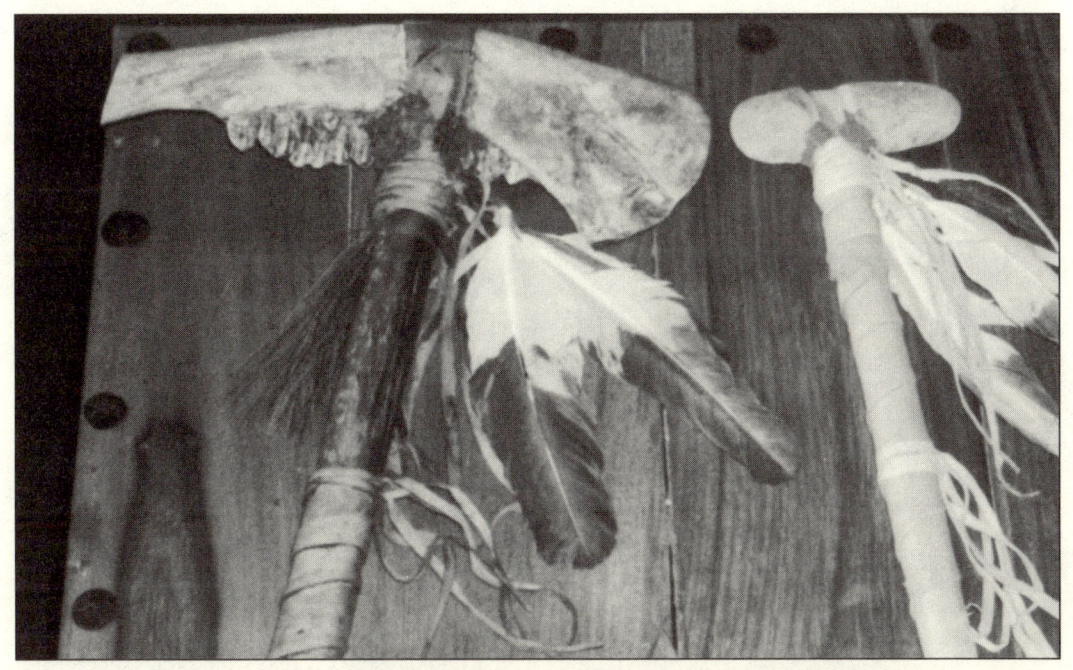

2-5. The jawbone of a horse was often used as a war club. *(Photo Peter Fiduccia)*

EDGE TOOLS

The Plains tribes used the large buffalo scapulas and shoulder bones as hoes, spades, and mattocks. The flat blade edges were sharpened and used as knives. Bones were also often carved into scoops and spoons (fig. 2-6).

One of the more common uses of bones was as hide scrapers and grainers. The sharp edge of a rib bone was used as is or in some instances serrated to produce teeth to "grain" or cut into the fat and meat to remove it from the hide. Deer or elk leg bones were often sharpened on one end and used as scrapers, grainers, or as stretching tools for tanning hides.

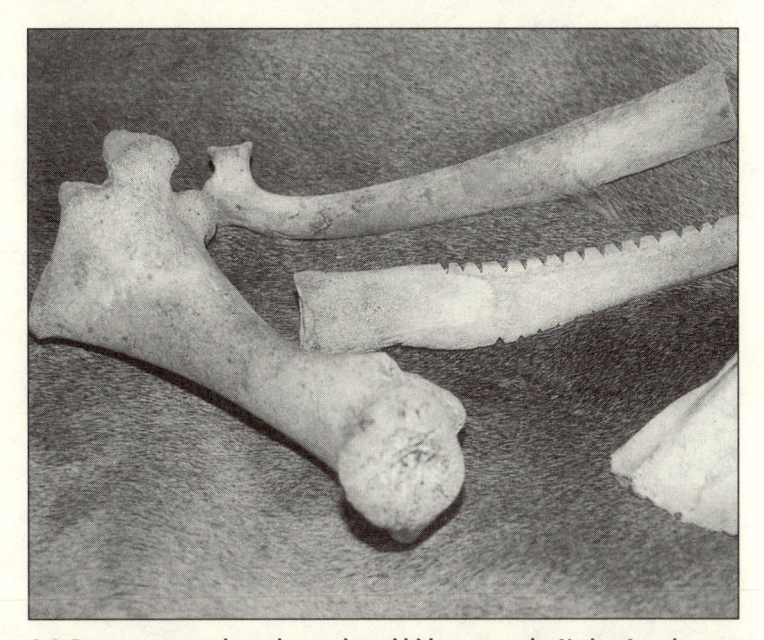

2-6. Bones were used as edge tools and hide scrapers by Native Americans.

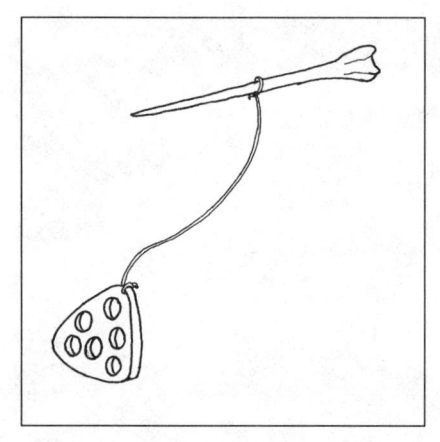

Antler, Bone, Horn & Hide

Games

Deer bones were also sanded into a variety of shapes and used in games of chance. Deer ankle bone became dice, normally tossed in a basket. Ring and pin games were also created from deer bones (fig. 2-7).

Musical Instruments

Musical rasps were common rhythm instruments and were simple notched bones, either a shoulder blade or ribs. A wooden stick was rubbed along the notches to produce the sound (fig. 2-8). Whistles and flutes were also made from the hollowed out bones of turkeys, ducks, and geese.

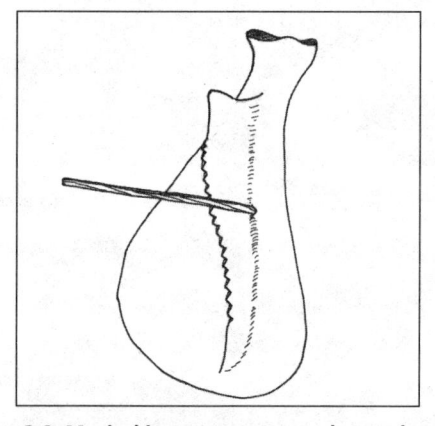

2-7. Bones were made into a variety of games and toys.

Breastplates

Bone hairpipe breastplates were originally designed as "armor" by the Plains Indian warriors. These days breastplates provide ornamentation for powwows and ceremonies. The originals were created from bones taken from the animals and birds of the area. Later versions were made from cow bones and trade beads from factories in the East.

Authentic bone hairpipe is still available from the Orient or Brazil. It tends to look too white and "new," but it can be antiqued simply by steeping it in a pan of hot tea. Remove the bone hairpipe when it reaches the "ivory" coloring that looks more original and then dry it on paper towels. Synthetic bone hairpipe in different lengths is also available.

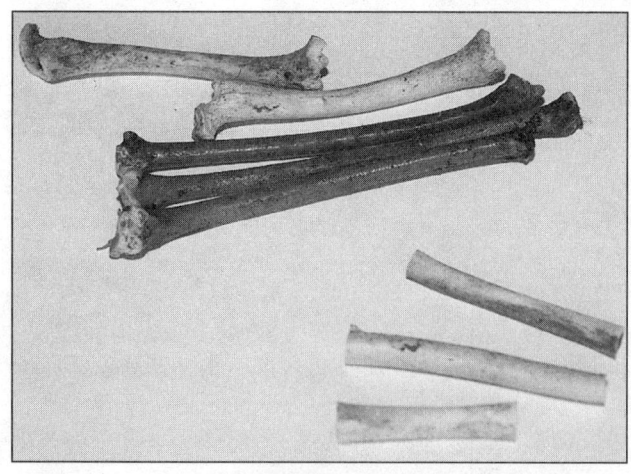

2-8. Musical instruments were also made of bones.

Bone hairpipe can also be made from the long wing bones of wild turkey or large geese. Boil the bones to clean them. Cut the ends from the bones, lightly round and taper each end, then use a stiff wire to push out the bone marrow (figs. 2-9 through 2-11).

Sinew was used to thread together the original breastplates and chokers, and you can purchase sinew or make your own from deer. The latter is not especially hard to produce if you have

2-9. The bones of many small animals and large birds can be used to create breastplates and chokers.

BONE PROJECTS

the original materials, but it does take some time. In deer, sinew is found on the legs and the loin. The loin produces the longest and easiest pieces to work with. Separate the tendon or sinew from the meat using a sharp but flexible boning knife. This is done more easily by starting the cut with the sinew on top, then turning the loin over so the sinew lies on the bottom and slicing along a smooth flat surface, much in the same manner as cutting a fish fillet from the skin. Incidentally, this will also make the deer loin much easier to prepare and cook. Then use a knife to remove any meat that may be attached to the sinew. Tack the strip to a piece of board and allow it to dry. The sinew should dry thoroughly, which will take several days to a week, depending on weather and temperature.

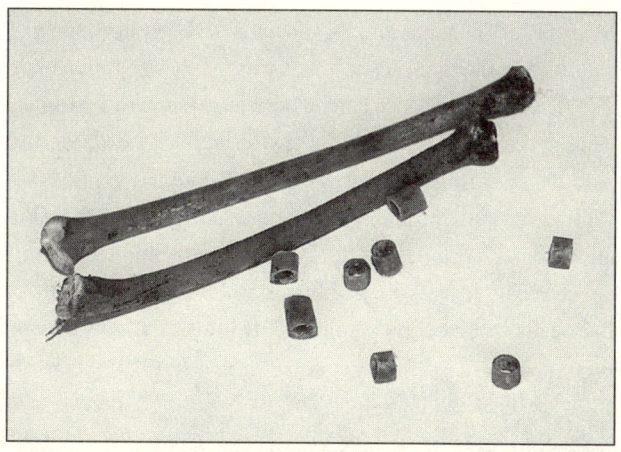

2-10. The bones are cleaned and sawn into the lengths needed.

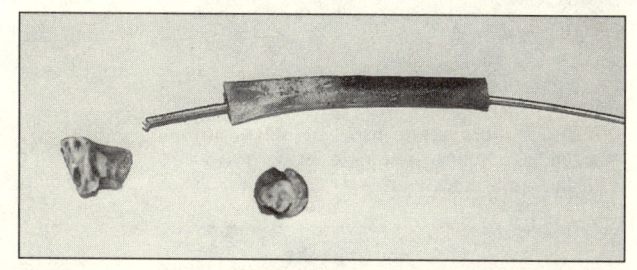

2-11. The marrow is then cleaned from the center of the bones. Shown is using a stiff wire to remove the marrow.

To make sewing material from the dried sinew, grasp one end and twist back and forth until you can get a strip broken off. Continue to twist back and forth and tear strips or threads away in the same manner as tearing small strips of cloth from a large piece. The threads of sinew can be stripped off in the size and thickness needed. Artificial sinew, made of tiny nylon threads waxed together, is also popular for these projects.

Breastplates were made in several designs, but the most common Sioux style utilized short bone hairpipes in the center and long bone hairpipes on either side of the short ones. Leather thongs were run vertically to support the sinew threaded through the hairpipe bones. Trade beads or "crow" beads were used to tie off the outside ends of the sinew and also added decoration.

The exact number of bones you'll need to create a breastplate depends on the length of the breastplate. A length of forty bones makes approximately a 20- to 21-inch breastplate. You'll need seventy-six to eighty, 4- to 4-1/2-inch-long pieces and half that number of short, 1- to 1-1/2-inch pieces. Measure the length you need and add or subtract the bones as needed.

If you are using natural bone hairpipes, make sure the sinew or thong used to thread the bones together will go through the hollow center. Authentic bone hairpipes usually have less consistent and smaller holes than the synthetic products.

Lay the three leather thongs for the sides and center parallel to each other, in approximately the positions they'll be in the finished breastplate. Tack their ends to a work board slightly larger than the finished breastplate. Then measure the distance between the bone locations. Use a sharp awl to punch holes in all four leather thong pieces for each row. At the top, punch holes only in the two outside thongs.

The hairpipe bones can be held in place with real sinew, artificial sinew, or even very thin thongs. Thread the lacing through a glass or wooden bead, through the second from the top hole in the outside thong, through a bone hairpipe, through a glass or wooden bead, through the first inside thong, through a bead, through a short bone hairpipe, another bead, the second center thong, another bead, a long bone hairpipe, the last outside thong, and finally through another bead. Then tie the lacing off.

Repeat until all lines of beads and bones have been threaded. If leather thongs are used to thread the beads in place, they can be left long as added decoration. The bottom ends of the four leather thongs can also be left long for decoration and beads can be added to these as well.

Tie two more leather thongs through the holes at the top of the outside thongs with a bead on either side of the holes. Tie these thongs around the neck to hold the breastplate in place.

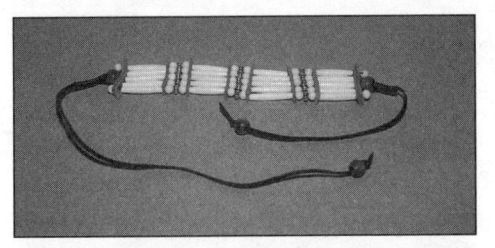

2-12A. Chokers were used as neck armor. Shown is a typical example using synthetic hairpipe and beads with leather spacers.

2-12B. Waxed thread is used to string the choker. A pillow makes a good work surface for threading beads. It can be used in your lap or on a table.

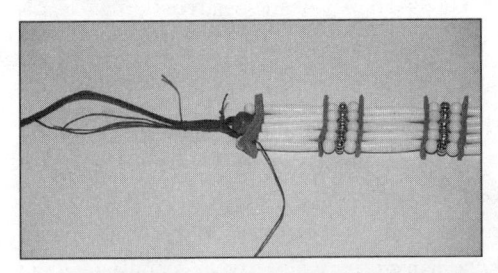

2-12C. A much neater method of finishing the choker is looping the tie thong back around the large bead and whipping waxed thread around the two pieces of tie thong and the three center strands. Clip all ends.

CHOKERS

Chokers were used as neck armor by warriors and ornaments by both men and women. Surprisingly good at stopping arrows, knives, and even bullets, chokers became a popular ornament of mountain men as well (fig. 2-12A). The design of chokers varies a great deal and may include numerous decorative items as well as bone hairpipes. Chokers may include wooden, brass, or glass trade beads, pieces of fur, bits of abalone or other shells, and the claws from different animals (fig. 2-12B). Tube-style chokers are the most common type. With this style, items are threaded onto imitation or genuine sinew in the same manner as for the breastplate, alternating bone hairpipes and other objects (fig. 2-12C).

TURKEY WINGBONE CALL

The wingbones of wild turkeys were used by Native Americans to make turkey calls or "yelpers." Artifacts show some of these calls may have been made and used as early as 6500 B.C. Early settlers and mountain men also learned to make and use wingbone yelpers as well (fig. 2-13). Artifacts show the first calls used only one piece, the piece that is

2-13. Wingbone turkey calls were popular in early times and are still very effective today.

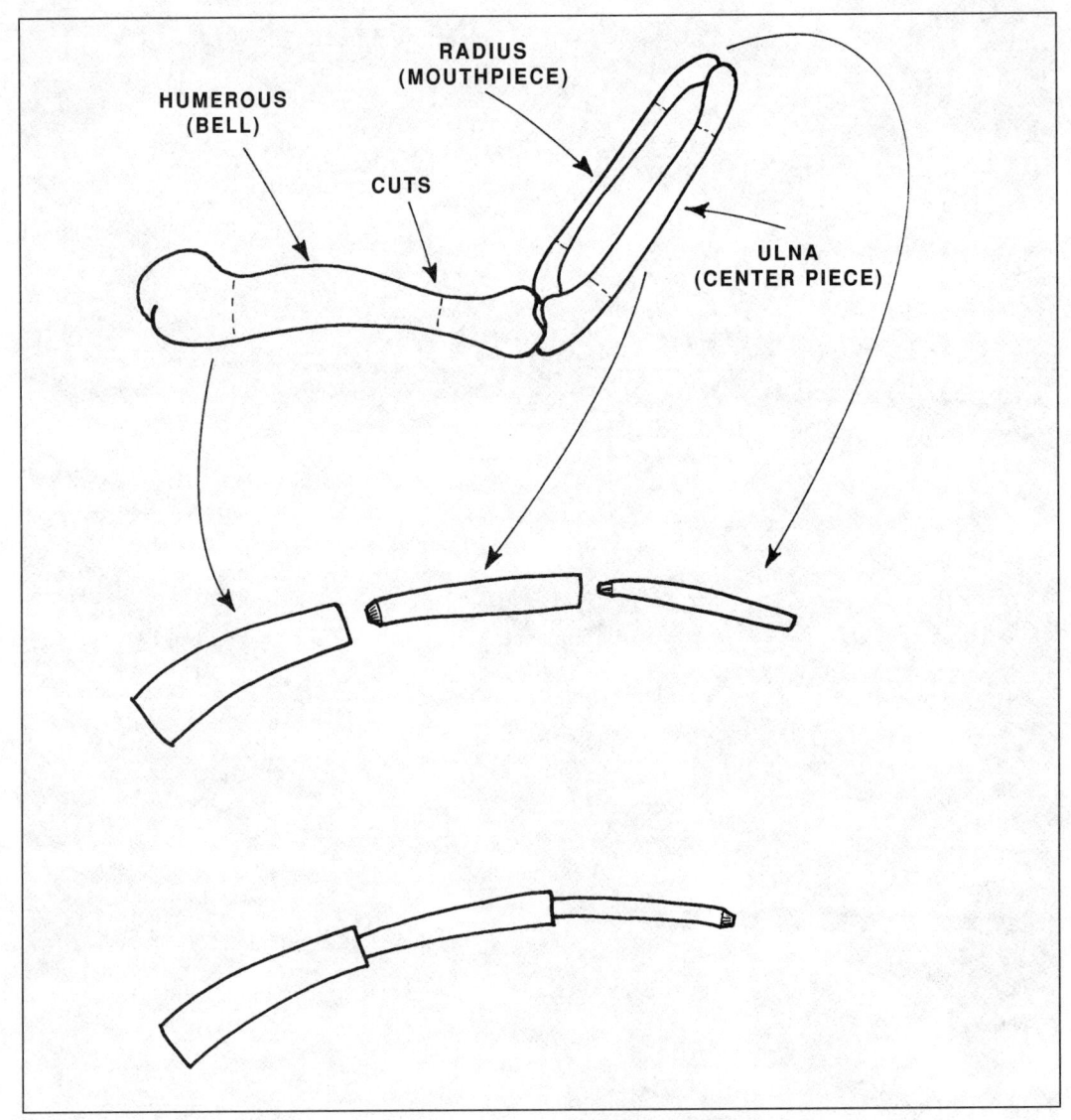

2-14A. The bones are boiled, cleaned, and hollowed out.

now called the mouthpiece. Later makers added a second extension, then a third. Trumpet-style bells made from cow horns were added in later years to produce even more volume.

Wingbone yelpers are just as effective for attracting wild turkeys today as they were thousands of years ago. They're also fun to make and use. One friend makes a number of the wingbone yelpers each year from his turkey trophies and gives them to friends.

The most commonly made calls these days utilize three bones from a single wing. These include the radius, which is made into the mouthpiece; the ulna, made into the center piece; and the humerus, made into the bell. The best bones for a call are those from a spring jake or a fall hen, where taking them is legal.

Before turning the bones into a call, pull off all the feathers and cut off all the meat. Then simmer

BONE PROJECTS

them to remove the remaining meat from the bones. This will take an hour or so to completely loosen all meat and gristle. Simmering the bones from both legs and wings makes a very good soup stock. After the first simmering, set aside the broth for turkey soup. (Do not use any subsequent batches of water with bleach.) There isn't, however, much edible meat on the wing bones. After simmering, remove all meat

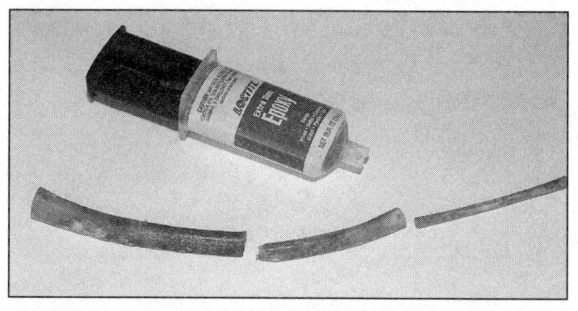

2-14B. The bone sections are cut, then glued together.

from the bones. Since you've simmered both wings, you might as well make two calls. They're easy to do.

Using a hacksaw, cut off the bones close to their ends (fig. 2-14A). It's best to keep the bones wet while cutting to prevent splitting them. Sand all rough or sharp edges. Then use a stiff wire, such as a coat hanger, to hollow out the bones and remove the marrow. A .22 rifle bore brush can be used to remove the marrow on some of the larger bones. Once the marrow has been loosened, blow out the loose particles. You may have to simmer the bones several times to get out all the marrow and open a clean passage through the bones. Adding a capful of laundry bleach to this water will help whiten the bones as well. Once all the bones are cleaned thoroughly, set them aside and allow them to dry.

When the bones are completely dry, lightly sand each and then insert the large end of the smaller (radius) bone about 1/4-inch into the smaller end of the larger (ulna) bone. You will probably have to lightly sand and shape the end of the radius to fit it properly. Then shape the small end of the ulna to fit into the humerus bone. Again, sand and shape until you achieve a nice smooth fit. You may also wish to further shape the outside of the ends to produce a smooth, rounded surface.

2-15. A leather thong is tied to the wingbone call for ease of carrying.

When you're satisfied with the fit of each of the bones, lightly mark across the joining surfaces of each joint with a pencil. Disassemble the pieces, then place a small bit of epoxy on the outside of the pieces that will be fit inside (fig. 2-14B). Be careful not to get the epoxy inside the ends of the bone openings. Carefully press the pieces together, aligning the pencil marks. Wipe away any excess epoxy and allow the glue to set thoroughly. Make sure the end of the mouthpiece is smooth and rounded. A light coating of polyurethane will help protect the call and give it a sheen. Again, be sure not to get anything in the hollow ends.

The call can be decorated with scrimshaw by lightly scratching the surface and then rubbing India or drawing ink into the scratches and quickly wiping it off with a damp cloth. A slight groove can be filed around the lower humerus joint and a leather lanyard tied in the groove. Or epoxy a fly-rod line guide in place to use to tie off the lanyard.

A wingbone yelper is primarily used as a locator call and can create yelps or clucks (fig. 2-15).

Antler, Bone, Horn & Hide

A wingbone call does take some practice to learn to use. The basic technique is to kiss or suck air through the call. This technique sounds simple, but it isn't. Position your lips together and insert the mouthpiece of the call about 1/4-inch into your mouth. Place the call a little to one side of the center of your lips. Hold the call about forty-five degrees downward and draw your breath in sharply, just as if you were puckering for a kiss. The vibration of the skin on your lips produces the sound.

It's also important to hold your hand properly in order to enhance the sounds. The bell end of the call should be placed at the top of your palm between your thumb and index finger. Use the rest of your fingers to create a "bell." You can also cup the fingers of your other hand over the first hand for even more control. Volume and tone can be varied by changing the bell shape of your hands.

You probably won't be able to make "turkey" sounds immediately, but after some squeaks and squawks, eventually you'll be able to produce yelps. Then you can learn to make other calls. The amount of pressure applied with your lips controls the pitch. More pressure produces higher-pitched sounds. Less lip pressure produces lower-pitched sounds. Volume is controlled by the amount of air sucked through the call: the more air, the more sound. Opening the bell of your hands also produces louder sounds. Once you learn to make the basic short yelp, then you can learn to sustain the sound for longer yelps and also to string a number of yelps together. You can also make clucks by sucking very quickly and at the same time pulling your tongue off the hole. Bringing an old tom into gun range with a wingbone call you've made yourself is the ultimate in turkey hunting challenge and fun.

Bone Knives

Bones can also be used as knife handles. Fixed blade, scaled-tang knives, as well as folding blade knives such as pocket knives, have traditionally used bone for handles. Pieces of bone can be fastened on the tang or case of pocket knives in the same manner as described for the stag handle knife.

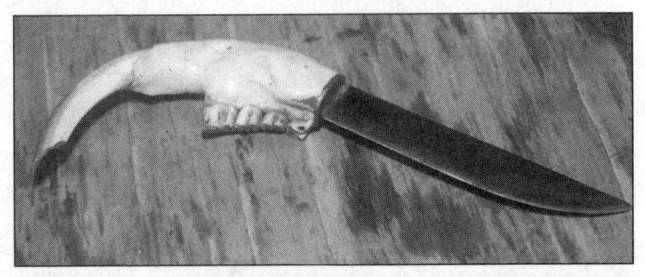

2-16. Bones can also be used for other unusual uses. Shown is a knife handle made from a beaver jawbone.

One of the most unusual knives in my collection is a beaver-jaw knife (fig. 2-16). The knife has a pointed tang inserted and epoxied into a beaver jaw, complete with a formidable tooth. A brass guard completes the unusual knife.

Skulls

The dried, bleached, and polished skulls of animals make very interesting conversation pieces and add to a hunting themed decor. Displaying polished skulls also allows you to show off trophies that might otherwise not be used. A prime example is a bear skull (fig. 2-17). These are quite impressive, as are those from cats like bobcat or cougar. Even smaller mammal and other predator skulls can be interesting. Cow and bison skulls, complete with horns, add to the popular Southwestern decor. Native Americans painted designs on skulls and used them as totems or identification markers.

Drying, bleaching, and polishing skulls isn't easy, and the first steps can be a bit smelly. First, remove

BONE PROJECTS

the skin and all meat and muscle that comes off fairly easily. Clean and treat the upper and lower jaw portions separately. Remove the lower jaw by cutting through the muscle joining it to the upper jaw. Then remove the tongue and jaw muscles. Remove the eyes and use a stiff wire with a hook on the end to work the brains out through the brainstem. This still leaves a fair amount of flesh and muscle on the skull. Simmer the skull in hot, but not boiling, water until you can remove as much of the flesh as possible. Do not boil the skull, or you may loosen the joints and allow the teeth to fall out or crack. This is especially important on smaller, more fragile skulls.

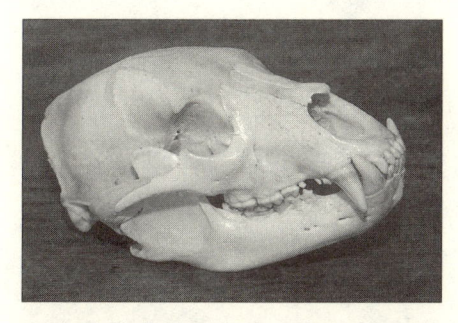

2-17. Skulls from animals such as bear are boiled, cleaned, and bleached for unusual decorative items.

Professional taxidermists use special beetles to complete the chore of removing meat and brains. You can use the same basic tactic. The home method just takes a bit longer. My first attempts utilized an old garden cold frame that was no longer in use. I placed the skulls on the ground in the cold frame, shut the lid and waited until the insects did their job. Actually, the method works quite well.

Another method is to build a wire cage of hardware cloth to hold the skulls and prevent pets and wild animals from running off with your would-be trophies. You will probably have to weight the cages down or tie them in place to something solid. A sunny location that is downwind of your house and your neighbors is the best choice. It will normally take about three to four months for a skull to be completely cleaned and thoroughly dried in this manner.

2-18. Animal skulls are often decorated with Native American or Southwestern designs.

Once the skull is cleaned, you can also use equal parts laundry bleach and water in a plastic bucket to bleach it. The process takes about two or three days for small skulls and up to two weeks for larger skulls. If the solution is to be used for more than a week, replace it with new solution at the end of the first week. You do risk softening the bones with this solution. For a safer method, use half hairdressers whitener and half forty percent hydrogen peroxide as mentioned for bleaching European mounts in chapter 1.

Regardless of the bleaching method, the next step is to use borax in water to remove any fat and grease that remains and to stop the bleaching action. Use about one cup of borax to two gallons of water. Simmer the skull in the water and borax solution for about fifteen minutes. Anytime the skull is immersed in simmering water, always check for teeth that have fallen out. Set them aside to be glued in place later.

Skulls can be left as is, given a coat of polyurethane varnish for a glossy look, painted with Southwestern or Native American designs, or bolted to display panels (fig. 2-18). ■

TOOLS NEEDED FOR

Horn Projects

- 1/8- to 3/16-inch tool-steel rod
- Antler or horn buttons
- Arkansas sharpening stone
- Artists brush
- Bandsaw, saber saw, or coping saw
- Brass screw
- Buffing wheel
- Camp stove or deep fryer
- Cloth, soft
- Coarse sandpaper
- Coat hanger
- Dowel
- Epoxy
- File
- Furniture wax, paste
- Glue, white craft, or plaster of Paris
- India ink
- Knife
- Lathe
- Leather gloves, heavy-duty
- Leather strap
- Masking tape
- Old, deep pan
- Pliers, basic and insulated
- Polishing compound
- Poster paint
- Rivet
- Sandpaper, medium and fine grit
- Scouring powder, fine
- Steel wool, extra fine
- Stropping abrasives
- Toothpaste
- Upholstery tacks
- Wire cage or basket
- Wooden dowels

3
HORN PROJECTS

Horn was a very common material and early people became very inventive in its use. Native Americans used horn from antelope, wild sheep, goats, bison, and later even cattle to create utensils, ornaments, and other items. Extremely tough, horn can be soaked, heated, and shaped fairly easily. It can also simply be cleaned and cut into different shapes.

Spoons made from the horns of mountain goats were common with the people from the Northwest coast as well as the Hopi and some Plains tribes. Some tribes used bison horn for spoons and cups. Others made musical rattles from cow or bison horns.

Early settlers found similar uses for horn and added their own, making mugs, napkin rings, shoehorns, bugle horns for military use, combs, run horns used to call back running dogs, jewelry, jewelry boxes, and containers for salt or explosives (fig. 3-1).

Years ago, the horns of mountain sheep and goats were often used. Today, with most sheep hunts costing several thousand dollars, most hunters prefer to mount their trophies rather than use them for projects. Cow horn, however, is still quite easily accessible, reasonably priced, and can be made into many items.

3-1. Horn has been a common material used through the ages. Any number of items have been and can be made of horn.

3-2. Although horn is available from many wild animals, the most common source is cow horns.

ACQUIRING HORN

Raw cow horn is available from suppliers of muzzleloading materials, including Dixie Gun Works. If you live in a rural area, you may be able to locate a slaughterhouse that can supply you with horns. Or talk to veterinarians. In some instances, they may dehorn cattle with large horns (fig. 3-2).

Antler, Bone, Horn & Hide

Horns are available in a wide variety of sizes, shapes, and coloring. If you intend to decorate the horn with scrimshaw, make sure it is lighter on the butt end so the design will show up.

Working with Horn

The best horns are those that have been seasoned at least a year or more. Fresh horns contain a semisolid, blood-filled core, which will eventually rot out. If you have fresh horns, place them in a wire cage or basket where pets and wild animals can't get at them and allow the core of the horn to rot, then dry out. A fresh horn will also shrink considerably as it dries out.

If you're in a hurry, boil the horn to remove the core. Do this outside, because it's a bit smelly and messy. The cooking unit of a fish deep fryer or a camp stove works quite well. Use a large enough pan so the horn can be totally submerged, but not a pan that will ever be used for anything but skulls, horns, bones, and the like. Bring the water up to a steady boil and, using pliers, lower the horn carefully into the boiling water. Simmer about an hour. Watch the water and replace it as necessary to keep the horn covered with water. Also watch that the water doesn't boil over. Using a pair of insulated pliers, remove the horn from the water and check the core. It should pull out fairly easily with a second set of pliers.

Once the core has been removed, wash the horn in clean water and set it aside to dry. With the core removed, drying will take about a month. Don't leave the horn where pets or wild animals can steal your future horn projects.

Once the horn has been cleaned, it can be shaped into numerous items. Horn can be cut quite easily with a hacksaw. It can also be boiled and then molded into items or pressed flat and cut into shapes.

Powder Horn

One of the most common uses of horn by the early settlers and mountain men was to hold powder. They created powder horns that were not only useful but also highly artistic.

In many instances, two powder horns were utilized, one for the main powder and a smaller one for the primer powder. Shown are examples of each (fig. 3-3). You can make your own powder horn fairly easily and decorate it to suit your style.

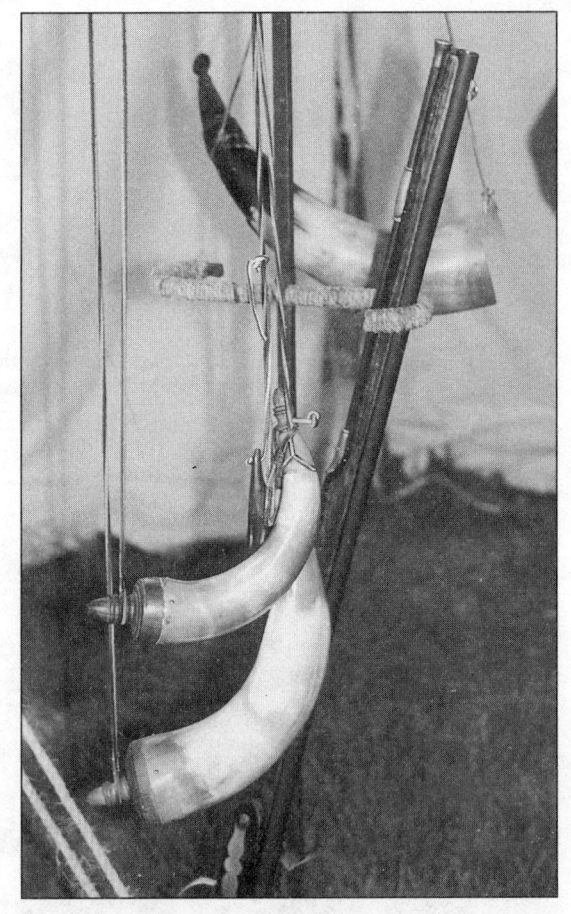

3-3. Powder horns are a popular project, especially for muzzleloaders and buckskinners.

HORN PROJECTS

3-4A. First cut the open-horn end square, then use a wire to determine the depth of the horn.

3-4B. Hold the wire outside the horn and mark the depth.

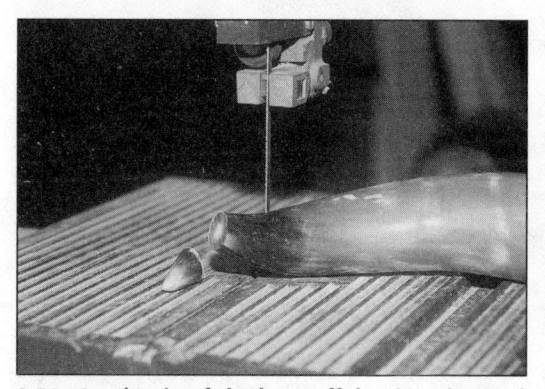

3-5A. Cut the tip of the horn off, leaving plenty of material inside.

3-5B. Bore a 1/8-inch starter hole all the way through the horn tip. Make a spout plug and bore the end to accept the plug.

Horn on some older animals, depending on the breed, may have rough scaling or checking on the outside, especially near the butt end of the horn. Clean this off first with the blade of a knife or coarse sandpaper. You may also find damage, such as cuts or deep barbed-wire scratches, but these can actually add to the uniqueness of the powder horn. Don't spend a lot of time on this initial cleaning. You just need to find out if the horn is structurally sound. Before you start to design your powder horn, you may need to use a hacksaw to cut off any butt portion that is extremely thin, scaled, rough, ragged or misshaped. Make sure the cut is square with the general curvature of the horn and not at an angle that will waste horn material (fig. 3-4A).

The next step is to determine where the solid portion of the horn ends. This can vary a great deal. Some horns may be hollow almost to the tip. Others may be solid for several inches back from the tip. Straighten out a coat hanger or use a similar piece of stiff wire and run it up into the horn cavity until it touches the solid portion (fig. 3-4B). Use a piece of masking tape on the wire to mark the depth of the cavity.

If the cavity ends within an inch or so of the tip of the horn, file the tip flat. If the tip is solid for several inches, cut it off about one inch from the end of the cavity (fig. 3-5A). Save this piece to make a powder measure (see page 49).

Antler, Bone, Horn & Hide

Bore a 1/8-inch starter hole in the end of the horn with a cordless electric drill and drill bit (fig. 3-5B). Make sure the bit does not go through the side of the horn. Keep it at the proper angle as you bore the hole. Once a starter hole has been bored, make a hole up to 1/4 inch in diameter, depending on the diameter of the end of the horn tip. Don't make the hole too large or it can weaken the horn wall.

Add a wooden plug for the butt and one for the tip, and you're finished. Most of us, however, prefer a bit nicer powder horn. This means a "fancy" butt plug and a stopper for the tip.

Butt Plugs

Butt plugs can be as fancy or as simple as you like. The simplest ones fit flush with the butt end of the horn. First, you'll need to sand the cut end of the horn. It will probably be uneven, regardless of how you cut it. Tack a piece of medium grit sandpaper to a work surface. Holding the horn upright and at a consistent angle to the sandpaper, smooth and finish off the end so it is even all around with no dips or irregular surfaces.

Paint a bit of poster paint on the butt end of the horn and quickly place it down on a piece of paper, making sure you don't move it once it touches the paper. Then clean the paint off the horn with cold water. This print will illustrate both the inside and outside edges of the butt end where the butt plug must fit.

3-6. Butt plugs are made for the large end. A wide variety of designs was utilized.

Butt plugs should be made of nice, smooth-grained, solid wood such as walnut, maple, or cherry (fig. 3-6). Cut the butt plug to fit inside the shape of the horn using a bandsaw, saber saw, or coping saw. You can also create a turning for the butt plug, using a lathe. This allows you to create a tie strap knob as well as a much more decorative butt plug. Any number of butt plug designs can be turned.

As horns are rarely perfectly round, the best tactic is to turn the plug to the outside diameter, then whittle or rasp and file down a short, 1/4- to 3/8-inch lip to fit inside the horn. Another tactic is to boil the horn for about forty-five minutes until it softens, then push the round plug into the butt end of the horn. The horn will usually shape itself to match the turned plug. Make sure you handle the hot horn with heavy-duty leather gloves. Allow the horn and plug to cool for about twenty-four hours. The plug will be solidly anchored in place once the horn dries around it. Many horn butts have quite irregular shapes. In that case, it's easiest to simply whittle the butt plug to shape.

Regardless of the shape of the butt plug, it should be anchored solidly in the end of the horn. If the horn and plug haven't been matched by boiling, epoxy glue can be used. Decorative tacks such as upholstery tacks can also be used to fasten the plug in place. Wooden dowels were also traditionally used on some horns. These are driven into holes bored through both the horn and plug, then sanded smooth and flush with the outside of the horn.

Now, a means of carrying the horn must be devised. A butt plug can be turned with a "nipple"

Horn Projects

3-7. In many instances, the small end of the horn is shaped to hold a shoulder strap.

on the outer end to hold a shoulder strap or you can use other means of fastening the shoulder strap. A horn or antler button can be filed into a knob shape with a groove and held in place with a brass screw. Other means include simply adding a brass screw eye or other type of fitting. Another method of fastening a shoulder strap is to leave an extension of an inch or two on the upper side of the horn. A shoulder strap can then be fastened to this extension with a rivet.

The next step is to create a means to hold the shoulder strap to the tip. This can be as simple as a groove filed in the tip (fig. 3-7). The groove should be about 1/8 inch deep and 1/8 to 1/4 inch wide. Or, you can create more elaborate designs by completely shaping the tip. Regardless, it's important not to file too deeply and cut through the tip material. Horns with thick tips allow more freedom in this design. Shown are several designs. If you really want to get fancy, consider creating a brass band

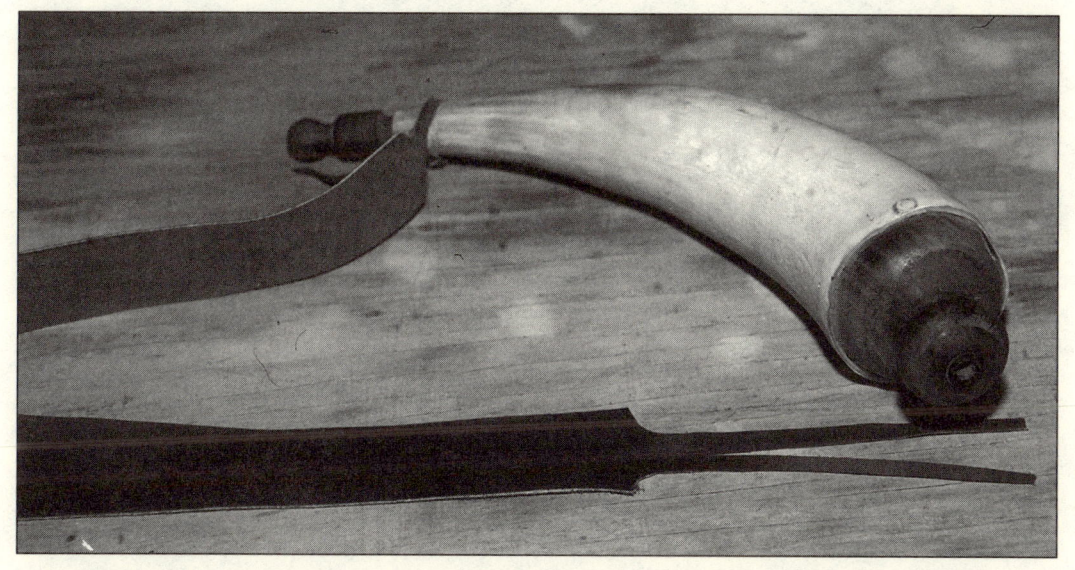

3-8. The small end of the horn is then closed with a spout plug. Many different varieties were used.

to fit around the tip in the groove with a brass ring to hold the shoulder strap.

After fitting the butt plug and shaping the tip, the horn should be well polished. This can be done with extremely fine sandpaper, followed by extra-fine steel wool. A fine scouring powder or toothpaste is used for the final polishing. A buffing wheel with polishing compound makes the chore easy. Once the horn is polished to a good sheen, give it a coat of paste furniture wax.

The open (tip) end of the powder horn is closed off with a spout plug. The end of the plug should fit snugly, but not too tightly, into the hole in the spout (fig. 3-8). Plugs can be turned or whittled into shapes as simple or as elaborate as you desire.

Scrimshaw

Many old powder horns were works of art, engraved with names, a variety of designs, even maps (fig. 3-9). This can be done quite easily with purchased tools, or you can make a homemade engraving tool as follows: Heat a piece of 1/8- to 3/16-inch tool-steel rod until it is red hot. Then bend the end, creating an L shape about 1/4 inch from the end. Grind the end to a very sharp point. Reheat the tip until it is red hot, then quench it in cold water to harden the point. Create a wooden handle for the tool by turning it on a lathe or simply carve a handle. Bore a hole in the end of the handle for the rod and glue it in place.

The point must be extremely sharp, and the best method of achieving this, as well as keeping the point sharp while scratching the design, is to use an Arkansas sharpening stone. Finally, strop the point using a piece of leather with stropping abrasives. The tool is used by holding it with one hand and using the thumb of the other as a steady rest. You'll probably want to at least add your name and the date you made the horn. After that, use your imagination.

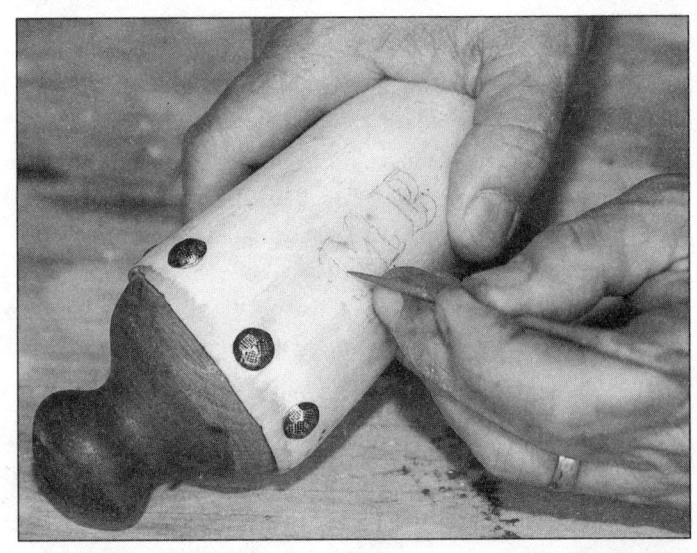

3-9. Decorating a powder horn with scrimshaw adds ornamentation and personalizes the horn.

Once you've scratched your design into the horn, apply a tiny bit of India ink with a small artist's brush to the scratches. Immediately wipe away the excess ink with a lightly dampened, soft cloth.

Shoulder Straps

As with other parts of a powder horn, shoulder straps can be as elaborate or simple as you desire. A leather strap with slits cut in the ends to fit over the tip and over the butt plate fixture is the simplest. You may wish, however, to plait the ends for a more elaborate strap.

Horn Projects

3-10. Shoulder straps are created out of leather and fastened to the horn.

Powder Measure

The tip cut from the horn during the first steps can often be made into a powder measure (fig. 3-10). A thong can be used to tie the measure to the powder horn or to tie it around your neck. Bore a hole through the tip to hold the thong. Hollow out the measure from the larger end, using a cordless drill and a drill bit. Use a black powder measure to measure out the amount of powder you should normally use. Then bore a hole, a bit at a time, until the powder fits in properly. Make sure the hole is the correct size to suit the measure of powder. Don't overbore or underbore. ■

PART TWO

LEATHER PROJECTS

Leather is one of mankind's most valuable commodities. It is used for shoes, clothing, and a wide range of other items. The projects in this section are for the most part items from the past. Many of these ideas are based on the excellent use made of leather by Native Americans. Several more-modern projects, such as knife sheaths and belts, are also shown.

TOOLS AND MATERIALS FOR
Leather Clothing Projects

- 12- by 16-inch piece of soft wood
- Buttons, antler or horn
- Decorations, such as paint, quills, or beads
- Hammer
- Lacing cutter
- Leather
- Leather-hole puncher
- Leather lacing
- Leather thongs
- Needle, darning or leather, and lacing
- Needles, leather, size 16 to 19
- Scissors, heavy-duty
- Sewing awl
- Sewing machine, heavy-duty
- Sinew
- Snaps and ties
- Thread, heavy, waxed (such as linen)
- Waxed linen thread
- Whetstone
- X-Acto or utility knife and blades

4
LEATHER PROJECTS

Leather has been a traditional clothing material throughout the ages and is still quite popular today as well. Naturally, styles have changed over the years. Of necessity, the clothing of old was very simply styled. The leather clothing of Native Americans consisted primarily of leggings and breechclouts. Leather shirts were worn by the warriors of some tribes, but primarily for special occasions. For the most part, Native Americans went bare chested, wearing animal robes in cold weather. Leather dresses were worn by women. Settlers and mountain men readily took to the buckskin mode of dress as well, simply because leather was a readily available material that could be home tanned and used to create very durable, although not necessarily comfortable, clothing (fig. 4-1).

MATERIALS

The primary leather of choice of the past was buckskin although the hides of other animals, including elk and antelope, were also used. Home-tanned buckskin is still a popular choice, especially with modern-day buckskinners. Purchased leathers can also be used for both

4-1. Leather has been a traditional and popular clothing material since man first used animal hides for protection from the elements.

old- and modern-style clothing. Commercially produced leather of the thickness used for clothing is either cowhide or in some cases goat- or sheepskins, which have much the same appearance as buckskin and are sometimes sold as "buckskin." Deer hides are also available for the traditionalist. Cowhides of the thickness needed are available as either top grain or splits made by machine splitting thicker

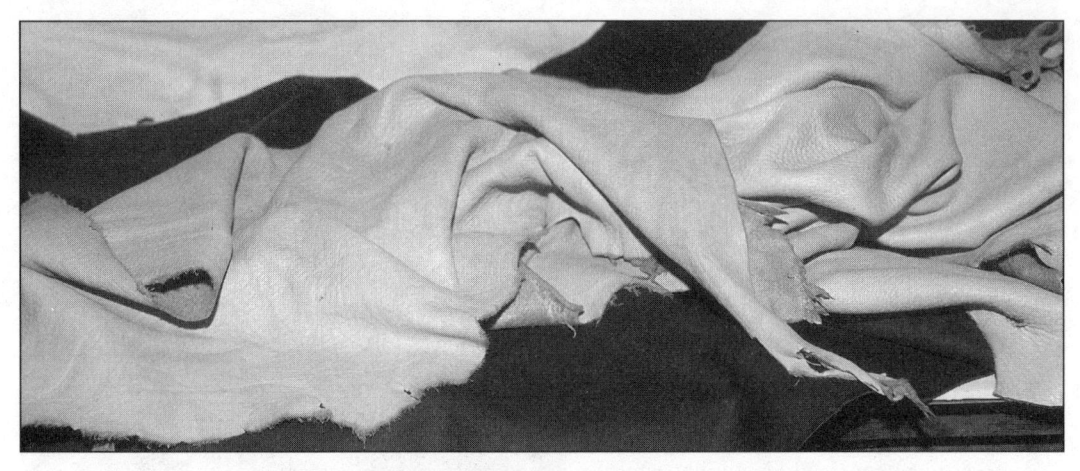

4-2. A wide variety of thicknesses, finishes, and colors of leather are available.

hides (fig. 4-2). Splits are the inner side of the hide and have a suedelike appearance on both sides. Top grain is the top layer of a split hide and still has the finished grain. Either can be used; splits, however, are more economical.

Full leather hides are sold by the square foot. Small-size skins run from four to six square feet; medium size skins from seven to eight square feet, and large from nine to ten square feet. Full deerskins are available in three common sizes: small, medium, and large. On the average, three large deer hides are required for a shirt for the average-size person with a shirt size of 15-1/2 to 16. Four small hides may be required. Normally, four medium-size skins are needed to make a pair of pants for an average person with a thirty-three-inch inseam.

Cowhides and the skins from other large animals are normally sold as half hides. These will range in size from ten to sixteen square feet. Usually only two half hides are required for a shirt and two half hides for pants. It's best to hold the hides up to the person being fitted to make sure enough length and width is available. Also, check the hides for holes. A hole in the wrong place can mean a lot of waste and require more work in laying out the garment. If in doubt regarding the amount of material, it's best to purchase an extra skin. You can, of course, piece together smaller hides for garments, but it's extra work, and in many instances creates less comfortable clothing.

If possible, buy hides that match. Not only should the coloring of the hides match but the thickness as well. This prevents the garment from pulling to one side because of the differences in the weight of the different hides.

The overall thickness of the leather is also important. The hide should not be so thick that you can't easily stitch or lace it or be so heavy that it will be uncomfortable to wear as a garment. On the other hand, extremely thin skins tend to stretch and become baggy with use. An extremely thin area in an otherwise thicker piece of leather is also cause for concern because it will be weaker than the rest of the garment.

Leather is available in a wide variety of thicknesses and is classified by ounces, which describe both the weight and the thickness. One-ounce leather refers to one square foot of leather that weighs one ounce. This leather is about 1/64 inch thick. Leathers from two to three ounces are most commonly used for clothing.

Leather Projects

Patterns

Full-size patterns are available from some companies for a wide variety of leather garments. You can also make your own patterns fairly easily. For instance, you can remove the stitching from a shirt that you like and that fits well and use this to create a pattern on heavy paper. Don't choose a garment that is tight fitting. It's best to iron the pieces flat before transferring them to the paper, and don't forget to add seam allowances to the pattern.

Many traditional Native American garments and those copied by the mountain men, however, consisted of hides simply sewed together without elaborate patterns. The shape of the hide was part of the design of the garment.

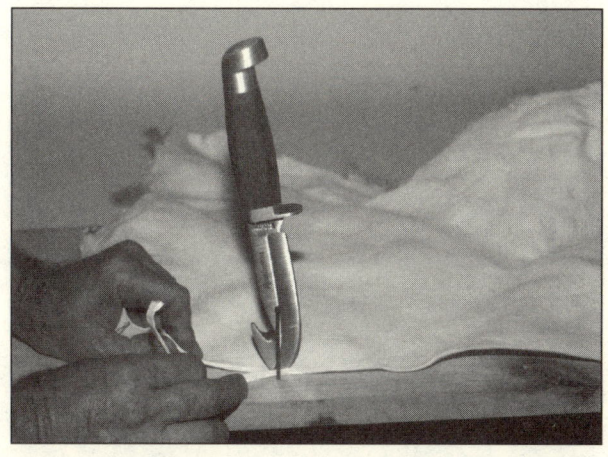

4-3. Leather clothing can be assembled with heavy thread or lacing. Lacing can be cut using a sharp knife and a nail driven into the board the width of the lacing desired.

Lacing or Stitching

Clothing can be assembled with either leather lacing or with heavy thread. Lacing can be purchased or it can be cut from the scraps left from cutting out the clothing. It should be cut from 1/8 to 3/16 inch wide using one of two methods (fig. 4-3). The first method is to use sharp, heavy-duty scissors and cut the lacing in a continuous circle. Another method is to drive a nail in a block of wood, start the lacing cut, then push the knife blade in to the wood and pull the leather through the space between the nail and knife edge. Or you can use a lacing cutter. As you cut lacing, pull and stretch it. Unless it is prestretched before using in the garment, lacing will stretch and become loose. Lacings can also break, and stretching will eliminate any weaker pieces before you begin to use them. (Additional information on lacing is on page 129.)

4-4. Lacing and thread can be stitched with a lacing needle. Thread can also be stitched with an automatic awl.

Waxed linen thread can be used to handstitch a garment together using a darning or leather needle. Thin skins can even be stitched using a heavy-duty sewing machine and a size 16 to 19 leather needle (fig. 4-4).

Any number of stitches or lacing methods may be used. The two most common, however, are the running stitch, sometimes called glover's stitch, and the whip stitch. If the pieces are sewn together wrong side out (or inside out) with a running stitch, then turned right side out, the stitching is fairly well hidden. If a whip stitch is used, the threads are exposed if the pieces are sewn with the right sides together. A whip stitch can also be sewn with the wrong sides together and a welt placed in the seam. The welt covers the stitching from the outside and also adds strength to the seam.

ANTLER, BONE, HORN & HIDE

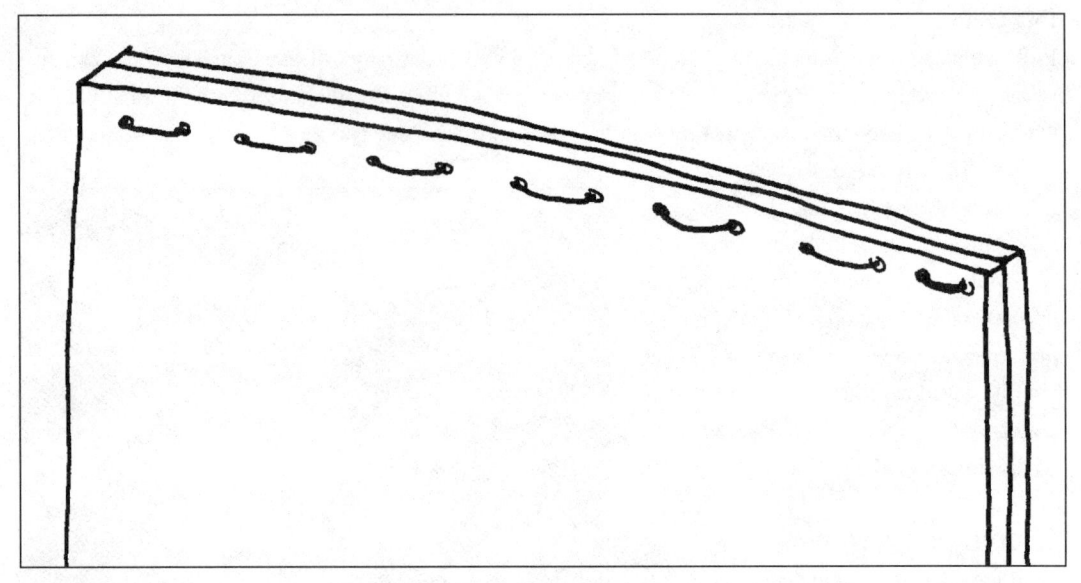

4-5A. Running stitch.

Running Stitch

To begin lacing with a running stitch, thread the lacing through both pieces and leave a small tag end. With a hole punched in it thread the opposite end of the lacing back through the next hole, run it through the hole in the tag end, and lacing (fig. 4-5A).

When lacing, pull the lacing firm after each stitch. Otherwise, it will be too hard to pull the lacing taut after several stitches. Do not, however, pull the lacing so tight the leather becomes puckered.

If you break a piece of lacing or must attach another piece, punch a hole in both the tag end of the existing lacing and the tag end of a new piece. Push the tag end of the new piece through the hole in the first piece. Then push the opposite end of the new piece through its tag-end hole and continue lacing.

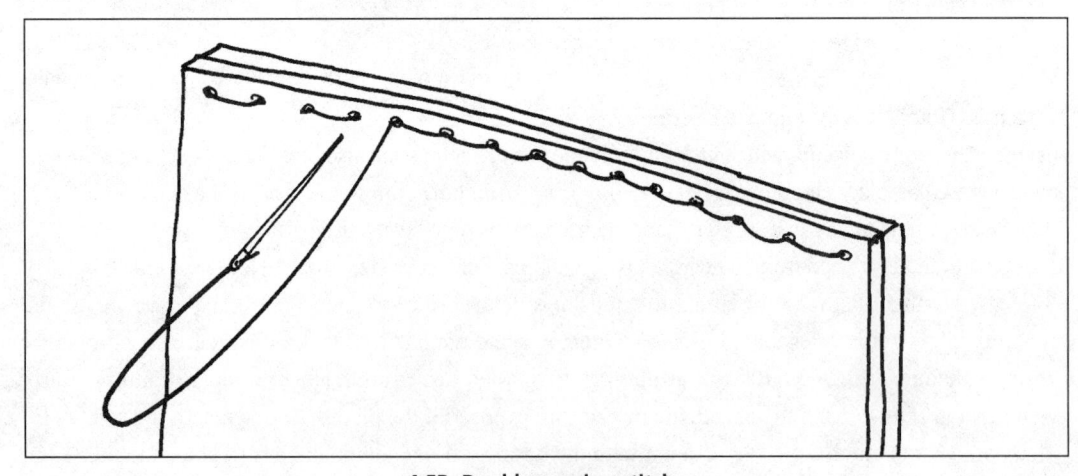

4-5B. Double running stitch.

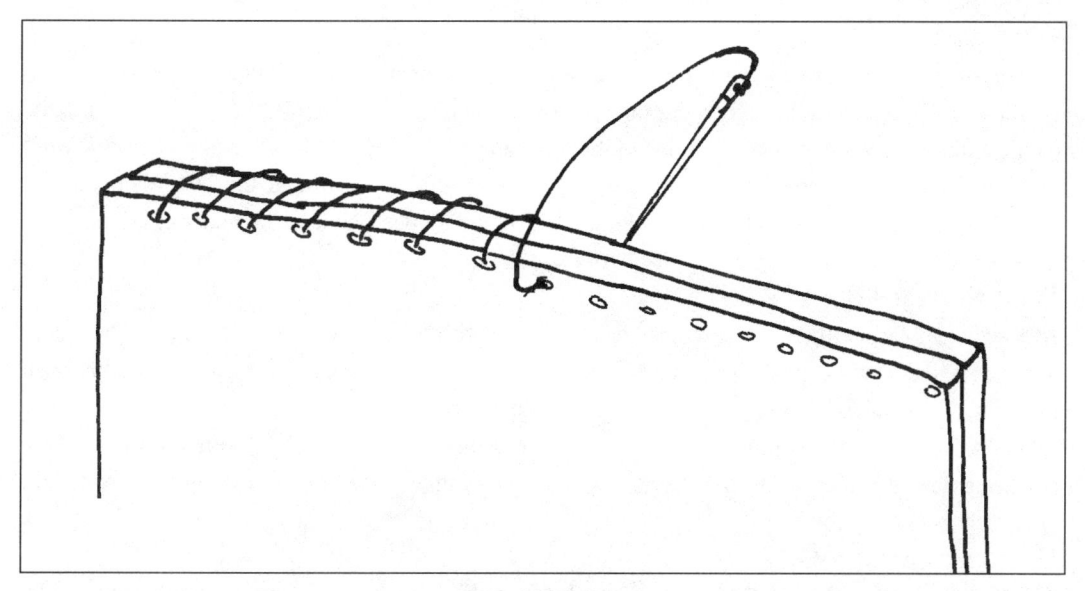

4-5C. Whip stitch.

Finish the lacing with a knot on the under or back side of the seam. If your stitching doesn't end on the back side, take the lacing back to the next-to-last hole to position the knot on the back. To make a knot, simply make a loop around the lacing between the last two stitches, push the tag end through the circle once and pull it snug. Repeat this knot, then go back to the next stitch and repeat again.

DOUBLE RUNNING STITCH

A double running stitch has a second row of running stitches added from the back (fig. 4-5B). The double running stitch is, of course, a stronger stitch than the single running stitch and should be used in places where extra strength is needed.

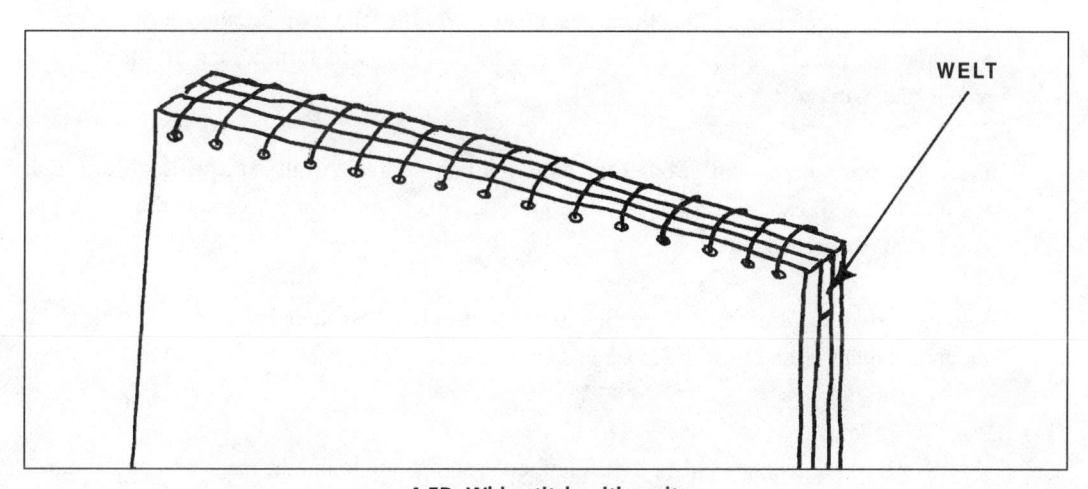

4-5D. Whip stitch with welt.

Whip Stitch

A whip stitch is also fairly easy and can be made with either thread or lacing. In this case the material is laid edge to edge with the right sides out (fig. 4-5C). The stitching begins in the same way but the lacing or thread is whipped over the edge of the seam and into the next hole. Finishing off with a whip stitch is done by bringing the lacing or thread back around and through the last stitch on top, encircling it several times, and making a knot. The knot is hidden between the material layers.

Whip Stitch with a Welt

As mentioned earlier, the whip stitch can also be made with the garment wrong side out. The stitch, however, will spread open when pressure is applied to the seam and the stitching will be visible from the front. A welt added to the seam keeps the seam from spreading as much and covers the seam (fig. 4-5D). A welt is a narrow piece of leather or material inserted between the two main pieces being stitched together. A piece of leather to cut into the fringe can be added to the seam in place of a welt.

Using a Sewing Awl

Another stitching method is to use a lock stitch sewing awl, such as the ones available from Tandy Leather. This device utilizes a needle with a groove in the tip and a spool of heavy-duty waxed thread. The awl can be used to quickly and easily stitch garments together as follows:

1. Pull about one inch of thread through the needle. Hold your forefinger firmly on the reel so it will not turn and insert the needle through the layers. This produces a short piece of thread on the back side of the seam. Pull this out to a length about twice the distance you will be sewing.

2. With the loose thread end in one hand, grasp the awl firmly with the other (continue to hold the reel firmly with your forefinger so it will not turn). Withdraw the awl until there is about one inch of thread between the material and the needle point. In this position you will begin the second stitch.

3. Release the awl and reinsert it at the proper distance for the length of the stitch desired. Slowly withdraw the needle partway, holding the reel tightly. This will form a loop on the opposite side of the material.

4. Insert the loose thread end through the loop, holding the reel firmly so it will not turn. Pull the needle and thread with equal force in opposite directions to form the stitch. You have just completed the second stitch.

5. Repeat steps 3 and 4 until finished. Sew with the needle in the same position at all times. Cut the thread, knot it, and tuck the loose ends out of sight.

Tools

Creating leather clothing requires only a handful of tools: something to cut the leather on and a needle or awl. Garments can be sewn using holes punched with a leather punch and leather lacing, with

LEATHER PROJECTS

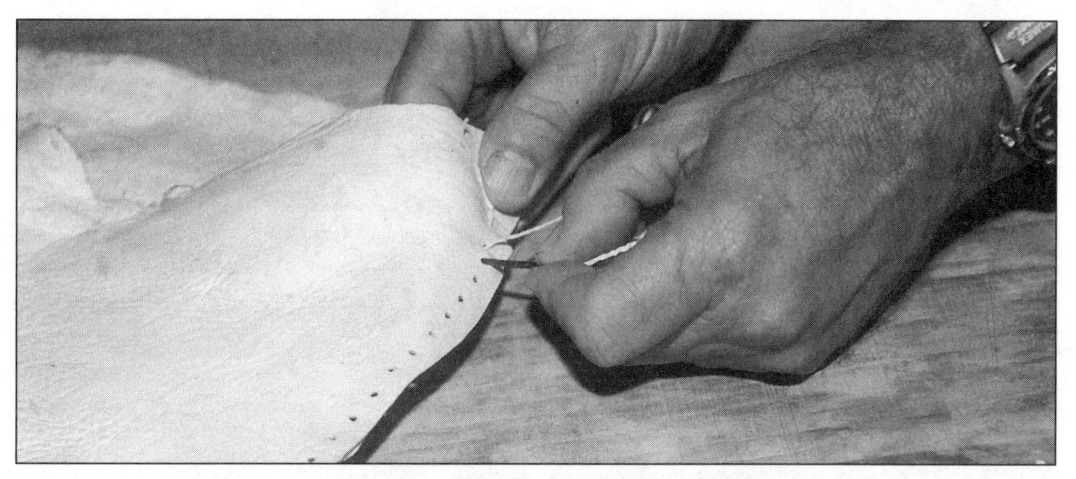

4-6. A lacing needle is used to thread the lace or waxed thread.

lacing needles, or with waxed linen thread (fig. 4-6). Traditionalists may prefer sinew, and artificial sinew is also available.

Other tools include an X-Acto, hobby, or utility knife and blades. Make sure you purchase several blades as they dull easily. You can sharpen these blades with a whetstone, but it's good to have several on hand. Heavy scissors can be used to cut lacing. You'll also need a leather punch or awl and hammer (figs. 4-7 and 4-8). A 12- by 16-inch piece of soft wood can be used to cut or punch holes on. A 3/4- by 2- by 12-inch piece of wood with a smooth straight edge can be used as a guide for cutting fringe and making other straight cuts.

4-7. Stitching holes can be punched with a revolving leather punch.

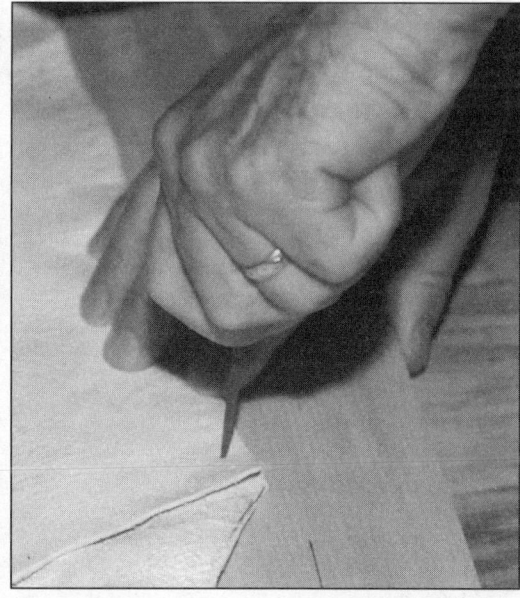

4-8. A leather awl can also be used to punch holes for stitching or lacing.

ANTLER, BONE, HORN & HIDE

4-9. The first step is to lay out the pattern or design of the garment on the leather.

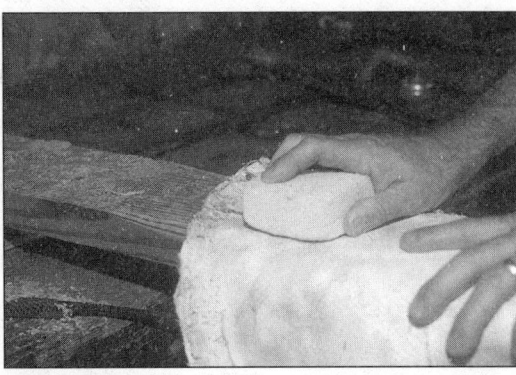

4-10. If using home-tanned skins, it's a good idea to sand or smooth the flesh side of the leather.

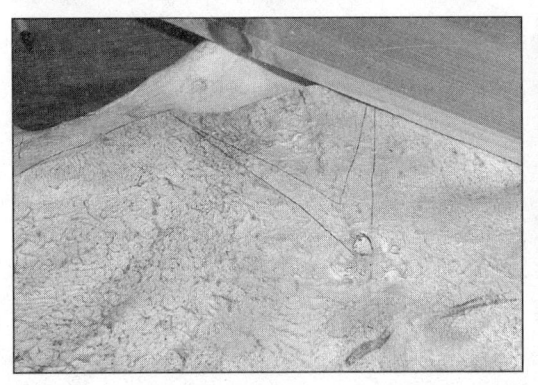

4-11. Move the pattern or design around on the leather to avoid bullet holes, cuts, and scars.

4-12. Using a piece of soft wood as a backer, cut the leather with a sharp hobby knife, from the back side.

Basic Clothing Construction

The first step is to lay out the leather, grain side down, and lay the pattern pieces in place (fig. 4-9). Wherever possible, butt straight sides of the pattern pieces together to utilize one cut for two pieces. This not only saves work but leather as well. Work around any holes in the leather, and make sure there are no flaws in the areas to be used (figs. 4-10 and 4-11). Tape or pin the pattern pieces in place, then use a sharp knife on a smooth cutting surface to cut out the pieces (fig. 4-12). Cut from the back side and hold the leather secure so it doesn't wrinkle or slide.

Fringe

Fringe can be applied to garments in two ways and traditionally both methods were used. The edges of some garments simply had fringe cut along the edges (figs. 4-13A and 4-13B). More elaborate styles also utilized cut-edge fringe. But, in many cases, the fringe was an additional piece sewn in place. For this technique, it's a good idea to cut the fringe piece to the appropriate size, sew it in place in the seam, and then cut the fringe. In this way you'll be sure the fringe piece is of the correct size and shape and yet you won't have to worry about keeping all the fringe end out of the way while you sew the seam.

LEATHER PROJECTS

Fringe should be cut about 1/8-inch wide. Wider fringe, looks awkward and narrower fringe tends to rip and tear off easily. Fringe can be cut with a pair of heavy-duty scissors. Or lay the piece out flat and use a straightedge and sharp knife to cut the fringe.

LEATHER GARMENTS

Following are some typical items of leather clothing.

SCALP OR WAR SHIRT

War shirts were some of the earliest clothing designs (fig. 4-14). They consisted usually of a sleeveless poncho and were worn only by noted warriors. The sides were left open or in some instances tied with lacings. Scalp or war shirts were made either from two skins of elk, deer, antelope, or sheep or from one larger skin. The shape of the shirt resulted from the natural shape of the skins. Sleeves were added to more modern shirts.

To make the one-piece war shirt, simply fold a large skin together in the center with the front legs meeting the rear legs. Cut a hole in the fold that your head will fit through. This hole should be cut slightly deeper in the front than the back. The area that hangs over the shoulders can be cut into fringe. The bottom can also be cut into fringe or simply cut

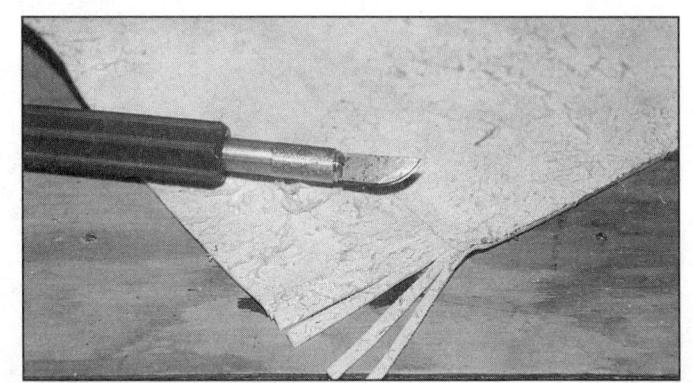

4-13A & 4-13B. Fringe is a decorative item on many garments. It can be cut with heavy-duty scissors or a sharp knife.

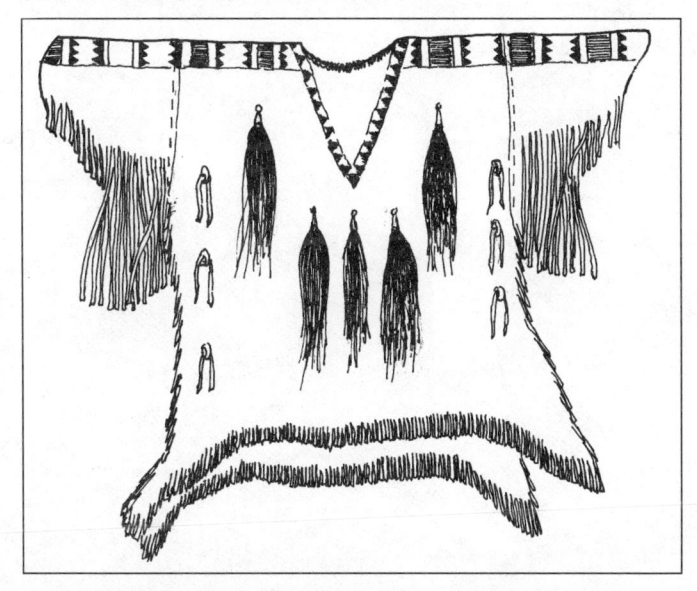

4-14. A very common early design of Native Americans was the war shirt. It consisted of either one hide or two hides laced at the shoulders and tied with thongs at the sides and under the arms. This one shows the hide sewn at the shoulders.

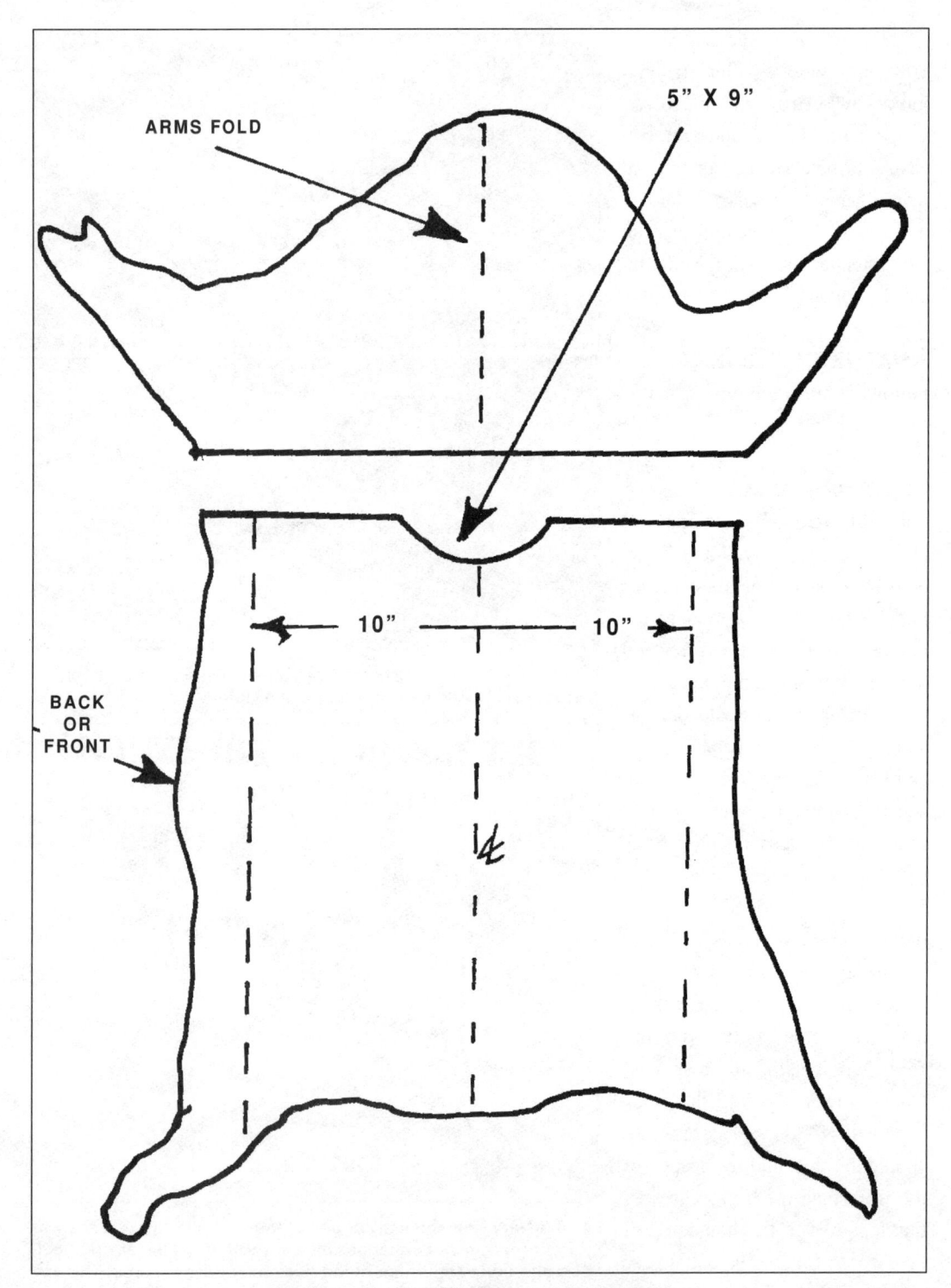

4-15. Four-piece war shirt pattern, using two hides.

Leather Projects

back to the sides. To hold the sides together, use leather thongs laced through holes in the front and back and tied in the back.

Another traditional war shirt design uses two hides joined at the shoulder (fig. 4-15). Cut the front and back from the two hides and make the neck hole cut. Trim the shoulder area on both sides to create a straight shoulder and join the two pieces with leather lacing across the shoulders.

In the past, fringe was often cut around all edges, and if small skins were used for the garment, fringed "tails" were sometimes sewn to the corners (fig. 4-16). Whether made from one or two pieces, these simple, but elegant shirts were commonly decorated with paint, quill, or beadwork.

Plains War Shirt

By the 1800s, the Plains style shirt was developed by the Crow, Blackfeet, Sioux and Cheyenne. These shirts typically featured long sleeves, sides that were sewn (instead of being held together with thongs), and a squared bottom. Tied-on fringe was often added to the lower portion of the shirt as well as around the top of the sleeves. This style quickly became popular with the settlers and mountain men as well. These elaborate shirts were quilled, beaded, or sometimes decorated with vivid paint designs. Pieces of ermine and other items were also used on these shirts for decoration (figs. 4-17 and 4-18).

Three to four hides are required for this shirt, depending on the size of the hides and the shirt size. The first step is to measure the individual with a cloth tape at the largest circumference, whether chest, stomach, or hips. Then add two inches and divide this number by two. This provides the width of both the front and back. Measure for the length as well. The shirt normally comes to about midthigh.

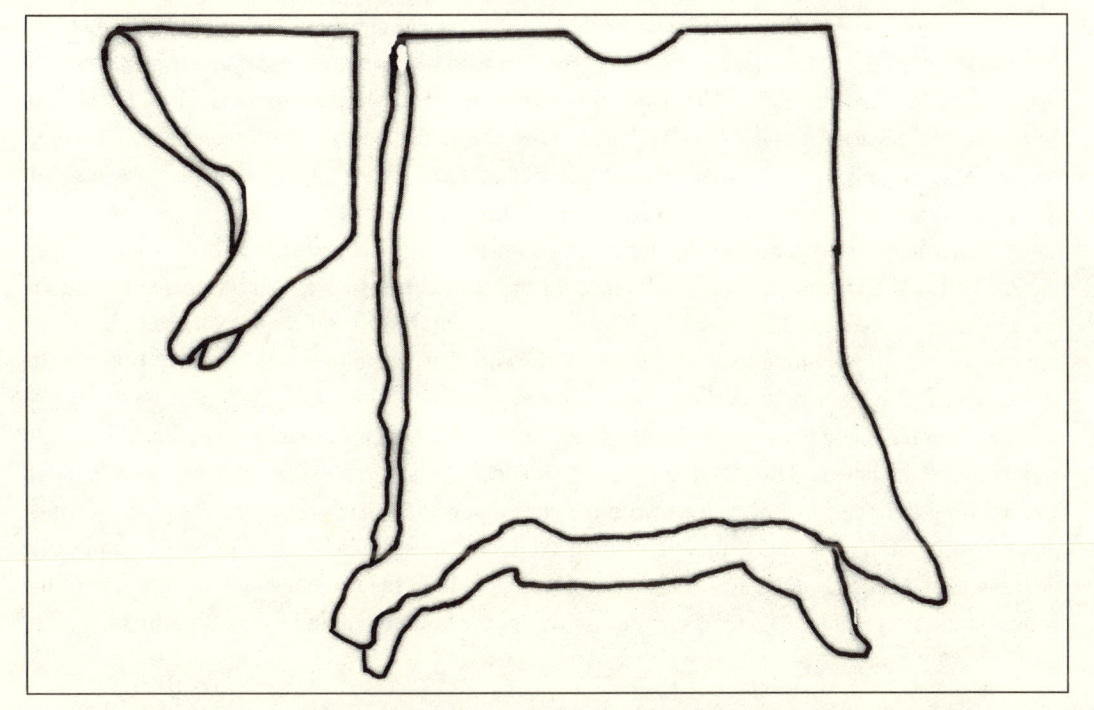

4-16. The neck or upper portion of each hide was folded and used to create the arms.

4-17. A later development was the addition of sewn sleeves and sides. Shown is a Crow shirt with ermine skins and quill decoration.

4-18. Pattern War Shirt with Sleeves.

Cut the front and back to the same approximate size, cutting the shoulders at a slight slope. Cut the relieved areas (or rounded areas) for the sleeves, then cut a neck opening that is deeper in the front than in the rear.

You can sew a piece of soft leather around the neck opening or cut a slit in the front and close the shirt with tied thongs. A more traditional method of making a Plains shirt consisted of leaving a neck flap of triangular leather from the tail of the animal. Sometimes the tail itself was also left on. This neck flap was folded down in front and was often decorated with bead or quill work. An adaptation of this method featured a triangular or rectangular piece of leather or in some cases trade cloth sewn at the front of the neck.

To find the circumference needed for the arms, measure the person's flexed biceps and add two inches. This will be the greatest circumference for the sleeve. The sleeves can be tapered toward the wrist as desired. Measure the sleeve length from the top point of the shoulder to the bend of the wrist. Sleeves should be fairly long to allow the elbow to bend. Cut fringe pieces to be added between the sleeve seams or at the shoulders if desired.

To assemble the shirt, sew the shoulders together, inside out, using a whip stitch and adding a welt between the layers. Sew the sleeves to the shoulder areas, wrong side out, using a whip stitch and inserting a fringe piece or welt between the layers. Sew the sleeves together, along with a fringe piece or welt, wrong side out with a whip stitch. Continue the seam down the side. A fringe piece or welt can also be added to the side seam. Sew the other side in the same manner. Finally, cut all the fringe on the fringe pieces. Cut the shirt square across the bottom, adding fringe if desired.

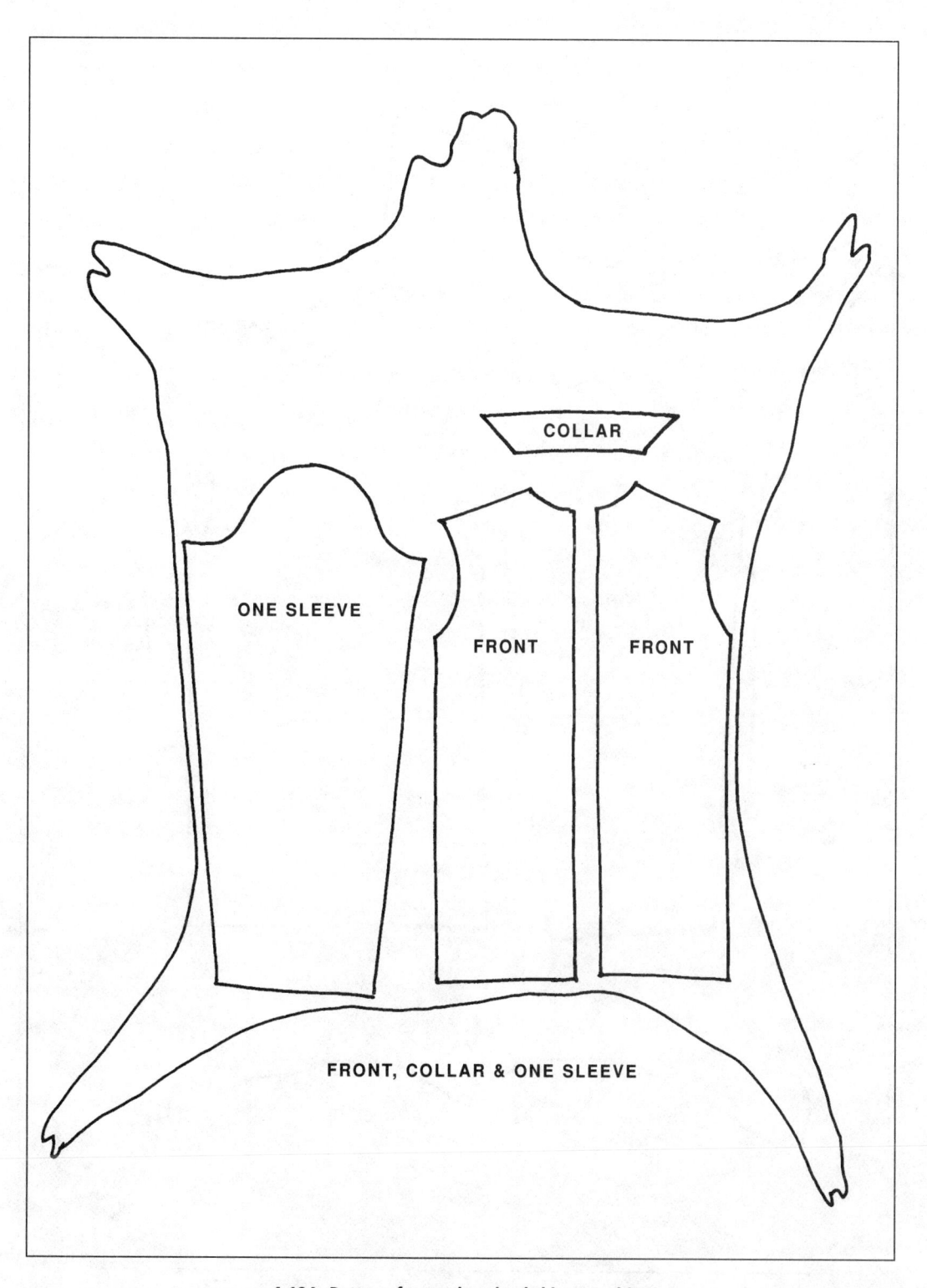

4-19A. Pattern for modern buckskinner's shirt.

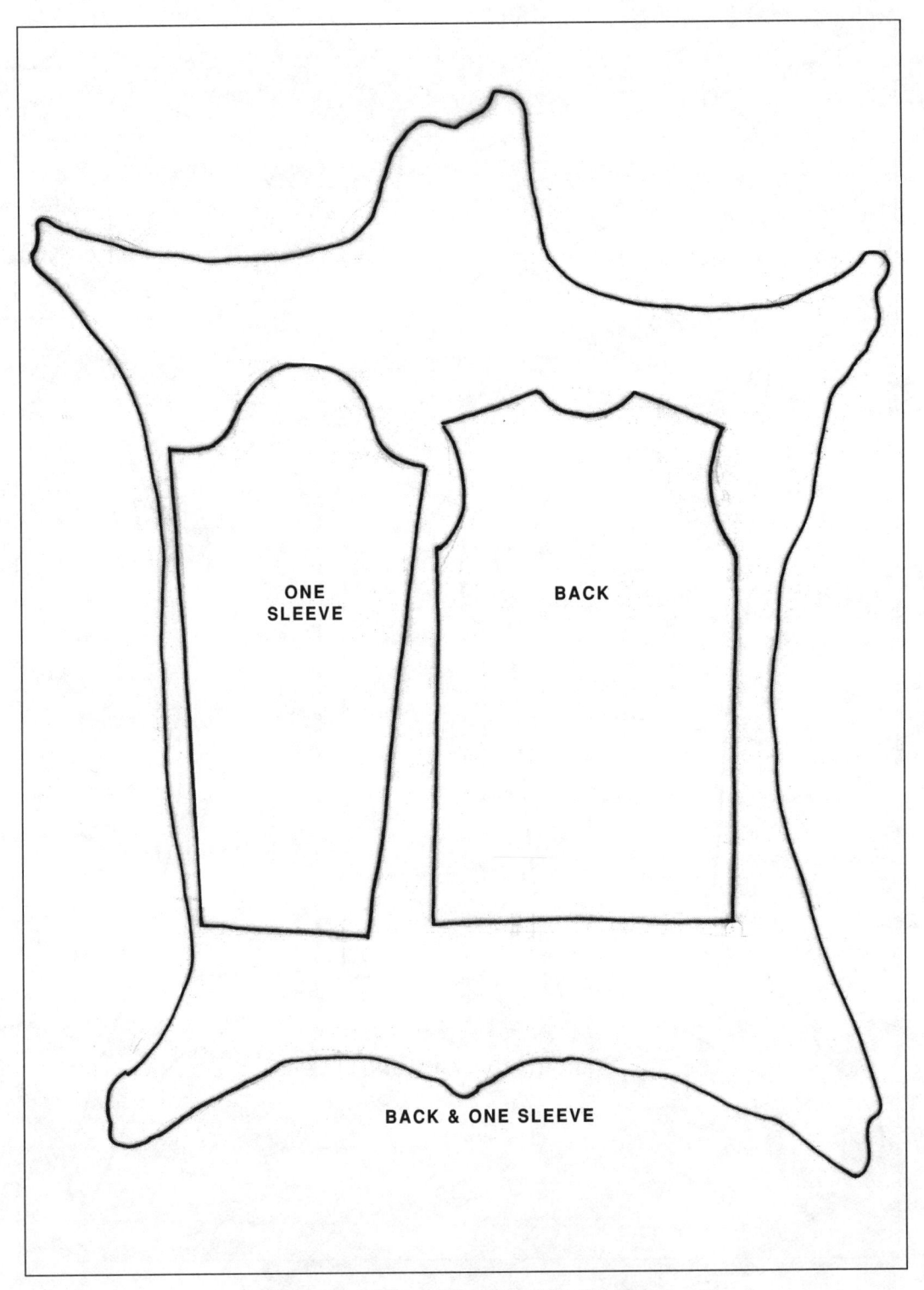

4-19B. Pattern for modern buckskinner's shirt.

66

LEATHER PROJECTS

BUCKSKIN JACKET

The settlers and buckskinners often wore an open jacket over a homespun cloth shirt. The construction of the jacket is basically the same as for the plains shirt, but the front consists of two pieces closed with thong ties or buttons (figs. 4-19A and 4-19B). The jacket also has a simple collar. Traditionally, these jackets were either laced with thong or sewn with waxed threads. Fringe pieces were laced or sewn in as the garment was constructed. The mountain men copied much of the decorations of the Plains tribes on their jackets as well (fig. 4-20).

LEGGINGS

Leather leggings were the covering for the lower portion of the body for both Native American women and men of the Plains and Woodland tribes (fig. 4-21). The leggings for men extended from the hip to the heel, while the leggings for women typically came only to the knee.

4-20. Mountain men quickly adapted the long-sleeved shirt as have modern buckskinners.

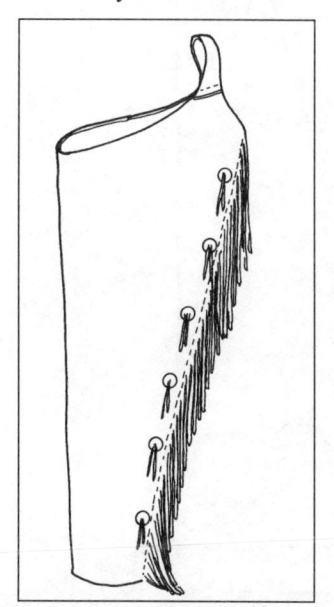

4-21. Leather leggings were common apparel of Native Americans. A wide variety of styles existed.

Each legging was made from a single animal skin folded over and sewn or laced together down the side. The rear legs on the skin were used to tie the leggings to a waist thong. Some Plains tribes utilized the neck skin as a trailing piece. Although the leggings could be tapered from thigh to ankle, some tribes made them more square, like chaps.

The first step in making leggings is to measure from the top of the person's thigh or hipbone to the ankle (fig. 4-22). Fold the rear legs of the skin over and fasten them together with a thong. Measure the overall length of the legging from the top of this loop. To determine the circumference of a tapered legging, measure around the thigh and the ankle. Add two inches to the length for the break at the ankle, then add two inches lengthwise for the seam. Mark this taper on the outside of each side of the legging. With wrong sides together, sew along the marked line with a double running stitch. The excess material outside of the seam can either be cut off or cut into fringe. Finally, add quill or beadwork as desired.

Men also wore breechclouts of either leather or trade cloth over the leggings. These breechclouts were simple pieces folded over a leather belt or thong tied around the waist (fig. 4-23). The leggings

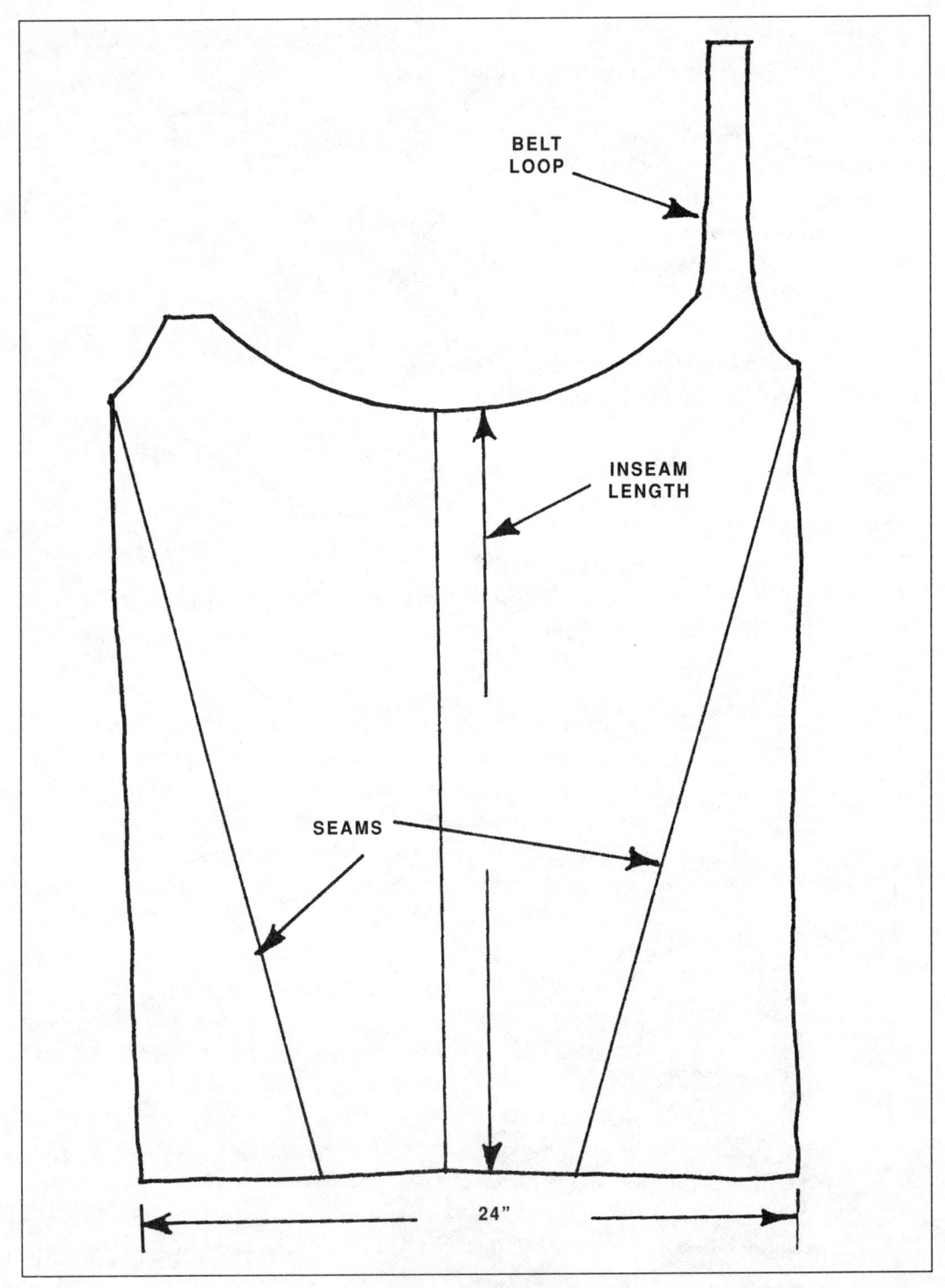

4-22. Legging pattern.

Leather Projects

were attached to the same waist thong.

Breechclouts are also very simple to make. Simply cut a piece of leather to a rectangular shape. The length is about fourteen to eighteen inches each for the front and the back flaps plus the length needed for the crotch area. The width should be about fourteen to sixteen inches. This piece is then wrapped between the legs and held in place with the waist thong.

Leather Pants

Leather buckskinning pants can be made in the same manner as the shirts. To start, either purchase a sewing pattern or take apart a pair of pants that fit well. Leather pants shouldn't be too tight, but they also aren't as loose as dress slacks. They should fit more like a comfortable pair of old jeans (fig. 4-24). When laying out the pattern on the skins, the top of the pants should

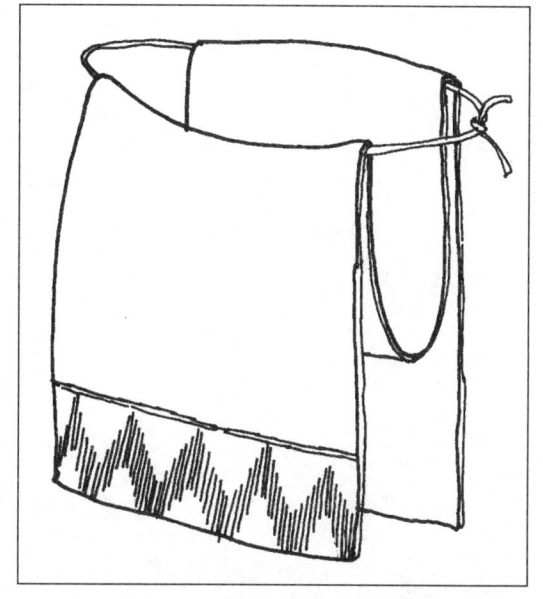

4-23. Breechclouts of either leather or trade cloth were utilized with the leggings. All were often beaded or quilled.

be at the neck end of the skin and the ankle at the tail of the skin. It will take several skins to make a pair of pants, depending on the skin sizes and the pants size (figs. 4-25A and 4-25B). If the skins aren't long enough, pants are usually seamed in the knee area and fringe added to the seam. If two pieces are needed for each leg, sew these together first. Cut the pants front with the fly piece attached to each side. Each fly piece will be folded under for extra support for the buttons and the button holes without an extra seam.

Cut the scooped front for the pocket and a one-piece inside pocket. Stitch the pocket lining directly to the inside of the pants with a running stitch around the edge of the pocket. Attach the front pockets and the rear patch pockets first, then sew the side seams from the inside with a whip stitch, adding a fringe piece or welt down the seam as desired.

With right sides together, stitch the front pieces together along the crotch seam below the fly opening with a double running stitch and a welt added for strength. Stitch the back pieces together in the same manner, adding a welt for strength. With

4-24. Mountain men adapted leggings into leather pants.

the pants turned wrong side out, match the crotch seams. Starting at the crotch, sew down each leg with a whip stitch or double running stitch. A welt can be added in the crotch and thigh area for added strength.

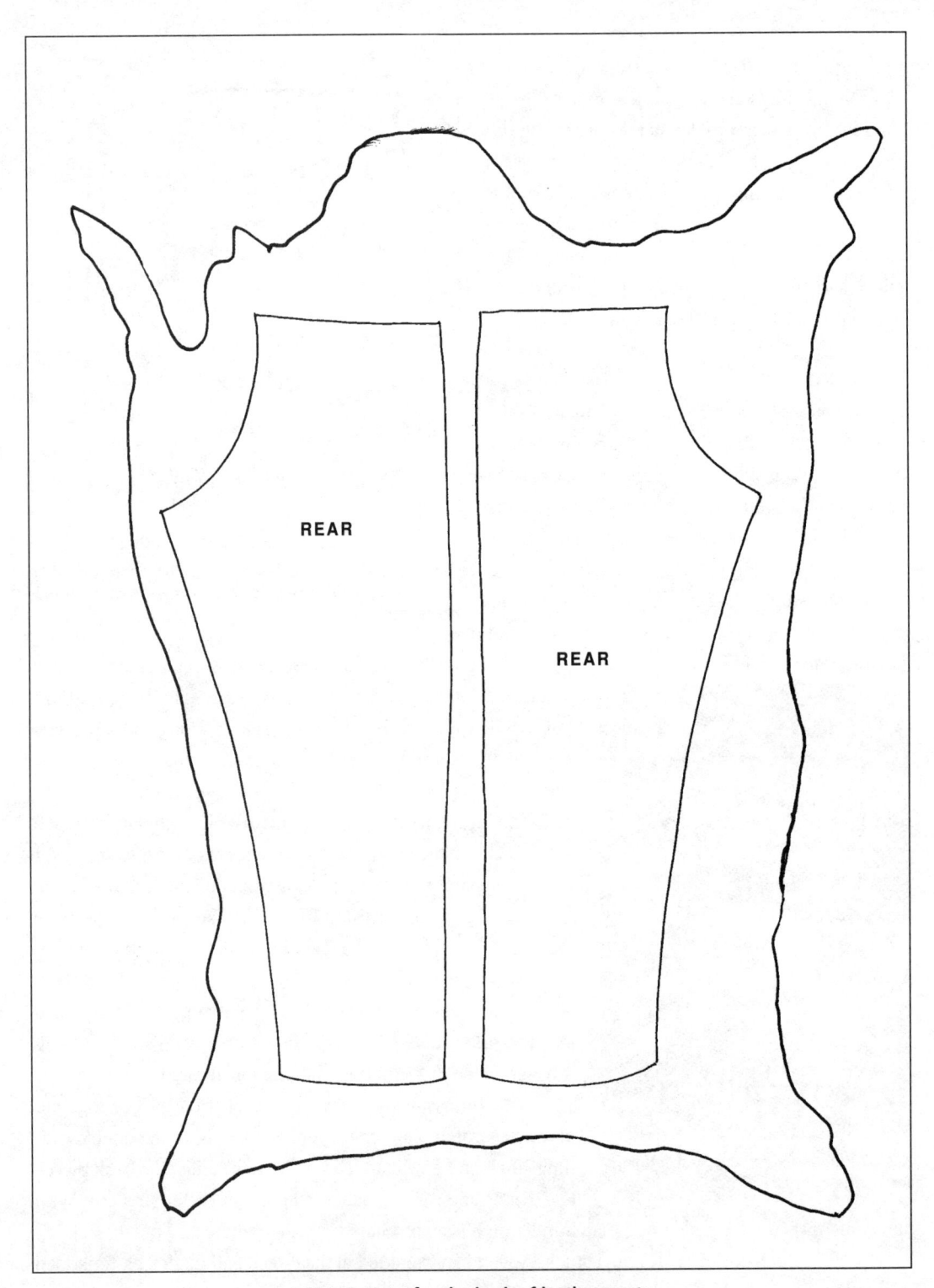

4-25A. Pattern for the back of leather pants.

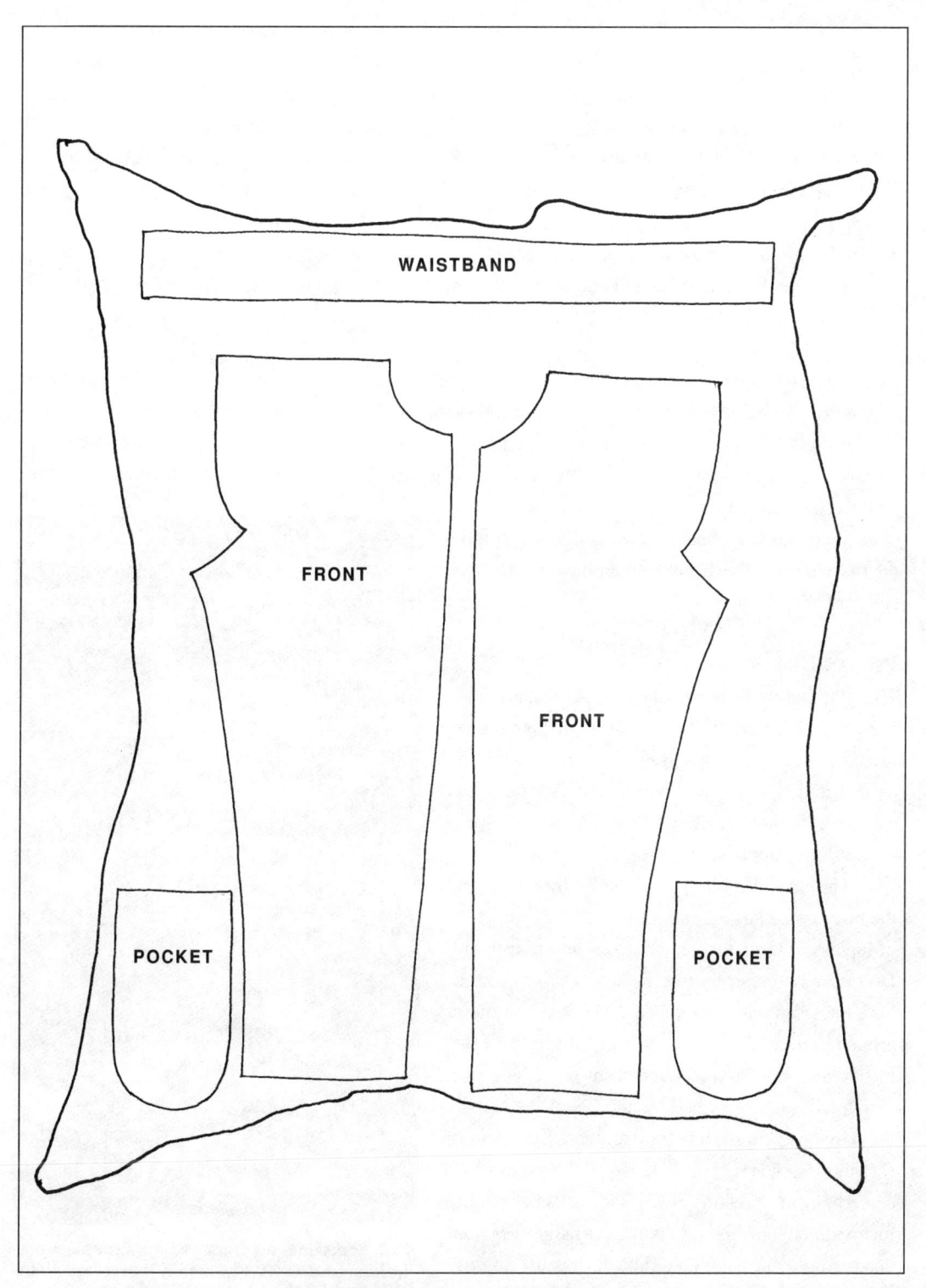

4-25B. Pattern for the front of leather pants.

Antler, Bone, Horn & Hide

Be sure to dry fit the pants as they are constructed and adjust as needed. Fold each fly piece back and stitch it from the outside with a running stitch. Cut holes for buttons and attach the buttons with heavy waxed thread. Be careful to not cut the buttonholes too large because the leather will stretch with use.

A double, folded over, waistband is best. Cut a strip of leather twice as wide as needed for the waistband and long enough to lap over and button in the front. Fold the leather lengthwise and stitch it to the pants with a running stitch, adding belt loops as needed. Stitch a second row of running stitches around the top of the waistband, sew in a button, and stitch in the tops of the belt loops. Cut a buttonhole on one end of the waistband and at the other end trim the leg bottoms to the correct length.

Skin Dresses

Skin dresses in a wide variety of designs were worn by the women of most Native American tribes (fig. 4-26). Some dresses were quite simple and others much more elaborate. The Plains design utilized two elk hides with the tails of the hide up in the neck of the dress. These tails were often folded down to create a neck flap. In later years, a yoke was added between the skins, but even those styles often left a loop of skin where the tail had once hung. Rows of beads were used as decoration on the yoke by the Blackfeet. Following are two styles of skin dresses.

Plains Dress

This dress style is extremely easy to make. You'll need two skins, from small to large, depending on the dress size. The skins used for a dress should be as thin and light as possible. Otherwise, the dress can be extremely uncomfortable. A one- to two-ounce skin is about right.

The dress width is determined by measuring the body at the largest circumference—chest, waist, or hips. Add three inches for seams and movement. Divide this number by two. This gives the width of both the front and back pieces. Measure the upper arm circumference with the biceps flexed. Add two inches and divide that number by two. The arm length will be determined by the size of the skins.

Lay one skin flesh side up and make the pattern for the back (fig. 4-27). To do so, mark a centerline on the skin. Then mark a neck opening just wide enough for the garment to slip over your head. Angle the shoulder line downward slightly. Mark one half the measurement for the upper arm

4-26. Buckskin dresses ranged from simple work dresses to dresses elaborately decorated with beadwork, quillwork, bones, and shells.

TAIL-CUT OFF OR FOLDED DOWN

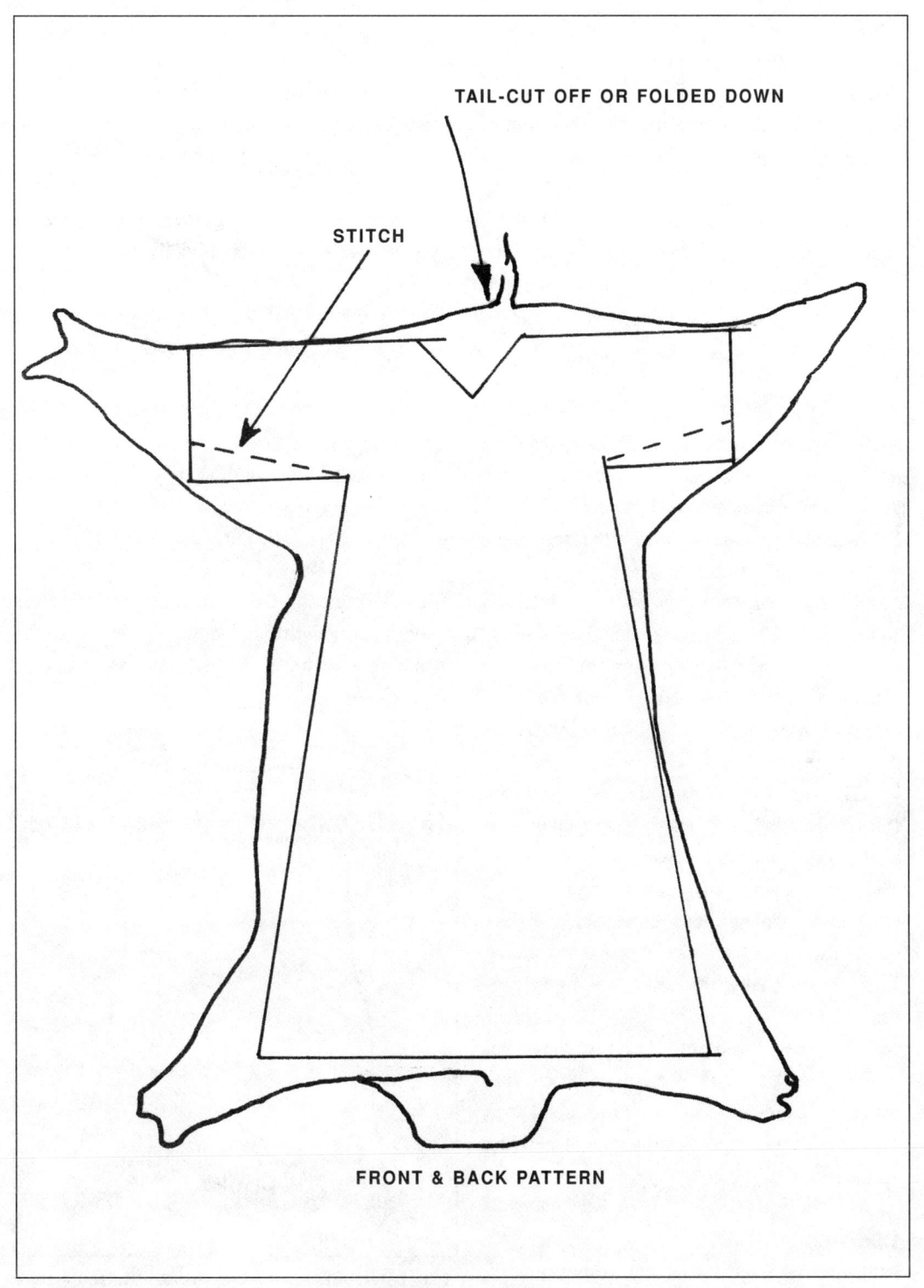

STITCH

FRONT & BACK PATTERN

4-27. Plains Dress Pattern

and draw a line with a straightedge. Repeat on the opposite side for the other arm. From the centerline of the back, measure out one half the width for the back on each side and mark. Then use a straightedge to mark the sides. The dress can be cut straight or flared from the hips down.

Mark the pattern for the front in the same way. The neck opening can be cut in the same manner as the back or the skin can be simply folded down in the old style.

The two pieces can be punched and laced or sewn together with a running stitch. With the pieces right side out, sew across the top of the shoulders, then sew under the arms, and finally down the sides with a running stitch .

Cut the material extending past the sewn area under the arms and sides into fringe strips. The sleeves and dress bottom can also be cut in fringe. Add beading or quill work as desired.

YOKE DRESS

Adding a yoke to the top of a dress makes it more comfortable and also adds more opportunities for decoration (fig. 4-28). With the yoke design, you can also add full-length sleeves to the dress if desired. Three large hides are required for this type of dress. Again, make sure the hides are extremely lightweight. One hide is used for the front and one hide for the back. The third hide is turned at ninety degrees and used for the yoke.

The side measurements for the front and back are determined in the same manner as the dress above (fig. 4-29). Remember that the yoke will add additional length. The bottom can be cut to the length desired after construction. In most instances, the yoke or top shoulder piece extends down equally over the front and back of the body pieces. The length can be adjusted there as desired.

The first step in assembly is to sew the sides of the front and back pieces together with a whip stitch and welt, sewing wrong side out. Then fold the yoke skin together lengthwise and cut a neck opening in the center. Sew the yoke to the front and back pieces using a running stitch. Traditionally, this seam was often concealed by beads or quill work.

The sleeves (the yoke piece hanging over the shoulder) and bottom can then be cut into fringe as desired. The underside of the sleeves can also be stitched or tied together, depending on the length of the yoke.

LEATHER VEST

Although we associate leather vests primarily with cowboys, later Native Americans also wore

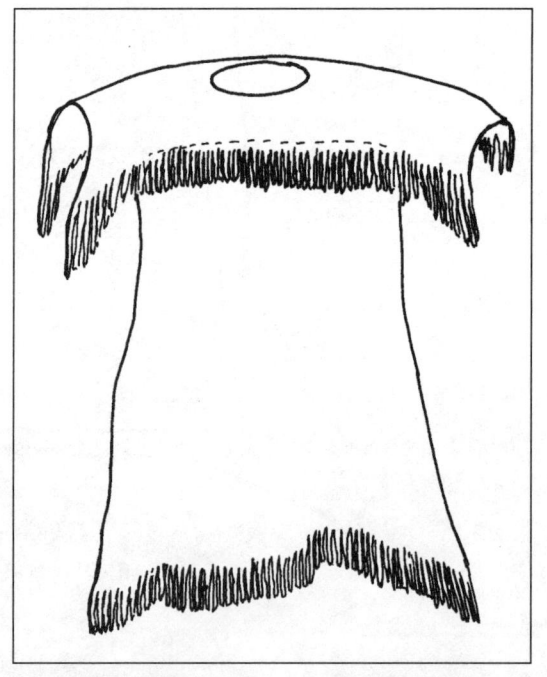

4-28. Later Native American dresses utilized a third skin as a yoke at the top.

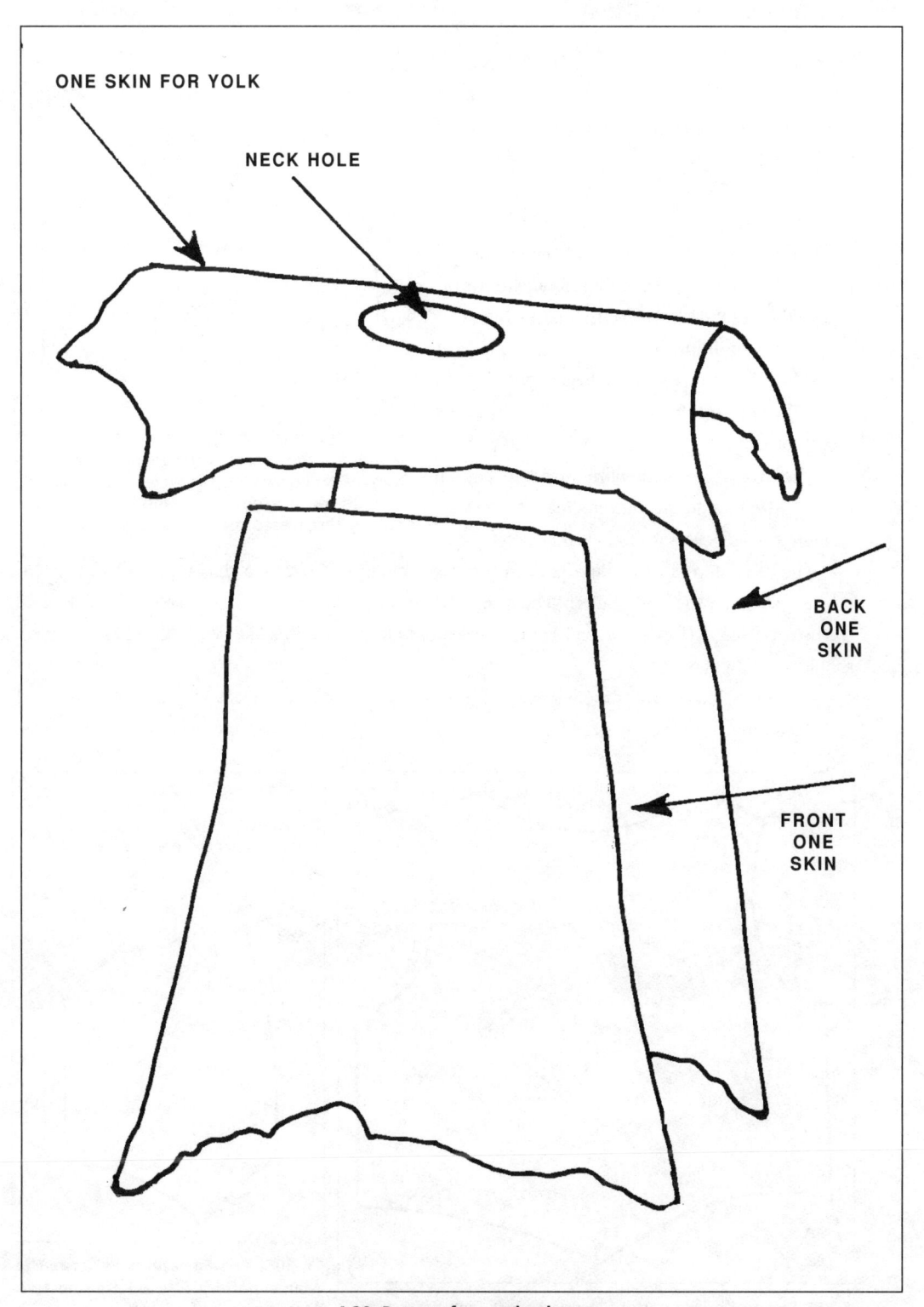

4-29. Pattern for a yoke dress.

them. Many of these vests were highly decorated, often fully beaded. Another popular style of the Old West was a vest made from the skin of unborn calves. I hunted with one cowboy-outfitter in Colorado who owned a handmade cowhide vest. According to him, the vest was invaluable. It protected him from thorns, brush, and other dangers while going about his work, and it also provided "layering" just as modern-day outdoor clothing does. Vests can be made of several different types of leather, depending on whether they are to be mostly decorative or purely protective.

The vest shown is a fairly standard pattern (fig. 4-30A). Add accoutrements as desired, including buttons, snaps, ties, even pockets.

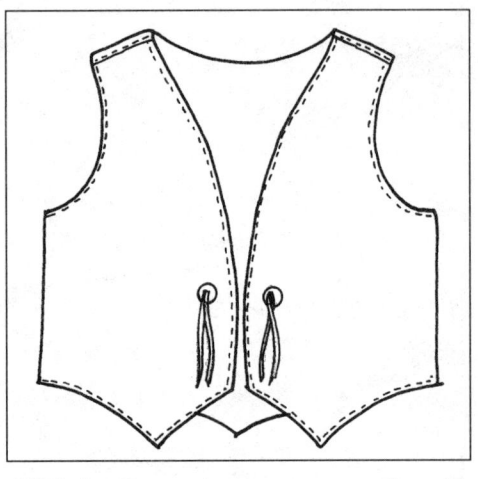

4-30A. Leather vests were very popular with Native Americans. They were often heavily beaded or quilled. The American cowboys quickly discovered their versatility.

The first step is to make a pattern. Disassemble an old oversize shirt or, better yet, an old unlined jacket for the basic pattern. The basic pattern shown utilizes a yoke with a single back piece and two front pieces (figs. 4-30B and 4-30C). These yoke pieces add needed fullness to the chest and back shoulder area without darts.

Cut all the pieces from the leather and join the back and front pieces with a whip stitch and welt, stitching from the inside. Place the yoke pieces so they overlap the back and front pieces

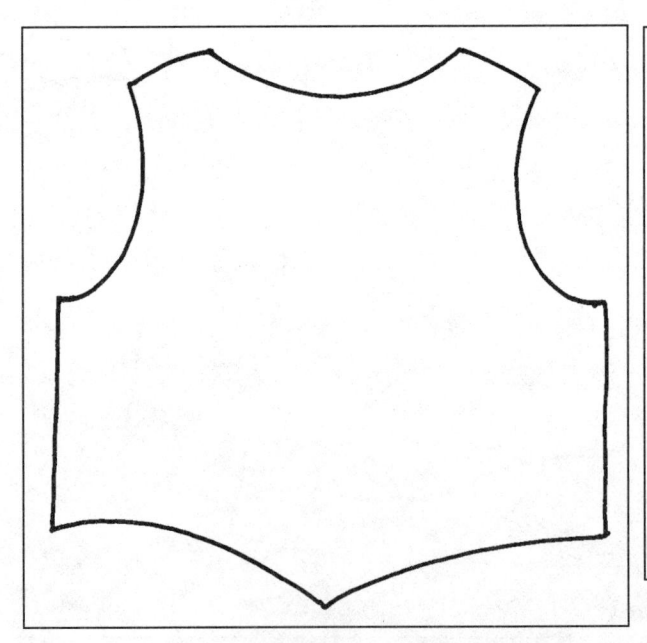

4-30B. Pattern for the back of the two-piece vest pattern.

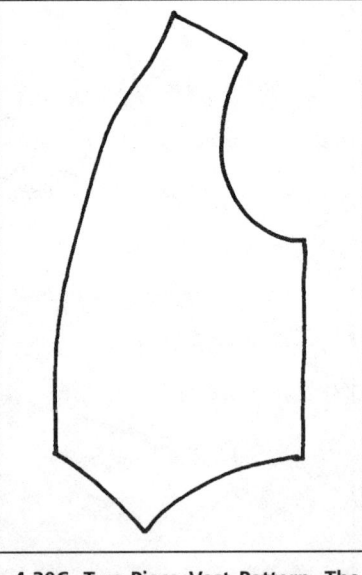

4-30C. Two-Piece Vest Pattern. The same pattern is used for the two front pieces of a leather vest.

Leather Projects

and attach them with exposed running stitches. The edges can be trimmed and other items added for decoration.

Chaps

Chaps were another extremely important item of clothing in the Old West. These leather leg coverings protected a cowboy from thorns, the sharp horns of longhorn cattle, and flying hooves during branding and other cattle-working chores. Chaps are just as important to today's cowboys, ranchers, and outfitters—anyone who has to deal day-to-day with horses and livestock (fig. 4-31). Typically, chaps are made of unsplit cowhides, although sheepskins were also used in the Old West. Chaps consist of a single piece of heavy leather cut using basically the same method as for cutting leggings. On chaps, however, the outside of the bottom portion extends further outward for more protection. The inner portion was once held in place with leather ties. These days, snaps are more often used. Chaps are fastened to a belt so both sides can easily be put on or removed at the same time. ∎

4-31. Leather chaps are just as important to today's cowboys as to yesterday's.

TOOLS AND MATERIALS FOR
Leather Footwear Projects

- Awl or rotary punch
- Cloth tape measure
- Cutting board, large plastic
- Felt-tip pen
- Four-hole stamp
- Glovers linen thread
- Heavy cloth
- Leather
- Paper
- Square
- Stiff cardboard
- Stiff paper
- Straightedge
- Tape to hold patterns in place
- Thong lacing
- Utility knife, skinning knife, or razor knife

5
LEATHER FOOTWEAR

Leather has been used for footwear since mankind first learned to utilize animal skins. Sandals were popular with many early peoples, including the Romans. Some Native American tribes of the Southwest also had sandals made with rawhide soles. Moccasins were popular footwear for many Native American tribes. The name comes from the Algonquin people on the New England coast and was picked up by the settlers. Several different styles of moccasins were developed, depending on the terrain and climate of the different regions. Moccasin styles representative of several regions are shown.

For the most part, moccasins were made of tanned leather with the hair or fur removed. The hides were commonly brain tanned, then smoked to produce a water resistant leather. The resulting leather was browner than tanned leather in the white stage.

MOCCASINS

It's fairly easy and fun to make your own footwear (fig. 5-1). Footwear can be made of tanned deer or elk skin, suede, leather, or leather or suede look-alike materials. Moccasins can be one piece or made with a rawhide or latigo sole. If you are purchasing commercial leather, a two- to three-ounce chrome-tanned cowhide is a good choice. Moccasins are usually made from the back area of the hide rather than the belly or flank because the back area provides a more sturdy leather. Split suede also makes great moccasins.

5-1. Center seam moccasins are the easiest to make, but the least comfortable because of the seam on top of the foot.

Regardless of the style of moccasin to be made, it's important to first make a sizing pattern for your foot (fig. 5-2). With some variations, this foot-size pattern can be used for all the moccasin styles. Make a pattern for one foot, then simply reverse the pattern for the opposite foot.

Place a piece of fairly stiff paper, such as a brown paper sack, on the floor and trace around your foot with a felt-tip pen. Mark a line through the approximate center of the foot (line A-A). This will be the overall length of the leather piece needed but will vary somewhat with the different moccasin

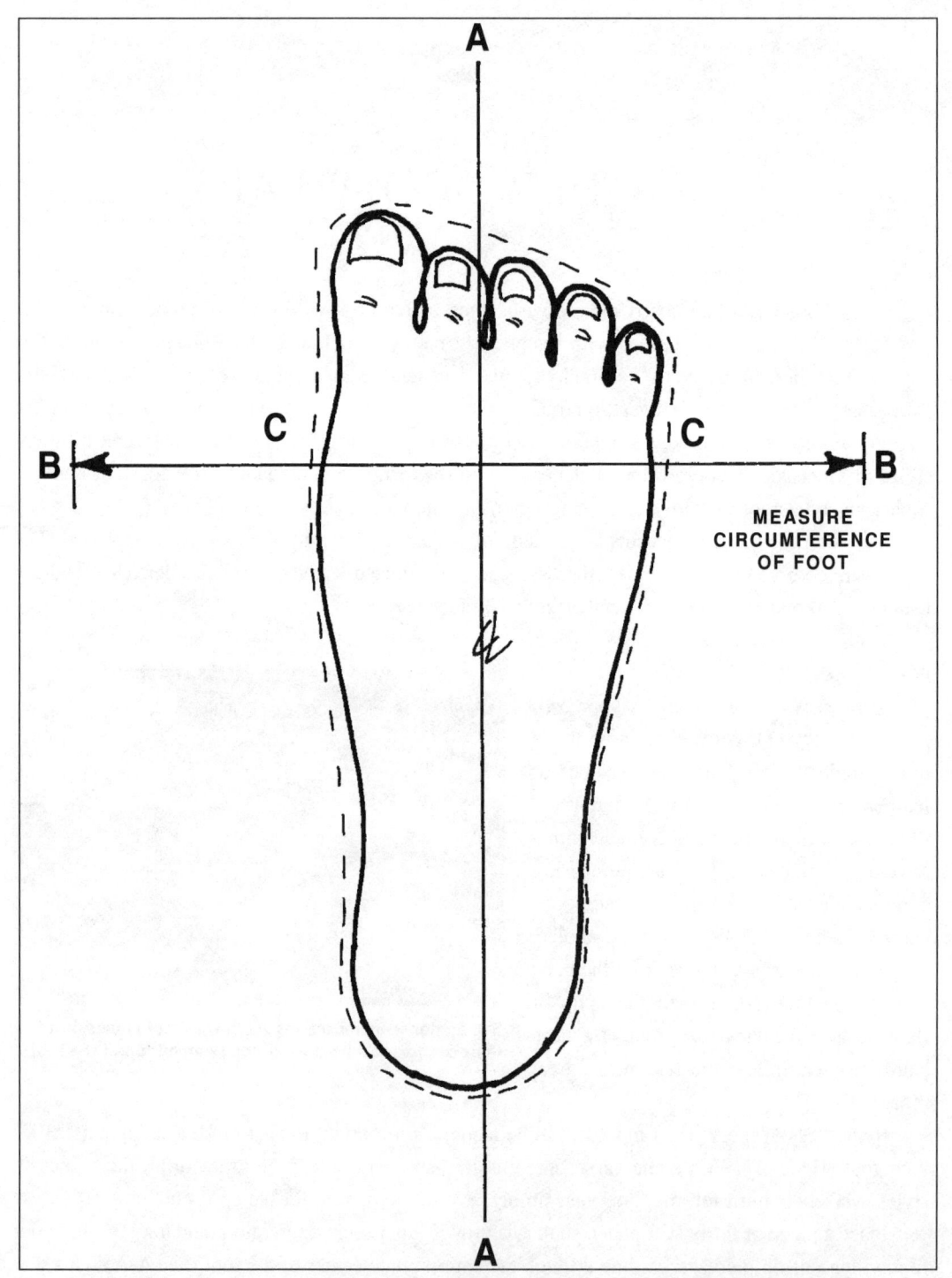

5-2. Before making moccasins, a sizing pattern should be made of your foot. Simply draw around your foot onto a piece of stiff paper. Line B-B is the circumference of your foot just behind the big toe.

Leather Footwear

designs. Use a cloth tape measure to measure the circumference of your foot at the widest point (usually just above the base of the big toe). Find the center of the measurement and mark it at line A-A. Mark the circumference of your foot at the ends of line B-B. Line C-C is the width of your foot plus one-half-inch at each side. Make a copy of your foot outline onto a piece of stiff cardboard and cut it out. Then reverse the pattern and cut a cardboard pattern for the other foot.

One trick is to first create the moccasins from heavy cloth, making sure they fit, then unstitch the cloth version and use the cloth pieces as patterns. This method is much easier than trying to rework the leather when the moccasin doesn't fit. Once you get a good-fitting pattern, save it for future use.

Now you're ready to start creating your moccasins. Lay the leather on a smooth flat surface you can use for cutting. A large plastic kitchen cutting board makes a good place to cut the leather without ruining a tabletop surface. Before cutting, lay the pattern on the leather and make sure there are no holes, gashes, or defects in the leather that could cause problems in the finished moccasin. Once you have the pattern in place, tape the pattern to the leather and mark around it with a felt-tip pen. Cut the leather using a sharp utility knife, skinning knife, or razor knife, following the pattern.

Stitching Styles

Most soft-sole moccasins are stitched together wrong side out. This not only somewhat conceals the stitching but also protects the stitching and provides longer life to the footwear. Whip stitching can be used, but the threads will be exposed. Adding a welt to the whip stitch conceals the stitching. A glovers stitch hides the stitching as well. More stitching details are included in chapter 4. Rawhide or heavy leather moccasin soles are usually stitched to the softer uppers right side out using a whip stitch thorugh lacing holes punched in the heavy leather. The whip stitch can be straight or at an angle. Adding a welt in the seam can provide a stronger, longer-lasting seam.

Soft-Soled Eastern Woodlands Moccasin Styles

The Eastern Woodlands moccasins were made from a single piece of leather and were traditionally

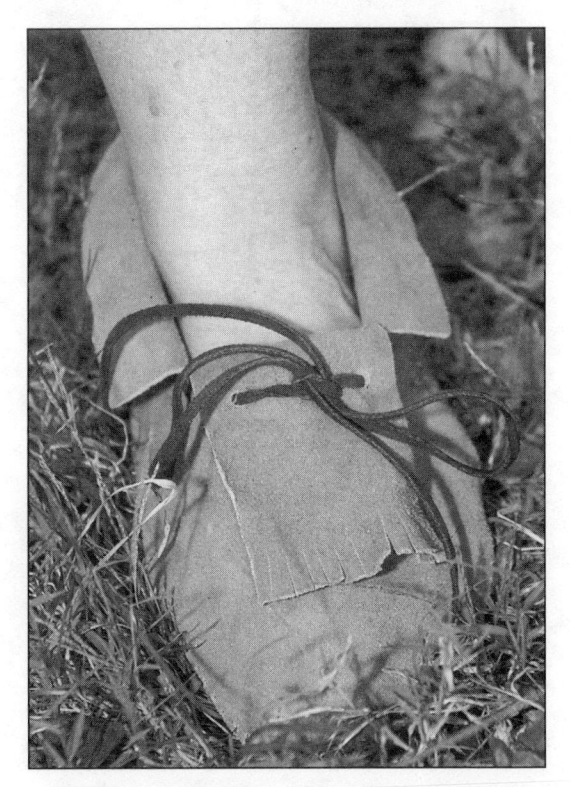

5-3. Some of the most common moccasins are side-seam style. These are fairly comfortable and easy to make.

made in three styles: with a center seam, a side seam (fig. 5-3), or a puckered toe seam. A cuff was often added by the Winnebago and Chippewa.

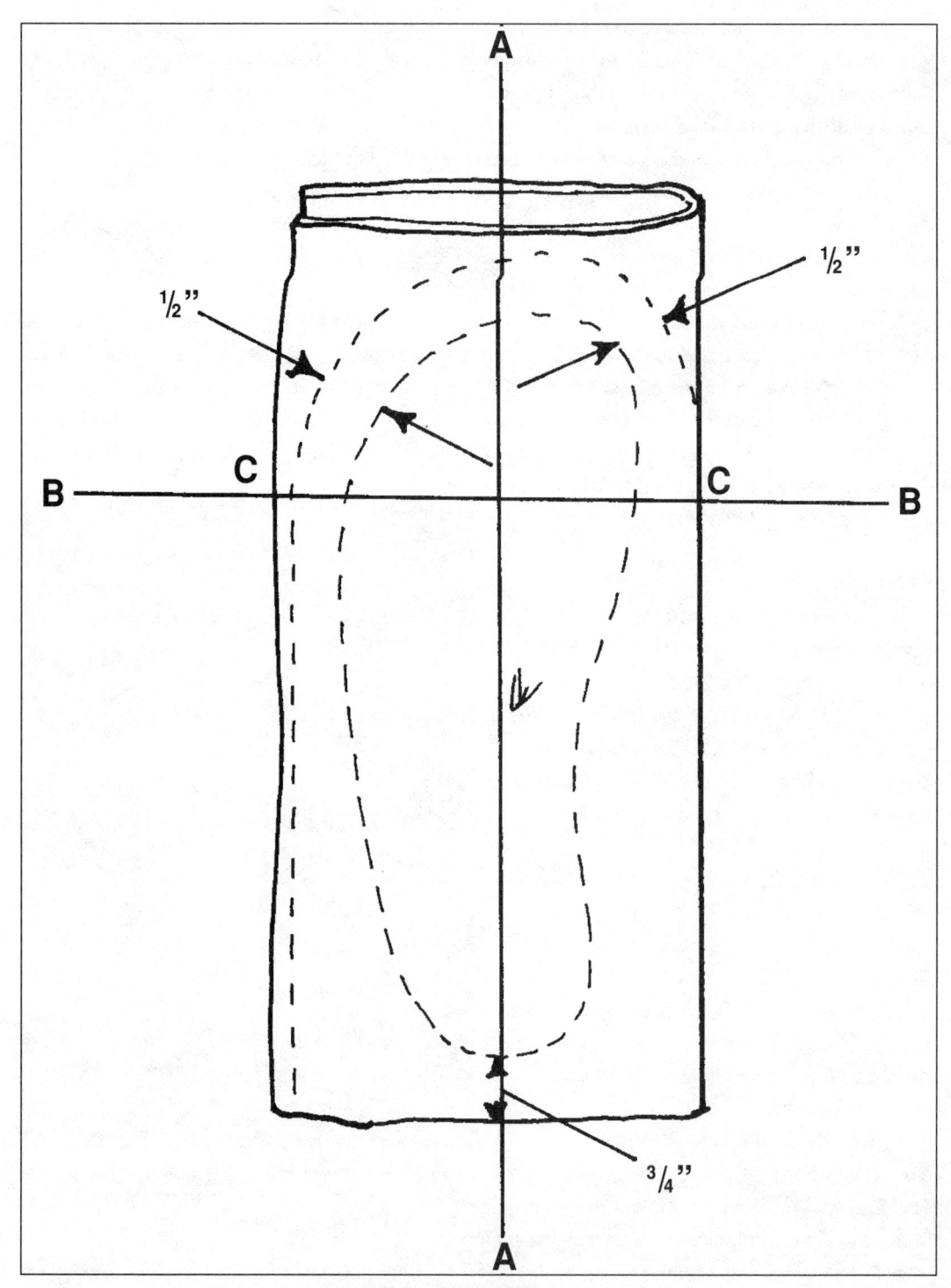

5-4A. Pattern for side-seam moccasin.

Leather Footwear

Side-Seam Moccasins

For side-seam moccasins, you'll need a piece of leather that when folded in half is large enough to cover your foot. Fold the leather over and place the cardboard pattern on the leather positioned with line B-B one-half inch from the folded edge (fig. 5-4A). Mark a line one-half inch outside of B-B for the outer side of your foot. Line A-A should be increased by one-half inch at the top for your toe and one inch at the bottom for your heel. Then mark an arc around your toe pattern and down to the side of your foot. Mark straight down to the end of the material. This is the basic pattern. Unfold the leather and cut one side. Refold and mark, then cut the opposite side.

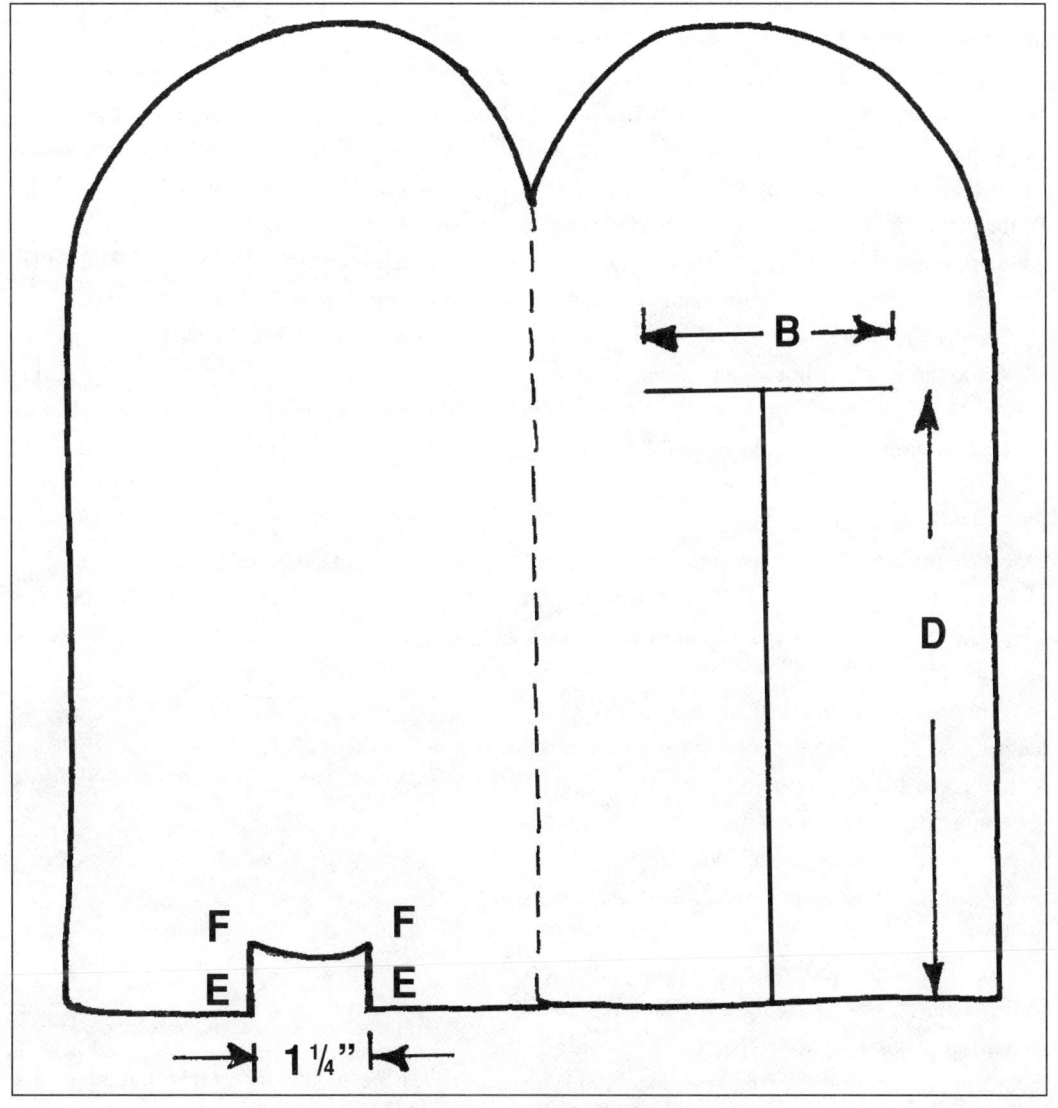

5-4B. Pattern for side-seam moccasin.

Unfold the cut piece of leather and lay it inside out. Position the cardboard pattern on the right side of the leather with the heel of the pattern about 3/4 inch from the bottom of the material and centered in the pattern (fig. 5-4B).

Mark line F-F about 1-1/4 inch long in an arc matching your heel pattern. Then mark from each end straight down to the end of the leather, line E-E.

Reposition the cardboard pattern on the left hand side of the leather piece. Remember, it must be reversed. Make sure the pattern is centered and positioned the same distance from the bottom edge of the leather. Turn the leather wrong side out (the lines drawn on the outside). Starting at the toe, sew around the side seam. A darning needle with natural sinew, artificial sinew, or waxed shoemakers linen thread can be used to sew the seam. If the leather is thick, you may also need an awl or small leather punch to create the holes for the thread.

Then turn the moccasin right side out, slip your foot into it, and check for fit. Continue to adjust and dry fit until you have the correct fit. Turn the moccasin wrong side out and sew up the heel, beginning at point F and sewing to point E on one side. Then stitch the other point F until both points E meet. Then finally, sew up the back of the moccasin going from the heel to the ankle. Stop and try fit the moccasin as you sew this seam to make sure you have the heel tight enough. You may want to gather or pull more material together or cut off some of the extra material at the heel for the best fit. One-piece, woodland-style moccasins should fit fairly snugly as they tend to expand with use.

In most instances, a tongue was traditionally added. The tongue should be cut in the basic pattern shown, to the width of line B, and sewn in place in the front between the side flaps. Cut thong lacing slits in the upper portion of the moccasin sides and around the back. Thread a piece of thong leather in place through the slits and use this to tie the moccasin in place.

Pucker-Toe Moccasins

Moccasins with pucker-stitched toes were also popular with the Woodland tribes of the East (fig. 5-5). In fact, the Chippewa tribe's name came from the phrase "people of the puckered moccasins." Other tribes who wore this type of moccasin included the Oneida and Iroquois. These moccasins were also soft-soled and fairly easy to make.

The pucker-toe moccasin consists of two pieces of leather, one making up the sole, sides, and heel with a second piece for the upper toe stitched in place. This style moccasin is actually a bit easier to fit than one-piece moccasins. A fairly soft piece of leather should be used in order to achieve nice, even stitching and puckering.

The first step is to lay the cardboard pattern on the leather with the inside facing up. Note the pattern is somewhat different from the previous side-seam moccasin pattern. In this case, a two-inch radius arc is marked from the tip of the toe to the inseam (fig. 5-6A).

5-5. Pucker-toe moccasins were popular with the woodland tribes of the East. These moccasins are more comfortable, but somewhat more difficult to make.

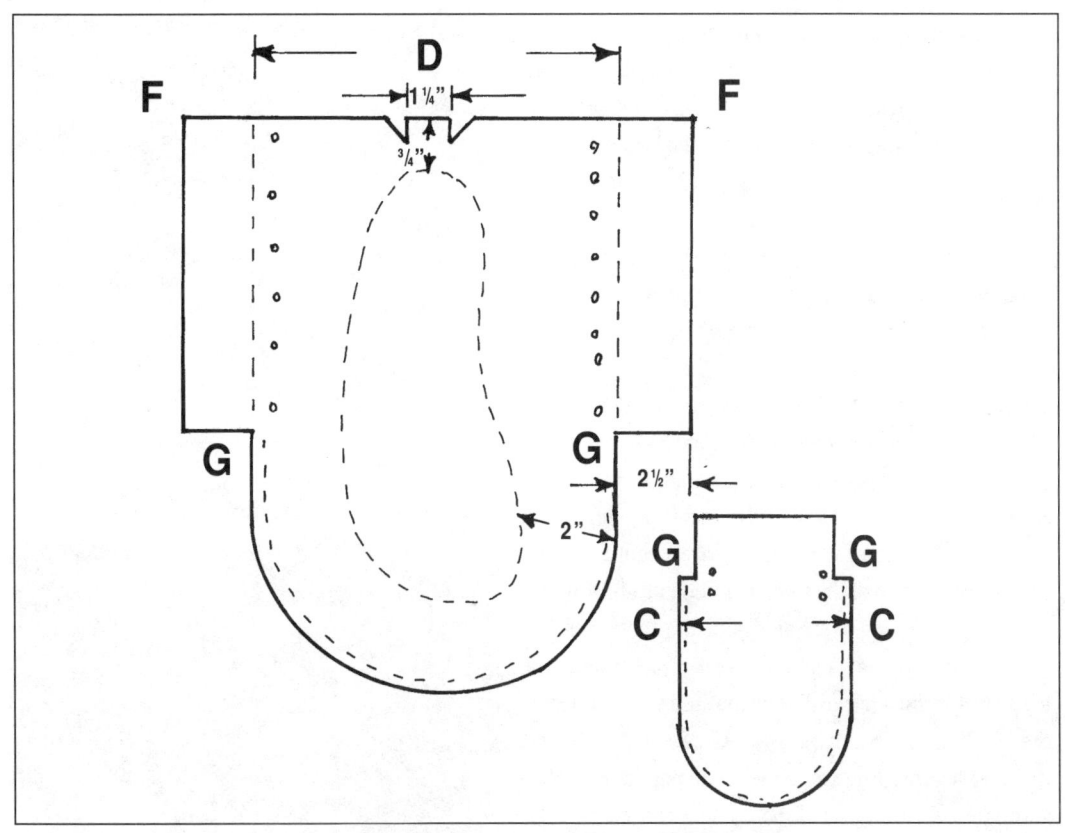

5-6A. Pattern for pucker-toe moccasins

The sides are also expanded approximately two inches past this line. Mark the heel cuts as shown in the diagram. Cut out the pattern following the lines marked. Use a straightedge and square to cut clean, straight lines.

Using the foot measurement, line B-B, from the original measuring pattern, determine the circumference of your foot at the ball of your foot area. The width of the top piece should be approximately the measurement of lines B-B less the measurement of line D. The length of the top piece will be from the end of the toe area to approximately the instep area plus two or three inches for a flap, if desired. The toe of the top piece should be rounded as shown.

Stitch the two pieces together starting at one corner and going around the toe area (fig. 5-6B). As the distance around the top piece is about half that around the bottom,

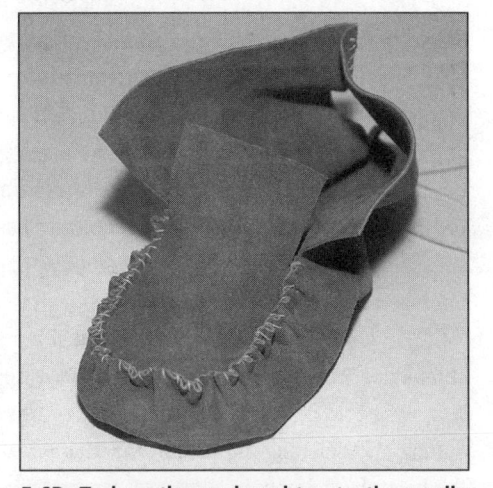

5-6B. To lace the puckered-toe to the smaller top piece requires counting stitches. Start by using a lacing stamp around the top piece, then count these and match the number of holes on the bottom piece. The hole on the bottom pucker piece will be spaced wider apart.

Antler, Bone, Horn & Hide

you'll need to pucker the bottom approximately every one-fourth inch. In order to do this, make the bottom stitches about twice as far apart as the upper stitches. Pulling the stitching tightly will pull the bottom material up over the top to create the puckered toe. After sewing the toe, sew up the heel (fig. 5-6C), then cut slits for the tie thongs and add them. Traditionally, the upper toe piece was often beaded, quilled, or embroidered before being stitched in place.

Center-Seam Moccasins

Moccasins with a center seam were primarily the footwear of the Woodland tribes and are very easy to construct (fig. 5-7). These moccasins are, however, somewhat less comfortable to wear because of the center seam on top of the foot. Traditionally, beadwork was often added to the toe alongside the center seam.

These moccasins are made of one piece of leather. A somewhat different method of laying out the cardboard pattern is used. Create a pattern by marking a centerline on a piece of paper. Lay the cardboard foot pattern directly over the centerline and draw around the foot outline (fig. 5-8).

Then flop the pattern to the other side of the centerline as shown and again mark around the pattern. Allow about one-fourth inch around each pattern, around the edge and along the centerline. Add one inch at the heel. Add flaps to each side from the instep area back to the heel. These side flaps are about one and one-half inches wide. Once the paper pattern has been

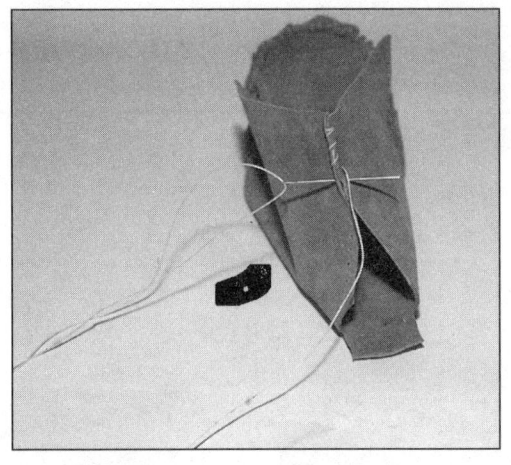

5-6C. Although not traditional, this heel is laced together on the outside for more comfort.

5-7. Footwear, including the moccasins of Native Americans, is one of the most common uses of leather. And it is one of the most popular projects of today's leather crafters.

determined and cut to shape, transfer the pattern to the leather and cut the moccasin outline. Both right and left moccasin are cut the same.

Sew the moccasin wrong side out. First fold the moccasin along the center, line D-F, and being stitching at point D. Sew to where the flaps meet at point E. Then stitch up the heel. Fold at F and begin sewing at F to points G. Note, the heel of this moccasin is rather pointed and a better fit is obtained by cutting and stitching the heel in the manner of the pucker toe and side seam moccasins. After stitching the heel, the pointed area at the floor could be folded up and stitched flat. Finally, punch holes for the lacing thongs following the dots on the pattern. Add the thongs and tie in front. The side flaps or toe area can be decorated if desired.

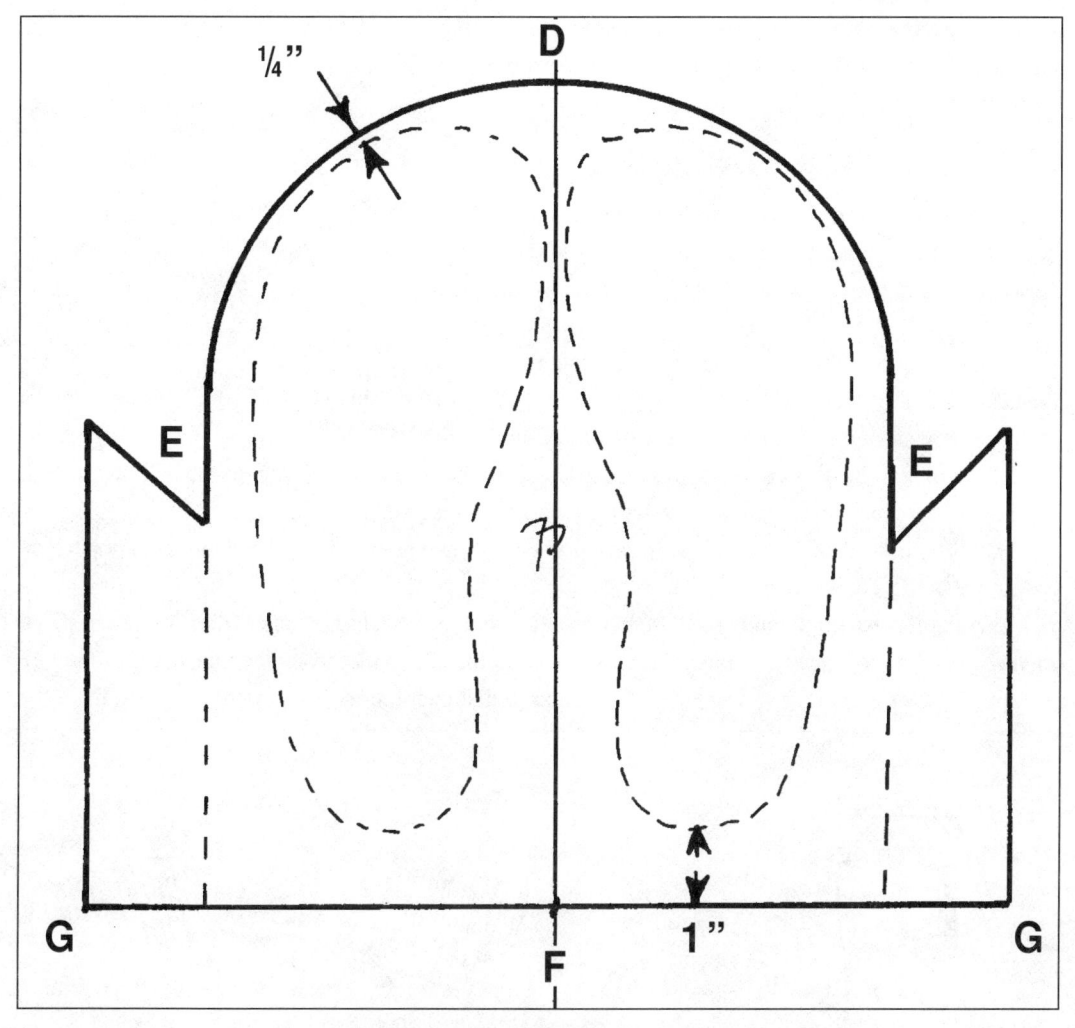

5-8. Pattern for center-seam moccasin.

PLAINS MOCCASINS

The moccasins of the Plains tribes, including the Blackfeet, Osage, and Sioux, were both soft and hard soled, with the hard-soled styles developed later. In some instances, the soles were attached to the outside bottom of completed moccasins; in other instances, the soles were sewn directly to the uppers. These moccasins were quite often heavily beaded or painted. Incidentally, the Blackfeet were given their name because of the coloring of their moccasins. The soft-soled moccasins were basically the same construction as the Woodland center and side seam moccasins.

HARD-SOLED PLAINS AND SOUTHWEST TRIBES MOCCASINS

Native Americans in the Southwest and some of the Plains tribes utilized rawhide soles stitched to buckskin uppers (fig. 5-9). Heavy harness leather can be substituted for rawhide in construction if desired. The hard soles protected the feet from the hard, rocky ground and from cactus. Some of these

ANTLER, BONE, HORN & HIDE

styles were low topped, others, such as those worn by the Kiowa and Apache, had higher tops for further cactus protection.

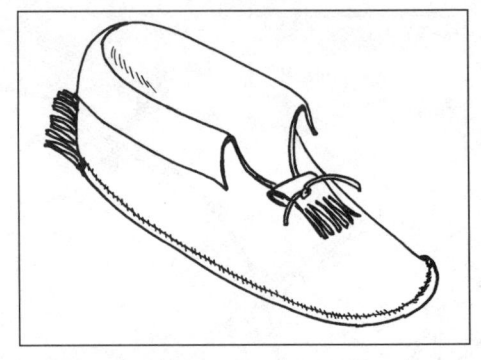

LOW-TOPPED HARD-SOLE MOCCASINS

The low-topped, hard-soled model has fringe at the heel. To create it, make the patterns on paper first (fig. 5-10). Two patterns are needed, one for the vamp, or upper piece, and one for the sole. The sole piece should be about one-fourth inch larger all around than the cardboard foot pattern.

Then transfer both patterns to the leathers and cut out the pieces. Line E-F is cut the approximate length of the foot from the heel to the ball of the foot. Line G-G is cut just slightly more than half the width of the foot at its widest.

Stitch the fringed heel area together from the outside. Stitch points D together and sew to point E on the outside with a double running stitch.

Sew the moccasin top and sole together wrong side out. Match the center front of the top piece to the center front of the sole. Match the center back of the sole with the center back seam of the top.

Begin sewing at the heel area and sew around to just past the instep on one side. Sew from the

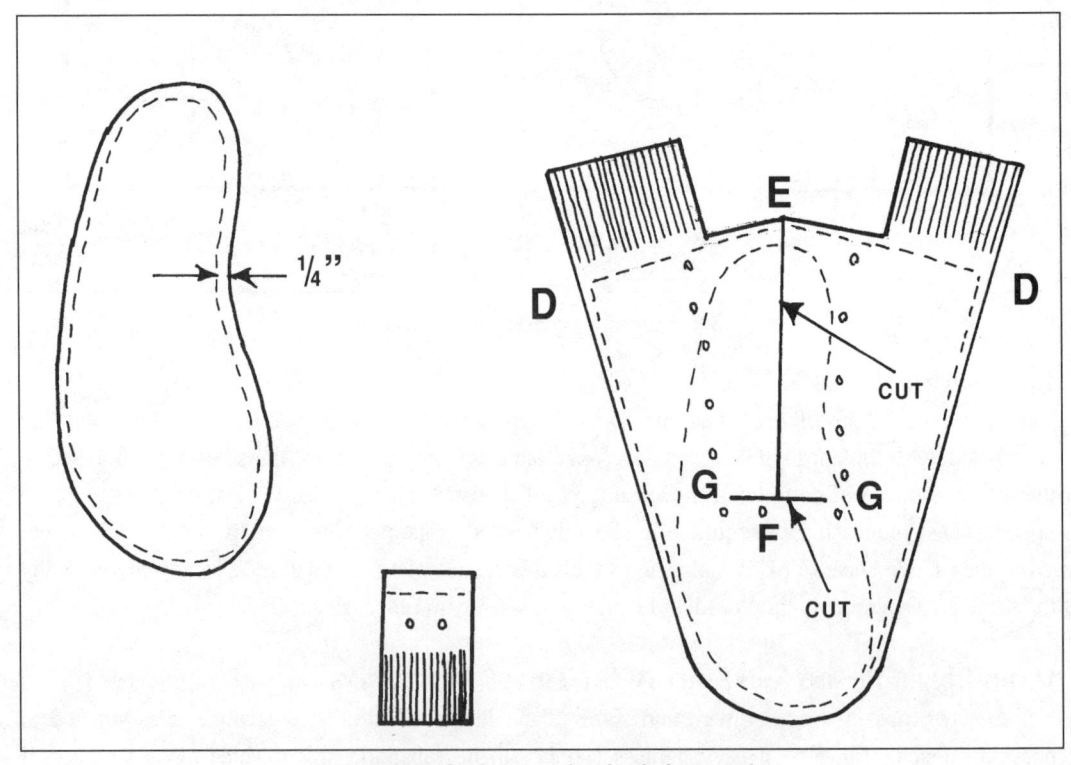

5-9. Hard-soled moccasins utilize heavy leather or rawhide for the soles. Shown is a low-top version.

5-10. Pattern for low-top, hard-soled moccasin.

Leather Footwear

heel forward on the opposite side. Then ease the front area of the top to the sole. The top will be slightly larger than the sole and is eased in evenly around the toe to add fullness for the toe area. After stitching, turn moccasin right side out.

Now add a fringed tongue. Cut this to the width of line G-G and to the desired length. Cut fringe on one end.

Sew the tongue in place with the wrong sides together so when the tongue folds forward the seam is between the tongue and the shoe top.

Finally, punch thong holes matching the dots on the pattern in the moccasin upper and in the tongue. Thread the thong through the holes and tie it in the front. Beading can be added to the flap edge or toe area.

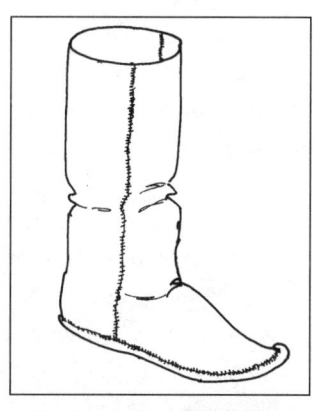

5-11. Moccasins of the desert country were often high-topped as well as hard soled.

High-Topped Hard-Sole Moccasins

The Apache, Salish (flathead), Arapaho, and Comanche moccasins were often high-topped and hard-soled. The Comanche and Arapaho women's moccasins were in fact, knee-high (fig. 5-11). The three-piece Apache moccasin utilizes a sole, front upper, and rear upper. In this case the sole

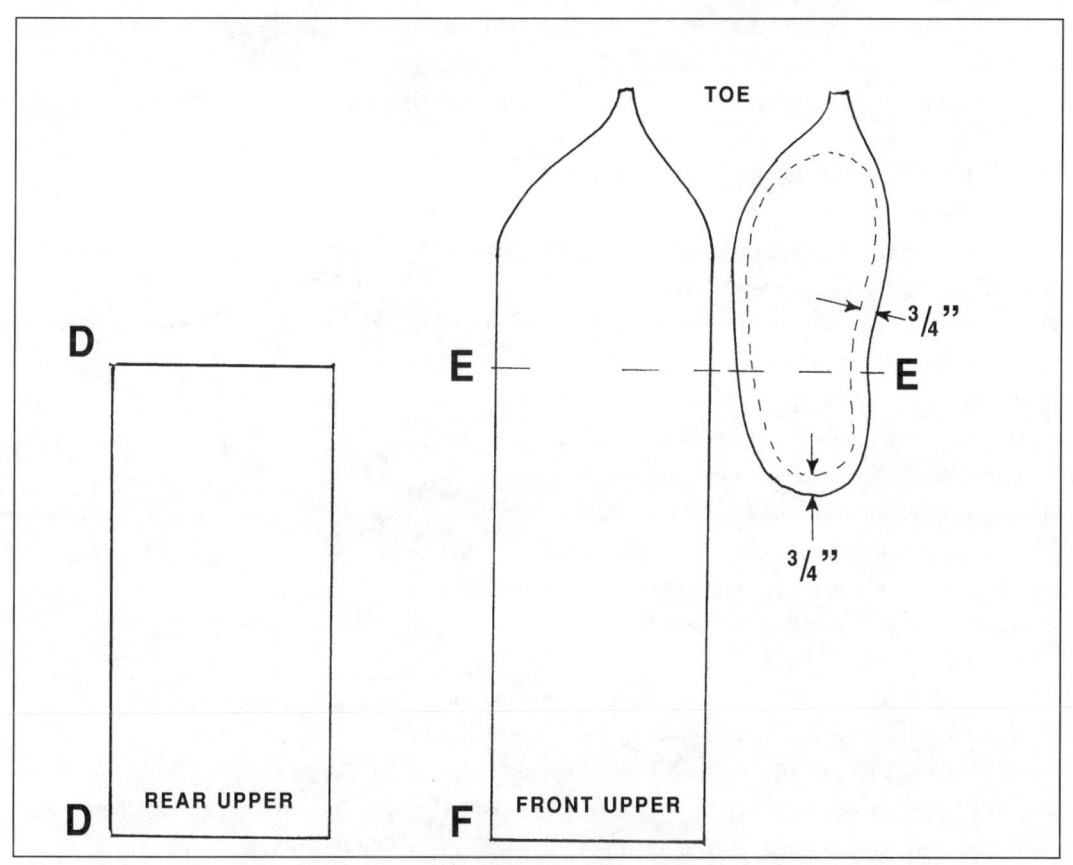

5-12. Pattern for high-top, hard-soled moccasin.

wraps up around the foot. Lay the cardboard foot pattern on the sole material and add about 3/4 inch all around the outside (fig. 5-12). Determine the height for the moccasin and make line D-D this height. Measure around the calf at the widest point. The back and front upper pieces will each be one-half this measurement plus one inch. The back upper will be the height desired and the width determined by the calf measurement. Note, if the calf measurement makes the back upper piece too wide to fit at the heel, the piece can be cut at a slight angle, narrowing the heel width as needed to fit the foot pattern and widening the calf area to suit.

The front upper is the height desired plus the amount needed from the toe of the pattern. The width of the front upper is determined by the calf measurement plus the amount needed to fit the toe area of the foot pattern. Again, this piece can also be cut at an angle to widen the calf area if needed.

Cut to sole to shape and size. Depending on the thickness of the sole leather, it may be necessary to skive the edge of the sole. Note this moccasin can be made with the traditional pointed toe or the toe can be rounded. Cut the front and rear upper to size and shape. Reverse this pattern to cut the right foot moccasin. These moccasins are not the same for both feet unless the toe is rounded.

This style moccasin is sewn together wrong side out and a welt can be added for strength around the sole. Begin sewing by matching the center front of the sole with the center front of the front upper piece and sewing from the center front around both sides to points E, easing the toe area as needed to fit. Sew the rear upper piece to the heel of the sole matching points D and F with points E. Finally, stitch up both side seams from the sole to the moccasin top. Turn the moccasin right side out.

SEMI-HIGH-TOPPED HARD-SOLE MOCCASINS

The Pueblo and Apache utilized semi-high-topped moccasins with a somewhat different design (fig. 5-13A). They feature a single vamp-and-upper piece fastened to a gathered sole (fig. 5-13B). These moccasins are also reversed for the left and right feet. The sole should be cut about one-inch larger all around than the original cardboard foot pattern because of the gathers (fig. 5-13C). Sew the two pieces together from the outside. This moccasin requires a bit of effort in sewing the sole to the upper as the sole has to be gathered to meet the upper.

Slightly moistening the sole, skiving the edge of the sole and pre-gathering on a basting thread can all make the chore a bit easier. Pre-gathering the sole also gives a better idea of the size needed for the upper piece.

Cut the upper and vamp piece to the pattern as determined by the drawing shown. Line F-G on the upper is the same as line F-G on the sole plus one-fourth inch on each side for a seam.

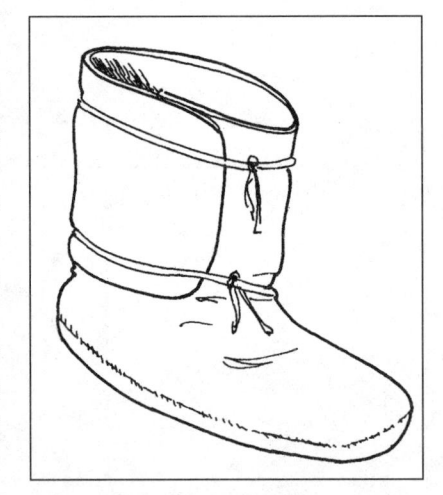

5-13A. Semi-High-Topped moccasin.

The length of line F-H-I is the length needed to stitch around the rest of the pre-gathered sole with point I meeting at point M. The length of line I-L is the height desired for the moccasin.

Mate points G, D and F on the upper with those points on the pre-gathered sole. I like to tie these

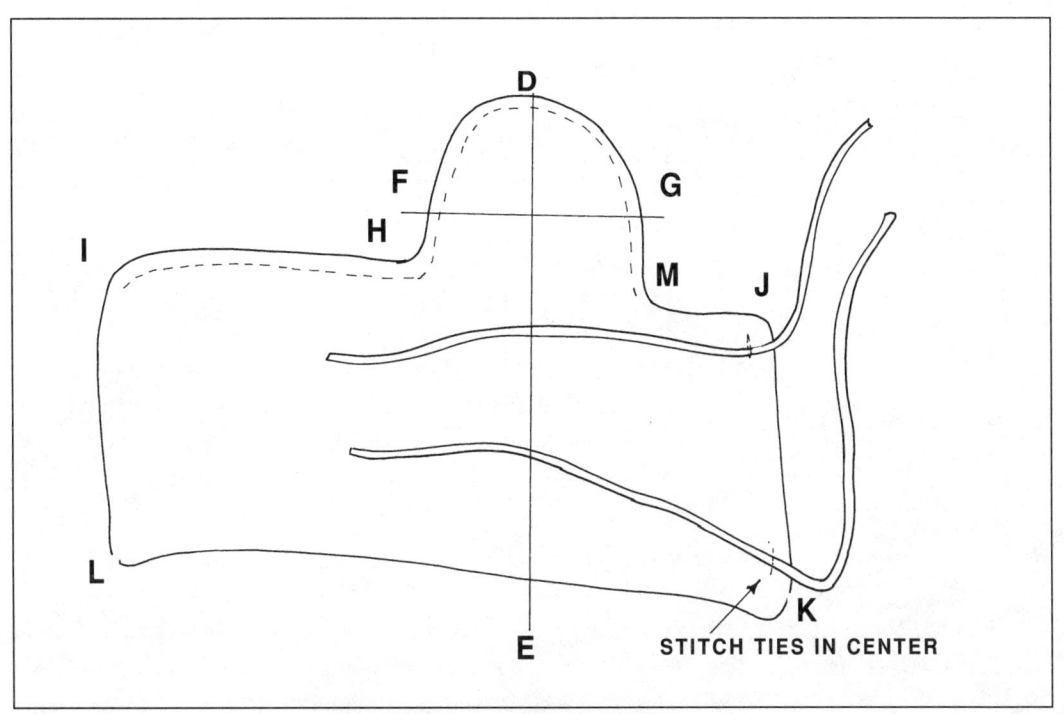

5-13B. Pattern for semi-high-topped moccasin.

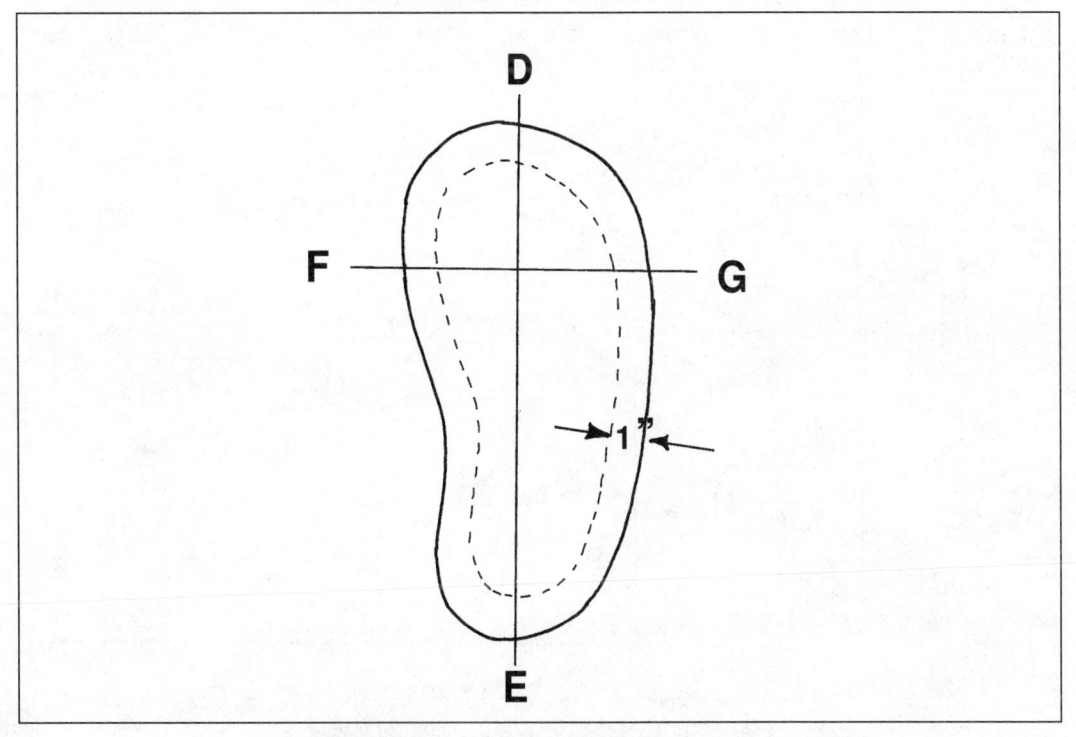

STITCH TIES IN CENTER

5-13C. Foot pattern for semi-high-topped moccasin.

Antler, Bone, Horn & Hide

points together by running thread through the stitching holes and tying. This way I can make sure the upper matches the sole before I begin stitching, cutting the ties as I stitch. With any gathered sole or gathered upper moccasin it is a good idea to tie together the upper and sole at the major points and then make the stitching holes in each area. This way you can be assured that the stitching holes will match. Stitch from point D to point M, then stitch from center point D to point I, stitching from the outside.

Side J-K is an outside flap. Tie-strings are added to this side, one toward the top and one toward the bottom. The ties are stitched to the moccasin in the center of the tie and then wrapped around the moccasin and tied buttons or snaps could also be used.

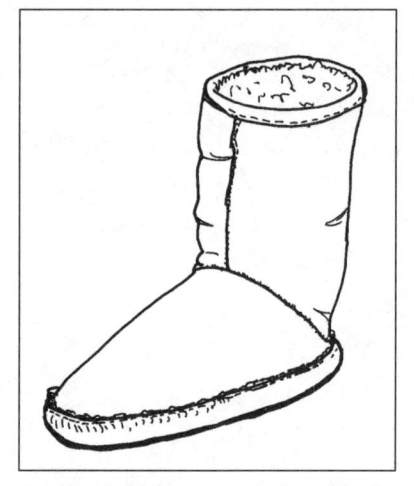

5-14A. Mukluks are made in much the same fashion as hard-soled, high-topped moccasins. They're somewhat difficult to make for a first-timer.

Mukluks

Mukluks are constructed similarly to mocassins. They utilize three pieces, in this case, the sole, a vamp, and wraparound upper (fig. 5-14A). Shown are the patterns for the three pieces and how to size them to your foot (figs. 5-14B and 5-14C). Sheepskin, with the wool on the inside, can be substituted for the sealskins used by Native Americans. Rawhide or harness leather can be used for the sole. Because of the puckering needed to gather the sole to the vamp and uppers, quite a bit of effort is need-

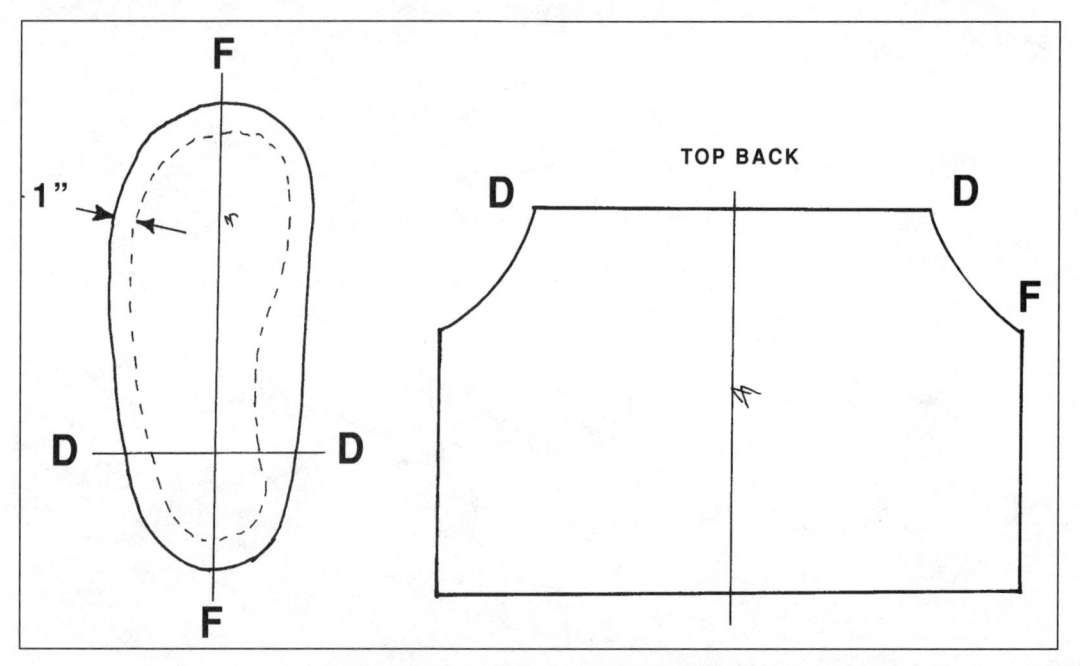

5-14B. Pattern for the sole and top back of mukluks.

FRONT VAMP

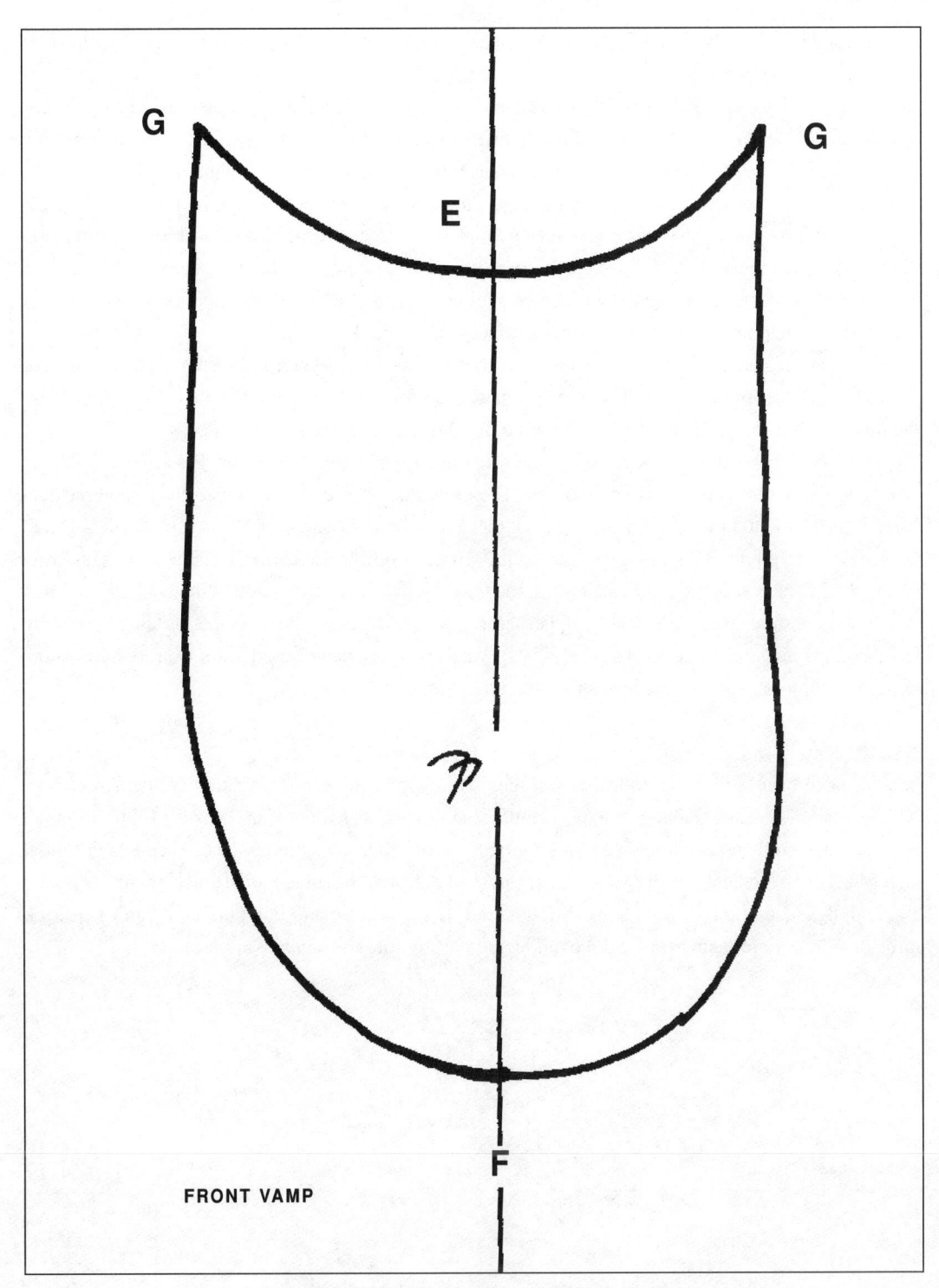

5-14C. Pattern for the front vamp of mukluks.

ed in the sewing. Slightly dampening the materials can make the chore somewhat easier. By adjusting the puckers of the material, the boot can be sized to fit your foot.

Cut the sole one inch larger all around than the original cardboard foot pattern. Mark a line F through the center of the foot pattern. Mark a line D across the rear of the foot approximately in line with the ankle bone. Match the length around the heel from D to D on the sole with the heel area length of D to D on the top back piece. The height of the top back piece is determined by the desired height of the mukluk. If you are making mukluks to go over the calf, check the calf measurements and angle the top piece, if necessary, to fit (see the instructions for high-topped moccasin). The width of the top back piece between points E is determined by the measurement of the front vamp between points G and E. The three points E meet in the center front of the mukluk.

The size of the front vamp is determined by the foot size. Match the center front F with the center front of the foot pattern F. The front vamp and the sole are then eased together with points G on the front vamp meeting the top back piece at points D on the heel area of the sole.

After cutting all the pieces to size, begin sewing. Again, sew inside out. Begin sewing at the center toe F and sew to points D on each side. Then sew the top back piece to the sole around the heel area from point D to point D. Sew the top back piece and the front vamp together mating points D and G and sewing to points E. As you sew these seams, sew in the leather tie strips (if desired) about half way up the seam. These straps should face toward the back because they cross around the heel and are then tied in place in front. Adjust the length of the straps to suit the height of the mukluks, as taller boots may require straps that cross and wrap several times. Finally, sew the center front seam from point E to the top. A tie thong can also be run through the top edge of the mukluk if desired.

Sandals

Sandals have been utilized as footwear for ages (fig. 5-15). Some Southwestern Native Americans wore sandals. The soles can be made of rawhide, sole or harness leather. Cut the soles 1/4 to 3/16 inch larger all around than the cardboard foot pattern. Sew a leather toe strap in place. Then attach sandal lacings between the heel and the arch area of the sandal. Stitch these lacings in place or simply punch a hole in the sandal, thread the lacing through, and tie the bottom end in a knot so it can't slip back through. Wrap these lacings around the ankle and calf to hold the sandals in place. ■

Leather Footwear

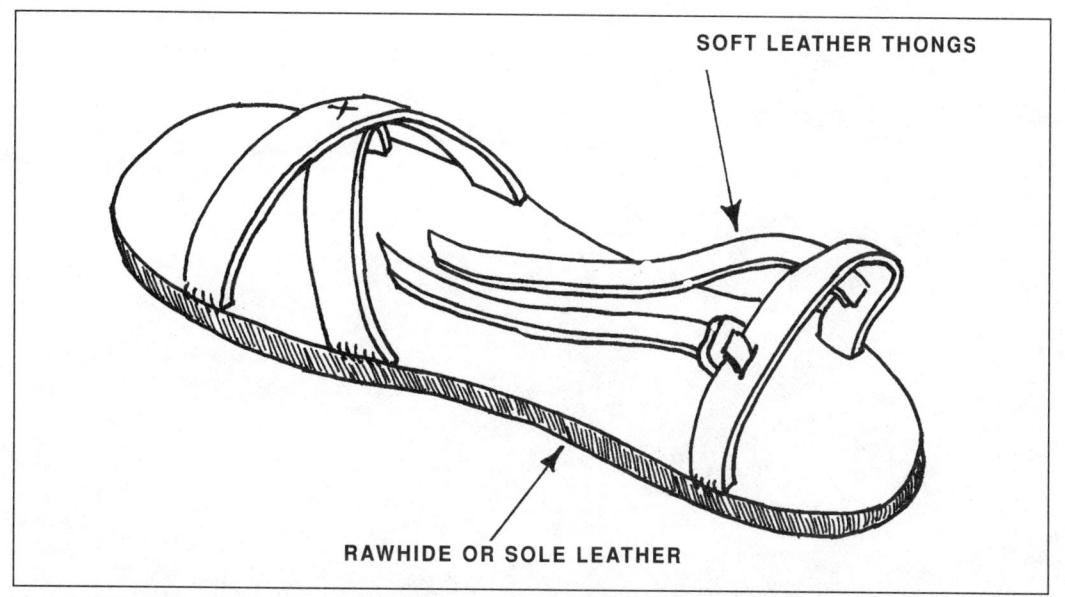

5-15. Sandals are easily made with heavy harness leather or rawhide for the soles and soft leather for the tie-thongs.

TOOLS AND MATERIALS FOR
Leather Accessory Projects

- Automatic stitching awl
- Awl or leather punch
- Backer board
- Bricks or rocks (to weigh down leather)
- Brown paper
- Buckle
- C-clamps
- Carabiner
- Clothespin
- Hammer, rounded or ball-peen
- Knife
- Lacings
- Lacing punch
- Leather, including soft suede or light buckskin
- Leather dye
- Leather thongs
- Metal snaps

- Paint, artists acrylic
- Peg, wooden or antler
- Plastic food wrap
- Rivet set
- Sand
- Shellac, white
- Sinew, simulated or real
- Split cowhide, 4-ounce and 6-ounce
- Stiff material, such as denim or canvas
- Straightedge
- Tracing paper
- Utility knife
- Waxed thread, heavy-duty
- Wire, stiff
- Wooden block
- Wooden peg

6
LEATHER ACCESSORIES

Leather accessory projects are fun. Many of these items make great projects for beginners learning to work with leather. And you can make any number of useful or decorative items. Some practical projects include leather belts, various types of knife sheaths, different kinds of pouches and bags, and rifle and bow cases.

BELTS

Some of the easiest leather projects are belts. Belts can be plain, tooled (see chapter 8), dyed almost any color you wish, and decorated in numerous ways. All the items needed to produce belts are commonly found in leather craft supply stores and catalogs. All you need for a basic belt is a piece of leather and a buckle. Strap leather or split cowhide is the most common leather used for belts. Strap leather is popular for heavier belts, and split cowhide is available in different weights. A nine- to twelve-ounce leather is a good choice for belts. You can often find belt blanks of different widths, ounces, and lengths (fig. 6-1).

You will also need a buckle. Again, a wide variety of shapes, sizes, and ornamentation are available.

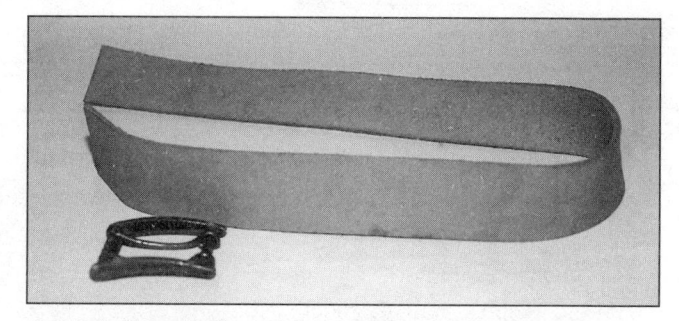

6-1. Belts are simple and fun leather projects. Strap leather is popular for making belts.

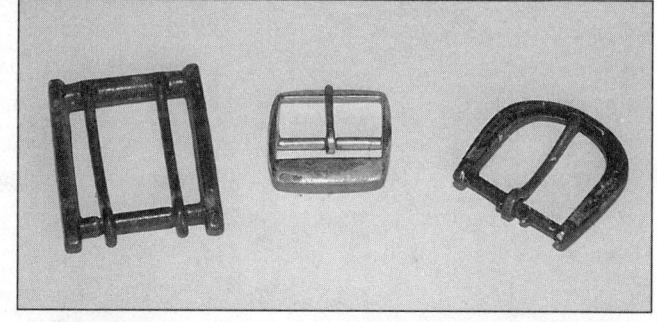

6-2. Belt buckles are available in a variety of styles, including regular or center bar.

Most buckles come in two designs—regular (the leather strap fastens to the end of the buckle and the tongue is located there) and center bar (the leather strap fastens to the center of the buckle and the tongue is located there) (fig. 6-2).

If you are cutting your own belt rather than using a belt blank, lay the leather out flat, flesh side

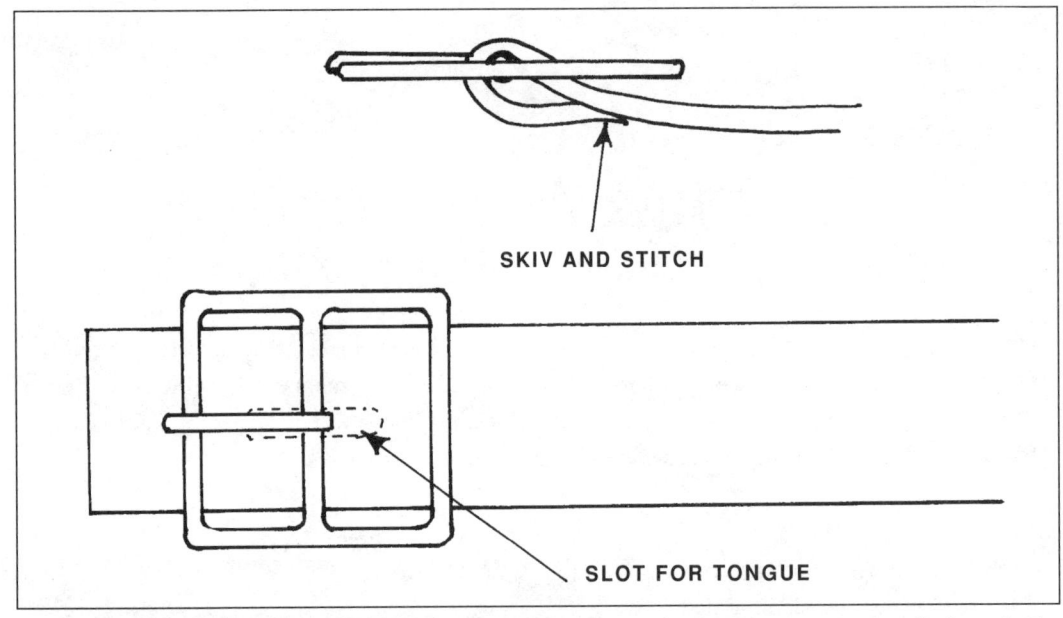

6-3. A center-bar buckle doesn't need a holding belt loop. The belt is cut to allow the tongue to fit through. The belt is then folded over the center bar, the end skived or shaved and the end of the belt is stitched in place.

up, on a smooth surface. Lightly mark the desired width and length using a ballpoint pen. Then, with a piece of soft wood as a backer board,, use a utility knife with a sharp blade and a straightedge to cut the leather. On heavy strap leather, it's best to make several passes, rather than trying to make the cut all in one pass. You can also clamp a metal straightedge down the leather with C-clamps to the board and assure a straight, smooth cut.

A center-bar buckle doesn't need a holding loop for the belt end. For a center bar buckle skive, or slice at an angle, back the end of the belt about one-quarter inch. Then lay the buckle on the end of the belt and mark the location of the center bar. Mark the belt on both sides of the center bar where the tongue is attached (if the buckle has two tongues, mark for both). Punch two holes at these marks and cut between them to produce the slit for the tongue or tongues (fig. 6-3).

Insert the buckle tongue or tongues through the slit or slits, lightly moisten the end of the belt, and bend it back over the center bar. Mark the leather for stitching and lacing holes and punch the holes using a revolving leather punch or awl. Then stitch or lace the flap down to hold the buckle in place.

To fasten a regular buckle to a belt, first make a holding loop. Cut the loop to the correct size and shape as shown to fit properly over the belt (fig. 6-4). Then punch holes in the ends of the loop and stitch it together using waxed thread. Make a wooden block of the same dimensions as the inside of the

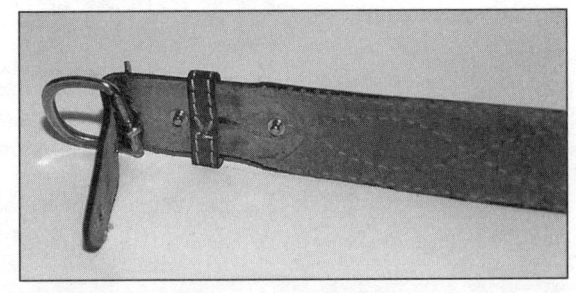

6-4. A holding loop is fastened between two snaps on a regular belt buckle.

Leather Accessories

finished belt loop. Moisten the leather and slide it over the block. Allow the loop to dry.

Position the buckle in place on the belt and mark the location of the tongue. Punch holes and cut between them to produce a slit for the tongue. Slide the loop over the belt, position the buckle in place with the tongue protruding through the slit, and mark the leather for stitching holes on either side of the loop. Stitch or lace the belt end in place.

Shotshell Belt

One of the most unusual belts I've seen was made for me by a friend. It utilizes a regular buckle and is decorated with spent shotshell ends (fig. 6-5). Holes were drilled at regular intervals along the main part of the belt, as well as on the buckle loop. The brass ends were removed from spent shotshells and the outer edges ground off, leaving only the thick butt portion. The shells of the primers, still left in the brass, were then pushed into the holes. Small washers were pushed over the caps and then their edges peened down over the primers to hold the shell ends in place.

6-5. The unusual belt shown has spent shotshells embedded into it for decoration.

6-6. Western-style buckles utilize a welded bar on the back and a hook for the belt holes.

Western Belt

Western-style buckles often use a welded metal bar on the back and a hook on the front to hold the buckle to the belt (fig. 6-6). These are quite simple to install. Loop the belt end over the metal bar, punch holes, and stitch the loop, lace it, or even rivet it together.

Tongue Holes

The final step in the assembly of any belt is to punch the buckle tongue holes in the opposite end of the belt. Place the belt around you and locate the position for the holes. Then add a hole or two on either side. Punch the holes using a revolving leather punch.

Decorating belts is half the fun. You can tool them as described in chapter 8. You can also use lacing as decoration. Lacing punches make this chore easy (fig. 6-7). Punch lacing slits along the top and bottom edges of the belt and run a lacing of a contrasting color through the slits. Or you can use a variety of other lacing designs as well (fig. 6-8).

Another tactic is to dress the belt with metal ornaments, such as those used on harnesses. Called spots or studs, they are available in a wide range of sizes and shapes. They have metal ears on the back,

Antler, Bone, Horn & Hide

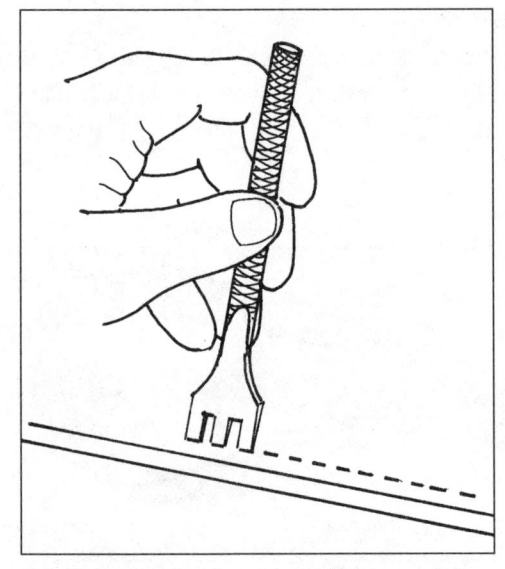

6-7. Belts can be decorated by using a lacing punch to cut spaced holes, then lacing is threaded through the holes.

which are driven into the leather and then folded over on the back of the belt. Studs may be purchased at leather crafts supply stores. For another interesting belt project, try the blind-braided belt on page 121.

KNIFE AND AXE SHEATHS

Some of the most popular leather projects are knife sheaths. A wide variety of styles, methods of construction, and leathers can be used to custom-build a sheath for almost any type of knife, axe, or machete. Knife sheaths are constructed in one of two ways. The first method uses heavy strap leather that is strong enough to withstand the abuse of the knife. The second method uses an inner liner of rawhide, molded around the knife blade. An outer decorative shell covers the rawhide liner.

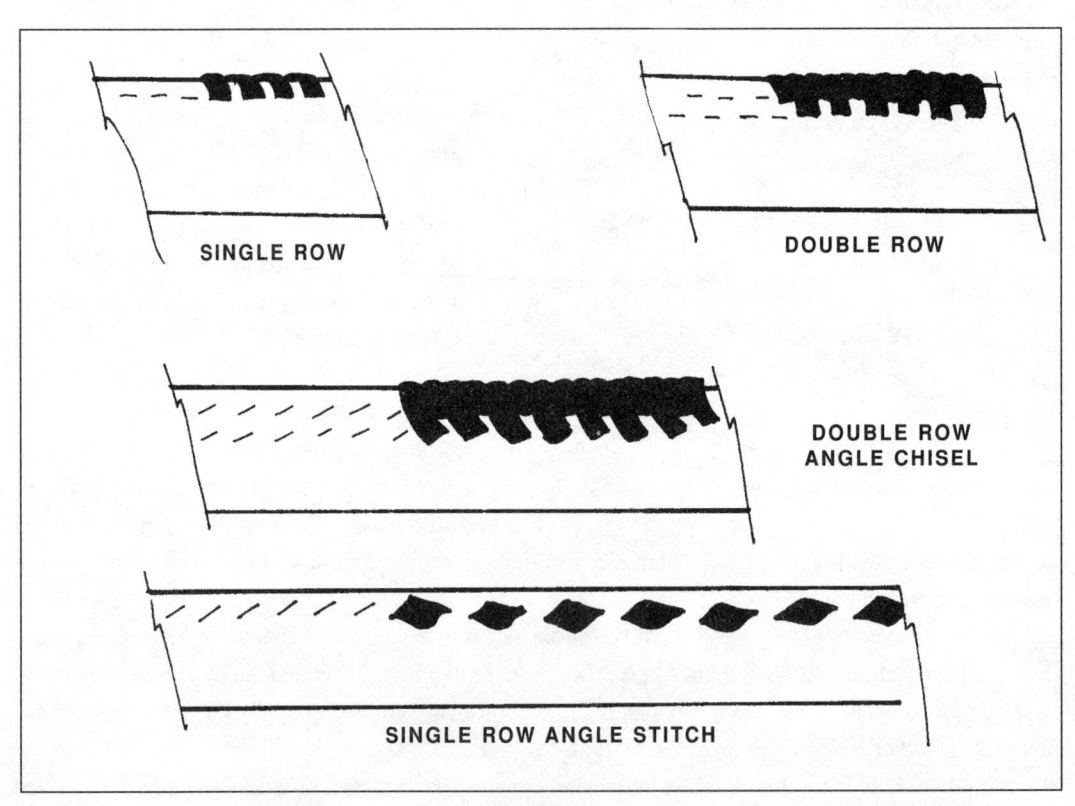

SINGLE ROW

DOUBLE ROW

DOUBLE ROW ANGLE CHISEL

SINGLE ROW ANGLE STITCH

6-8. Lacing patterns.

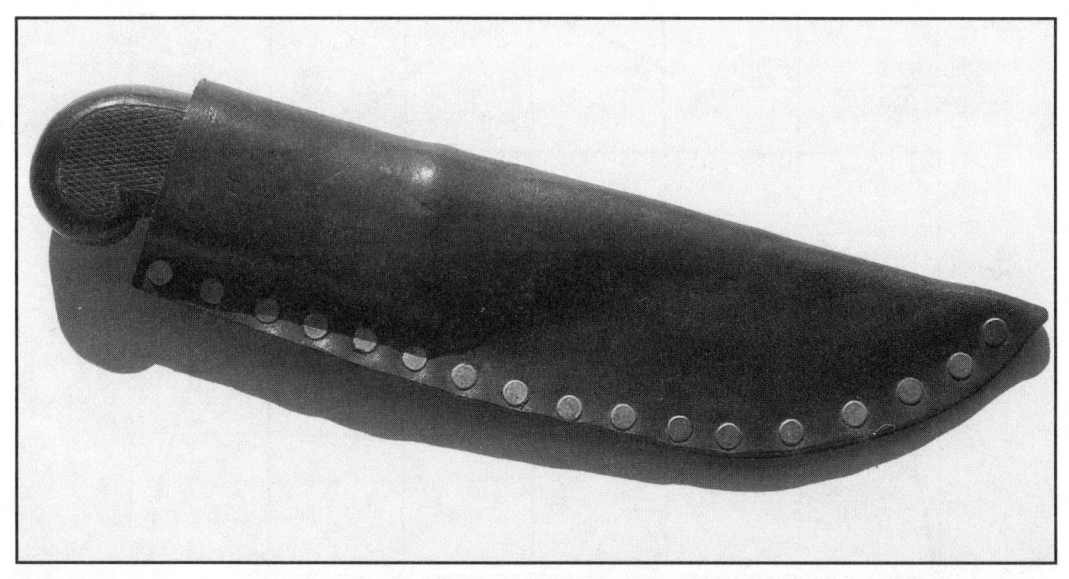

6-9. Knife sheaths are also some of the most popular leather projects. The riveted sheath is extremely easy to make.

ONE-PIECE RIVETED SHEATH

The simplest sheath is a one-piece design without a snap or other type of holder for the knife handle (fig. 6-9). Instead, this type of sheath is designed to hold the knife fairly deep in the sheath. Medium-stiff leather about 1/16 to 1/8 inch thick should be used. The first step is to position the leather flesh side up on a smooth flat surface. Lay the knife on the leather and trace around the knife up to almost the very end of the handle. Allow about 1/2-inch extra all around. This will be one side of the sheath. Trace the pattern with tracing paper, then flop it over to create a double pattern. Because this sheath fits over the knife handle, it's a good idea to wrap the marked piece around the handle and make sure there is enough room for the rivets on the upper portion before fastening the pieces together.

Place the leather on a wooden board or other cutting surface and cut the outline of the sheath with a sharp utility knife (fig. 6-10). Lightly moisten the leather and fold it together. Mark the locations for the rivets and punch them using a revolving leather punch. At the top of the back side, punch two holes the width of the belt to be used for the sheath. Punch two more holes spaced about an inch away in the same manner. Then cut between the holes to produce the belt loop.

Moisten the leather again and fold it together. Then fasten it with the rivets. Leather rivets can be installed quite easily in the prepunched holes using a purchased rivet set. Or you can make your own rivet set from a sawn-off bolt and a small block of metal.

NATIVE AMERICAN-STYLE SHEATH

The most popular Native American-style knife sheath is quite similar in design to the one-piece sheath, but different in construction. In most instances, Native Americans didn't wear the knife sheath on a belt but instead kept it in their clothing or on a thong tied around the waist.

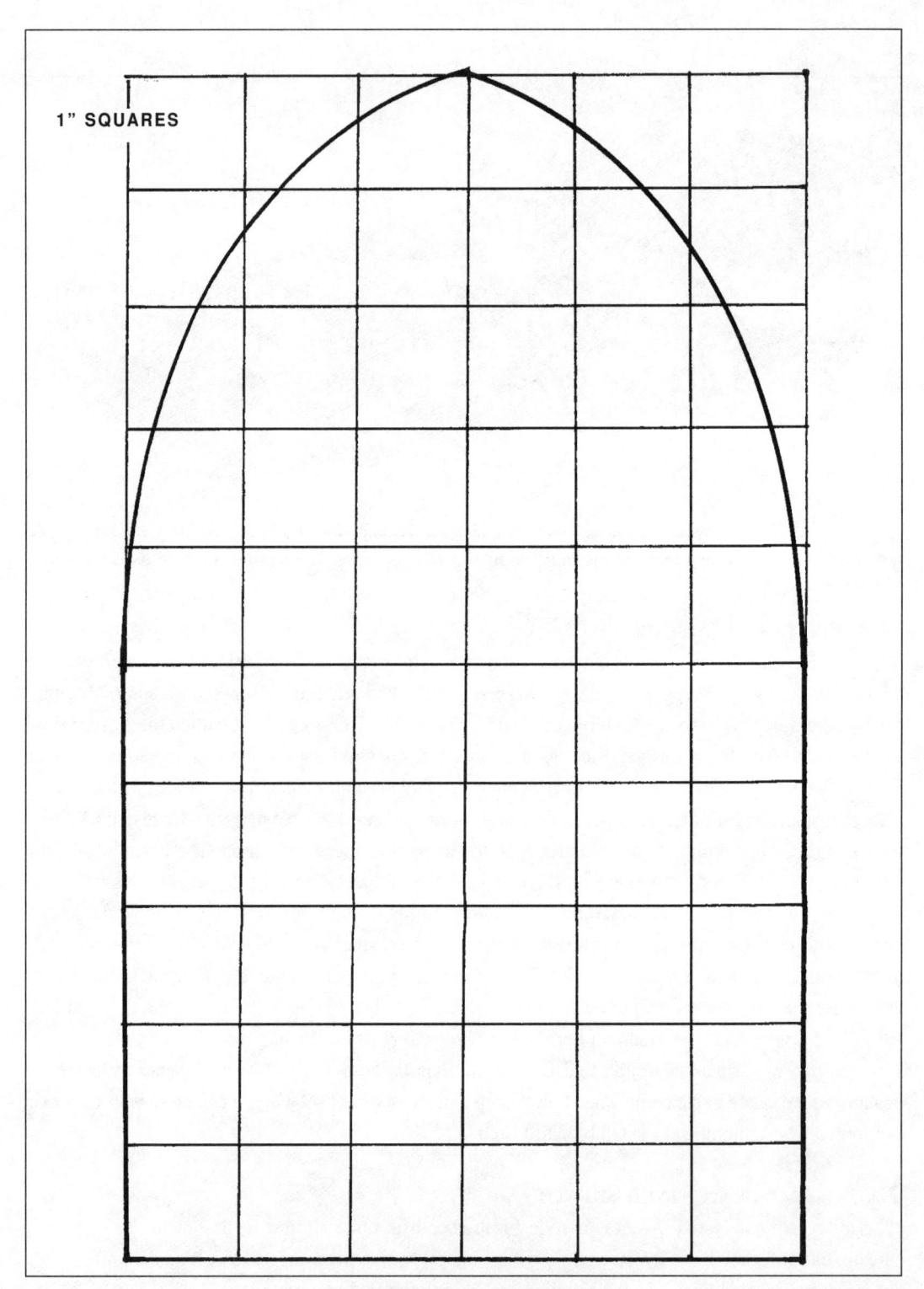

6-10. Pattern for a riveted sheath.

LEATHER ACCESSORIES

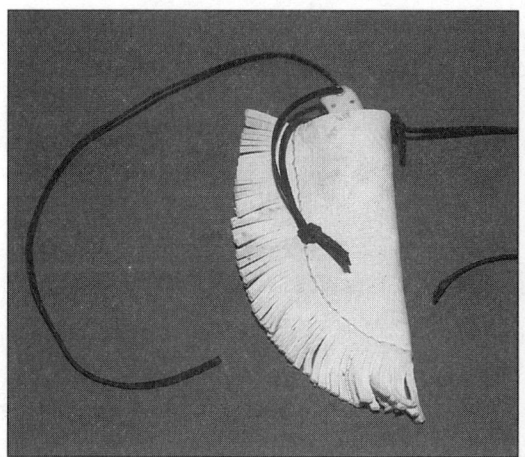

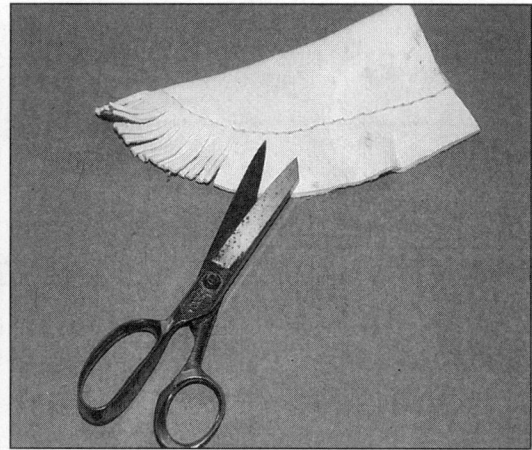

6-11A. & 6-11B. Native American fringed sheath was made to fit the stag-handled patch knife shown in chapter 1. Note it has a thong for tying around the waist instead of a belt loop. An inside rawhide liner protects the outer leather sheath.

Again, the sheath is made to fit almost up to the end of the knife handle (fig. 6-11A).

The sheath shown has a protective rawhide inner sheath covering the blade and an outer buckskin sheath. The first step is to construct the inner rawhide sheath. Lay the knife blade on the rawhide and mark around the blade up to the handle. Leave at least 5/8 inch all around. Repeat the pattern for the opposite side of the sheath. Soak the rawhide in water until it softens, then cut the sheath liner using a sharp knife. Fold the piece together and mark and punch stitching holes. Wrap the knife blade in plastic food wrap to protect it from the moisture, then wrap the wet rawhide around the knife to make sure it will fit. Rawhide shrinks when it dries so allow for shrinkage. If you are satisfied the sheath will fit properly, punch stitching holes in both sides of the folded material. Stitch the folded sheath together and then place it around the plastic wrap-protected blade. Mold the rawhide to fit the blade and allow it to dry.

After the rawhide has cured, position the inner sheath with the knife in it on a piece of leather for the outside covering. Mark around the inner sheath, adding 1/2-inch. Continue marking to within about an inch of the top of the handle. This creates half a pattern. Mark the other pattern half, fold the leather piece around the sheath and knife, and make sure the leather will fit around the knife handle. Then cut the leather to shape. Using a leather punch or awl, punch the stitching holes around both sides, making sure they match.

The outer sheath can be assembled around the inner sheath and fastened together with either waxed thread, simulated or real sinew, or with hand-cut or purchased lacing using a running or whip stitch. A tie thong is usually fastened to the back of the sheath and used to tie the handle in place. You can also make a waist thong to carry the knife.

Traditionally, these sheaths were beaded or sometimes painted. Fringe can also be added to the outer edge if desired (figs. 6-11B and 6-12). Cut a piece to match the shape of the backside of the sheath. Punch the edge and add it during the stitching or lacing process using a running stitch.

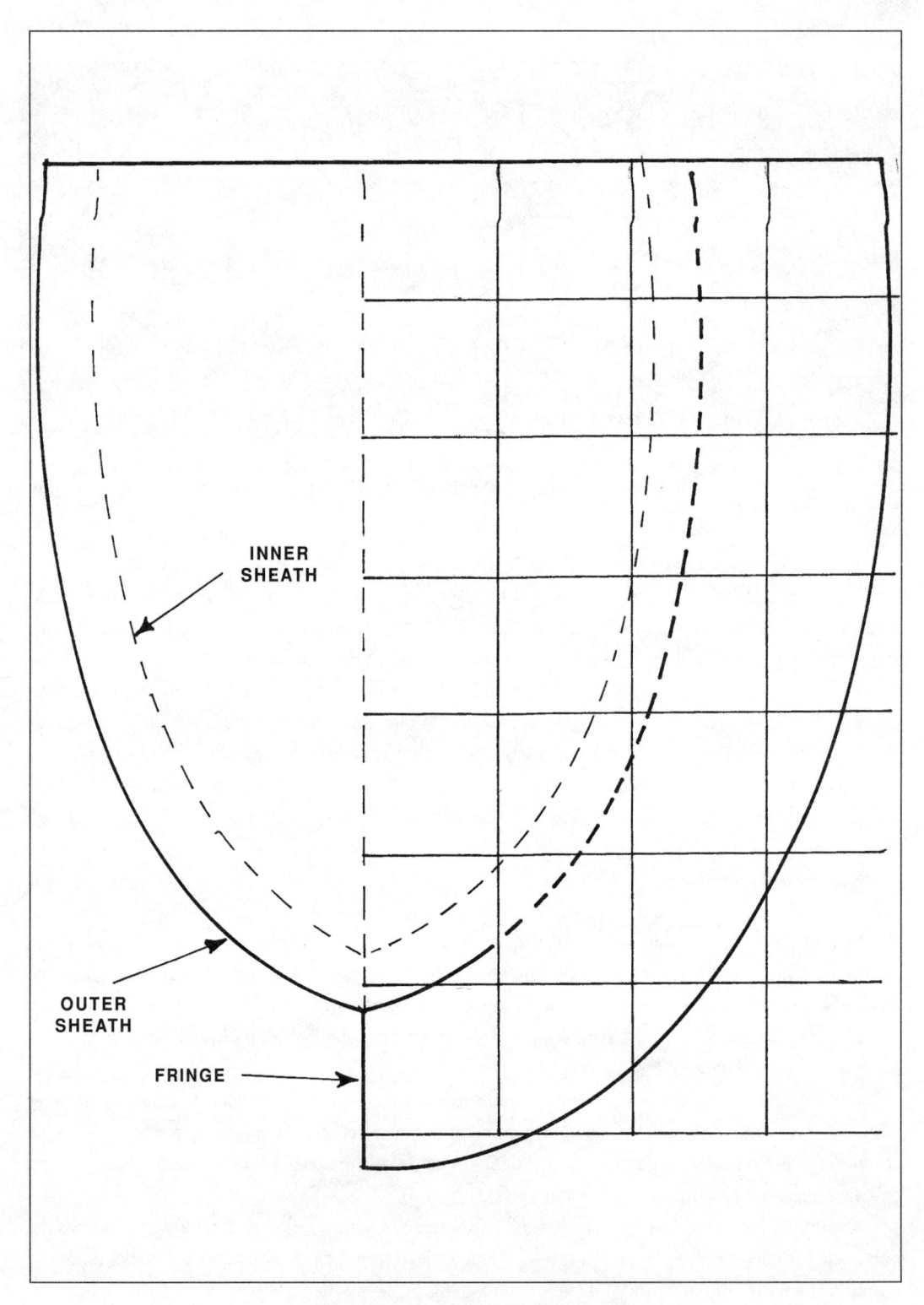

6-12. Pattern for a fringed knife sheath.

Modern-Style Knife Sheath

The sheath shown is more modern in style and construction. The sheath was made of 1/16-inch leather and dyed black. It is also stitched together using an automatic stitching awl and waxed thread. A handle loop with a snap provides a means of keeping the knife in the sheath (fig. 6-13).

To make this sheath, the first step is to lay the knife on a piece of leather, flesh side up, and mark around the blade, allowing about 1/2-inch on all sides. This creates one half of the pattern; repeat for the other half. Inside the sheath, continue the straight line from the top of the blade to the top of the handle to create the belt-loop holder. Double the length of these two lines, then mark a line at their tops to create the doubled-over belt loop. Then cut the handle strap to size and shape. Cut slits in the upper inner side of the belt loop holder for the handle strap (fig. 6-14). When all pieces have been cut to the correct size, dye the sheath and handle strap on both sides of the leather, using a good-quality leather dye.

Fold the bottom (blade) portion of the sheath together and, holding it tightly in place, use a sharp needle in an automatic awl to stitch it together. Space the stitches about 3/16 inch from the outer edge and about 1/8 inch apart. If you have trouble pushing the needle through both pieces of material, use a sharp awl to make starting holes.

The handle strap is threaded through the two slits at the top of the sheath. The strap

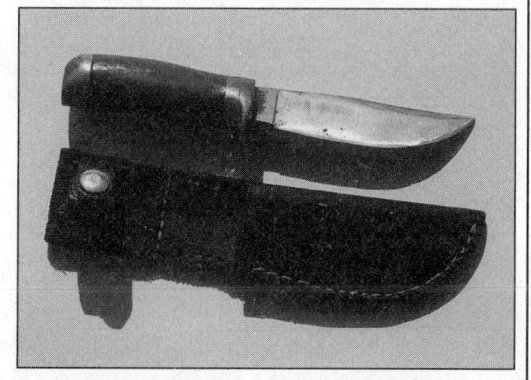

6-13. A more modern style knife sheath utilizes a stitched side and a strap with a snap to hold the knife in place.

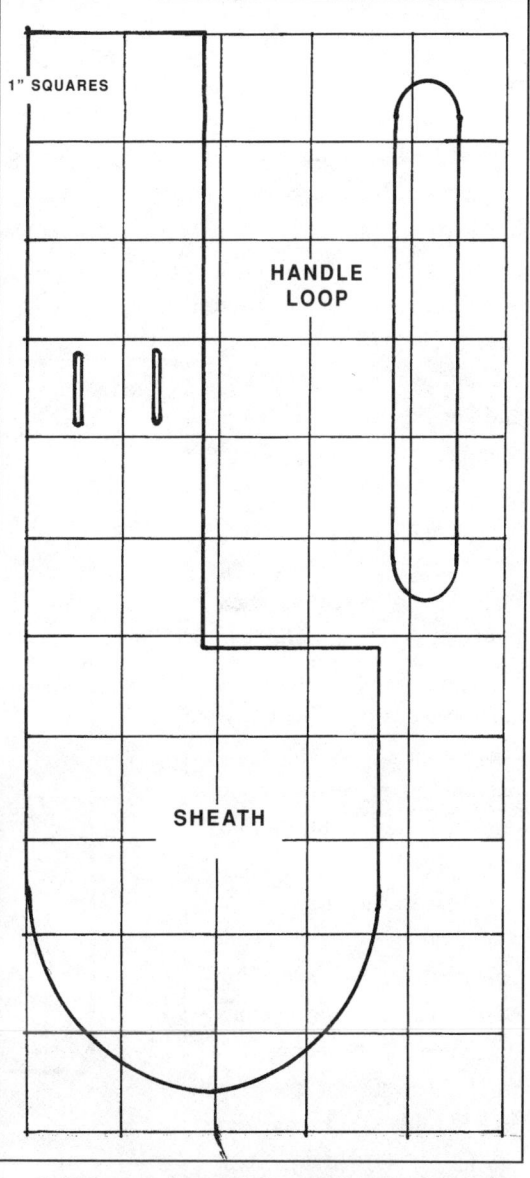

6-14. Pattern for a modern-style knife sheath.

Antler, Bone, Horn & Hide

uses metal snaps to hold the knife handle in place. Fasten the snaps in the ends of the strap using a rivet set. Then fold the upper portion of the belt loop back over until it meets the top edge of the blade on the back of the sheath. Stitch the belt loop in place using the automatic awl.

An alternate method is to use only a single-layer belt loop. Cut slits in the loop for the belt as described for the one-piece riveted sheath.

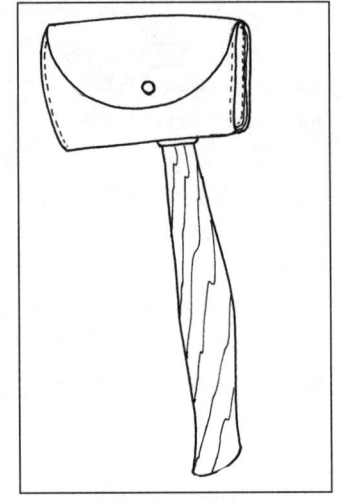

Axe Sheath

One of the most dangerous pieces of outdoor equipment is an axe. A sharp axe edge left uncovered can cause a nasty cut if you happen to bump into or hit it. And, left unprotected, the blade can also be dulled if the axe or hatchet bumps around in your truck. A sheath is the solution to this problem (fig. 6-15).

6-15. An axe sheath can protect the blade and user from a sharp knife edge.

Place the axe or hatchet head on a piece of leather, flesh side up. Add about 1/2-inch around the top, rear, and blade edge and mark for a pattern. Measure the thickness of the back of the head. Add this measurement to the rear of the pattern and draw a line that extends about an inch below the axe head. The bottom flap is fastened to the sides at the back to help hold the axe in place. Trace the pattern and repeat it for the opposite side of the sheath (fig. 6-16).

The sheath also has a flap to provide protection and hold the axe in place. This flap is a half-circle that comes down about halfway over the front. Measure for the flap and add this measurement to the top of the sheath. Mark the pattern well and cut it out

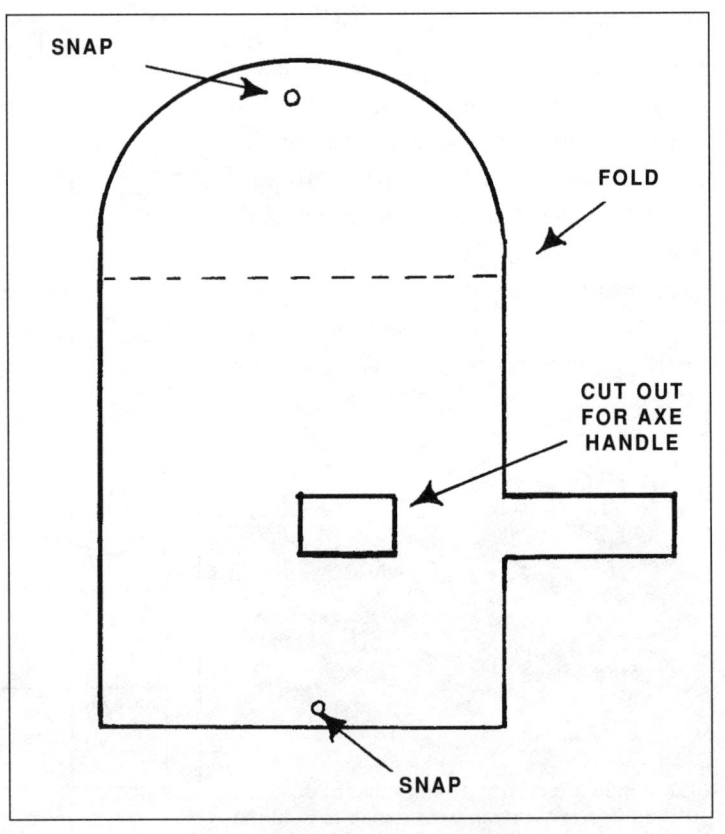

6-16. Pattern for an axe sheath.

LEATHER ACCESSORIES

using a sharp utility knife. If the sheath is for a belt hatchet, cut belt loop slits in the back portion of the sheath.

Fold the two sides together over the head and mark the handle location. Use a leather punch to punch lacing holes from the top down along the blade and around the bottom up to the handle. Punch matching holes in the opposite side. Punch two lacing holes in each side of the back bottom flap and punch matching holes in the rear of each side.

Fold the two sides together and lace or stitch the sheath together around the top, the blade edge, and the front bottom edge. Then bring the rear bottom flap up and lace it to the two sides. Install the snaps in the top flap and front side piece. Or, you can cut a slit in the flap and use a wooden peg and thong for the tie.

SHEATH FOR A FOLDING KNIFE, MULTITOOL, OR PLIERS

A leather belt case can easily be made to hold a folding knife, multipurpose tool, or even a pair

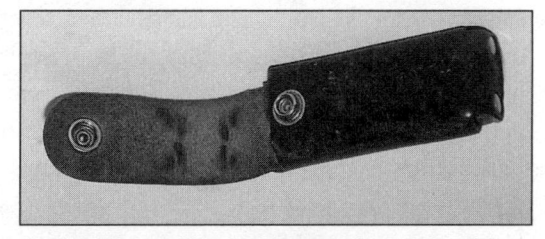

6-17. Folding multitools are extremely popular. Shown is a popular design for a sturdy leather sheath.

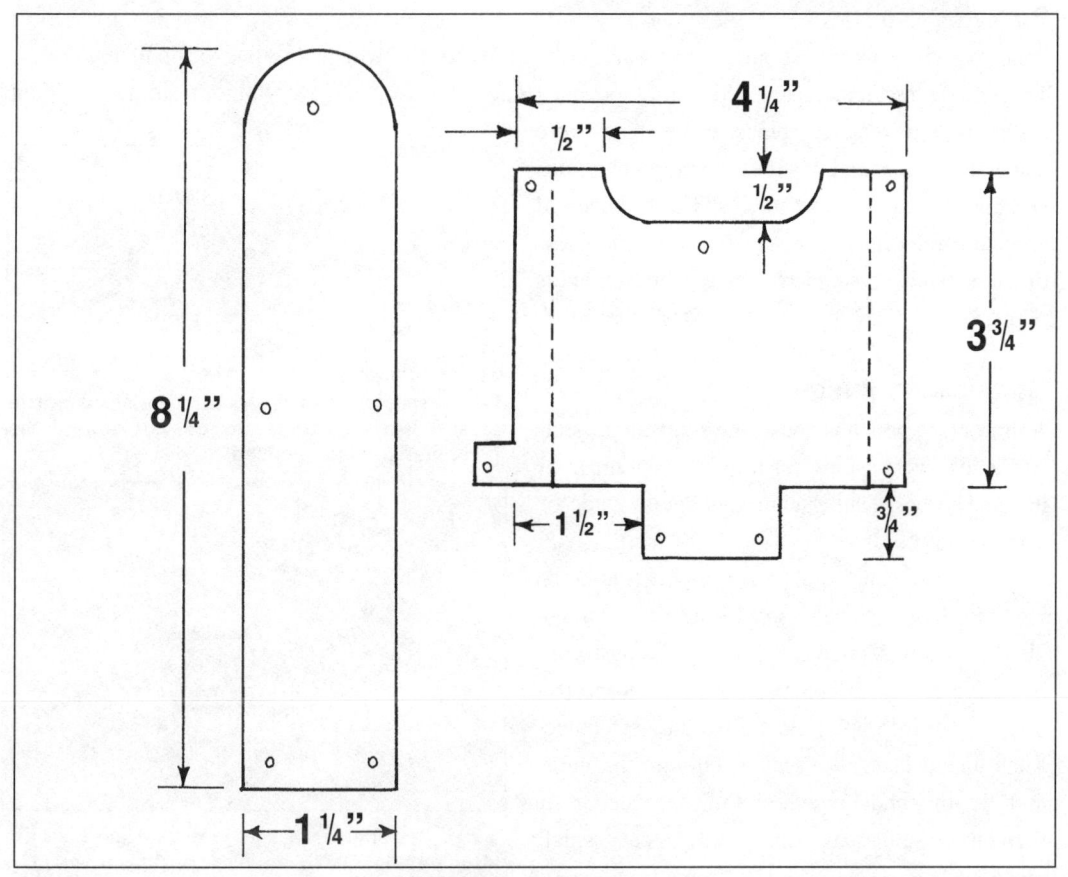

6-18. Pattern for a multitool sheath.

Antler, Bone, Horn & Hide

of pliers. First measure the knife or tool to be cased and make a pattern. The case consists of two pieces. The front, sides, and bottom are all one piece. This piece wraps around the tool and attaches to the inside of the back piece so it should be sized to the circumference of the tool. Lay out the knife or tool and add 1/2 inch to its length at the bottom of the pattern. The second piece forms the back, belt loop, inside bottom, top, and front flap piece. Lay out the patterns on a piece of leather, flesh side up, and cut the front piece to shape. Be sure to leave extra length on the back piece for the front flap.

The case is held together with leather rivets and assembly is extremely easy (fig. 6-17). First punch a hole on the front for the male snap and fasten it in place with a rivet set. Overlap the front and back bottom pieces. Punch and rivet them together at the bottom with a rivet in each corner. Bring the back piece up and fold the sides of the front piece over until they almost meet in the center of the back piece. Hold one hand around the sheath and try to fit in the knife or multitool. If the tool fits properly, punch and rivet the back piece in place only at the top corners with one rivet on each side. Finally, trim the top flap to suit. Position the top snap so it meets the snap on the front, punch a hole for the snap, and install it. The open back acts as a belt loop for this simple sheath (fig. 6-18). For a plier sheath, leave off the top flap.

POUCHES AND BAGS

Pouches and bags were extremely important to Native Americans, who had no pockets in their clothing. They made medicine bags and sturdy pouches and bags to hold everything from fire-lighting materials to ceremonial pipes. Many bags were elaborately decorated with beadwork, paint, feathers, bones, and other ornaments. The settlers and mountain men quickly discovered the usefulness of these handy containers. Today's buckskinners will also find many of these bags extremely useful.

DRAWSTRING POUCH

A drawstring pouch is one of the simplest projects and is also very handy for toting any number of items. The best leather choice is a soft suede or light buckskin.

The very simplest drawstring pouch is nothing more than a piece of soft leather, cut in a circle (fig. 6-19). A good size for a small bag would be twelve inches in diameter. Punch holes approximately one inch apart around the circumference. Then thread lacing or a thong through the holes and tie the ends together. Pull the lacing or thong to close the bag. This makes an easy, small medicine bag.

6-19. A simple drawstring pouch consists of a circle of soft leather. Lacing slits are cut around the perimeter and lacing added.

6-20A. Rectangular or square drawstring bags are also popular with today's buckskinners. The fringed model shown is decorated with beads.

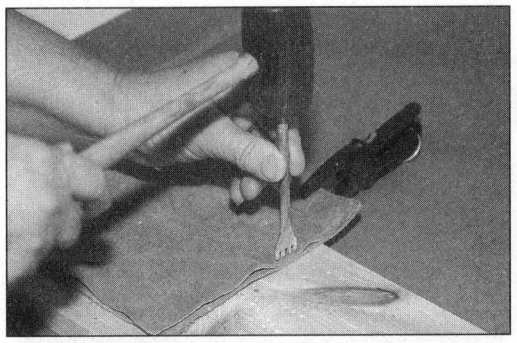

Leather Accessories

6-20B. After the bag is cut to size, a lacing punch is used to punch holes for the lacing.

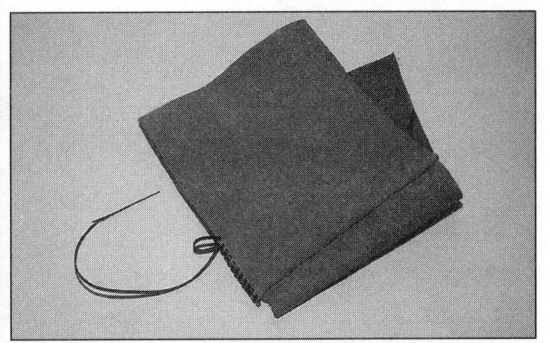

6-20C. Lacing is threaded through the holes using a lacing needle and a whip stitch.

A rectangular drawstring pouch can also be made in somewhat the same fashion (fig. 6-20A). Lay out the rectangular pouch pattern (sized to suit) on the leather and cut it with a sharp knife. Using a revolving leather punch, punch fairly large holes for the thong drawstring. The pouch has a fringe piece added around the bottom. Sew the bag wrong side out using artificial or natural sinew or waxed linen thread. The first step is to sew the side seam(s) (figs. 6-20B and 6-20C).

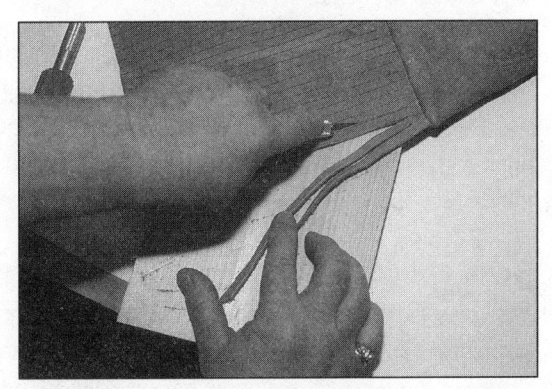

6-20D. Fringe is marked with a pencil and cut with a sharp knife.

This bag can be made from one rectangular piece of leather folded over with one side seam or from two smaller pieces with two side seams. Cut a fringe piece to size and place it along the bottom between the front and back pieces. Line up the bottom edge of all three pieces and sew them together. Turn the bag right side out. Cut a drawstring thong, thread it through the holes, and knot the ends together. Cut the bottom fringe (fig. 6-20D).

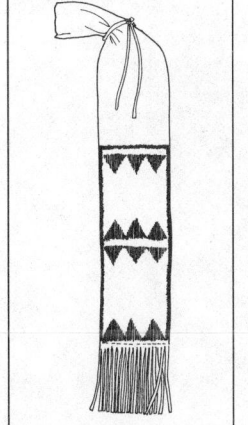

Pipe Bag

To Native Americans, a pipe was a cherished item. It was part of their ceremonies and also used for pleasure. Pipes were often kept in elaborate bags, typically decorated with beading or quill work (fig. 6-21). Construction is basically the same as for the previous drawstring pouch. The dimensions, however, are somewhat different. Typically, the dimensions are 6 by 24 inches, but they can vary according to the size of the pipe.

6-21. Pipe bags are popular projects with Native American afficionados.

Strike-a-Light Pouch

Both early settlers and mountain men used "strike-a-light" pouches, which were tied to the waist and often used to keep flint for fire lighting, as well

Antler, Bone, Horn & Hide

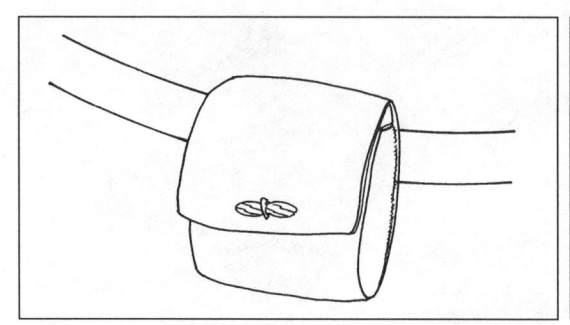

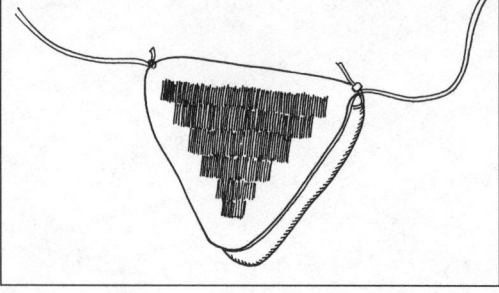

6-22. The strike-a-light is a small pouch carried on the waist. It once held flint for fire lighting as well as spare flints for muzzleloaders.

6-23. A neck bag carried valuables for yesterday's mountain men and is popular with today's buckskinners.

as spare flints for guns (fig. 6-22). To make a waist bag, use the same basic pattern and construction as the rectangular pouch. Eliminate the drawstring, however, and add a flap at the top of the back piece to fold over the front. This flap is held in place with a slit in the front and a wooden, antler or bone peg. Punch holes in both sides at the top and tie off a heavy-duty leather thong. This thong is then tied around the waist. It can also be attached to a belt.

Neck Pouch

Yesterday's mountain men often carried small items, including fire-starting implements, a small primer powder horn, and other items in a small triangular pouch tied at the neck. These pouches were copies of the personal medicine bags carried by many of the Native Americans and they were often beaded or quilled (fig. 6-23).

The pouch can be fastened with a drawstring, although traditionally, in most cases, a small flap came down over the front of the bag. Make the pattern as shown and cut the bag from extremely soft suede or lightweight buckskin. Sew it wrong side out using real or artificial sinew. Punch holes at the top corners and attach thongs to tie around the neck.

Shoulder Possibles Bag

Traveling with everything needed on their backs or in a pouch, mountain men often used a larger "possibles" bag carried across the shoulder (fig. 6-24). The bag shown is fairly large and carries quite a bit. I use it primarily for carrying black powder shotgunning gear when turkey hunting.

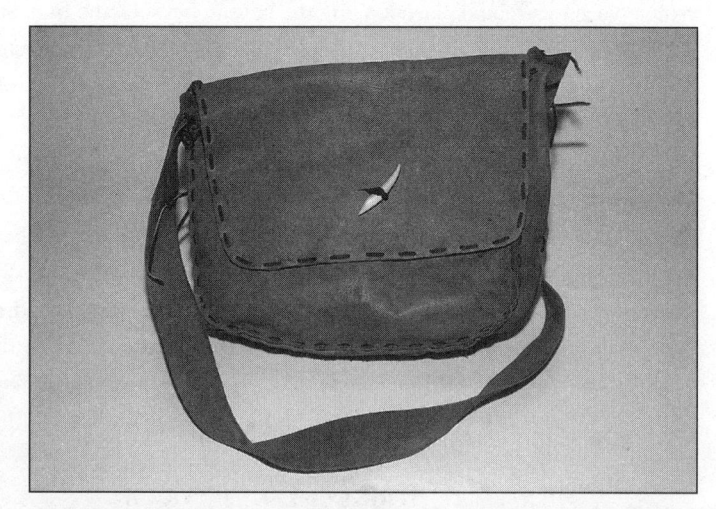

6-24. Probably the most important bag of the early trappers and mountain men was the "possibles bag." It carried everything "possible" needed to stay alive.

LEATHER ACCESSORIES

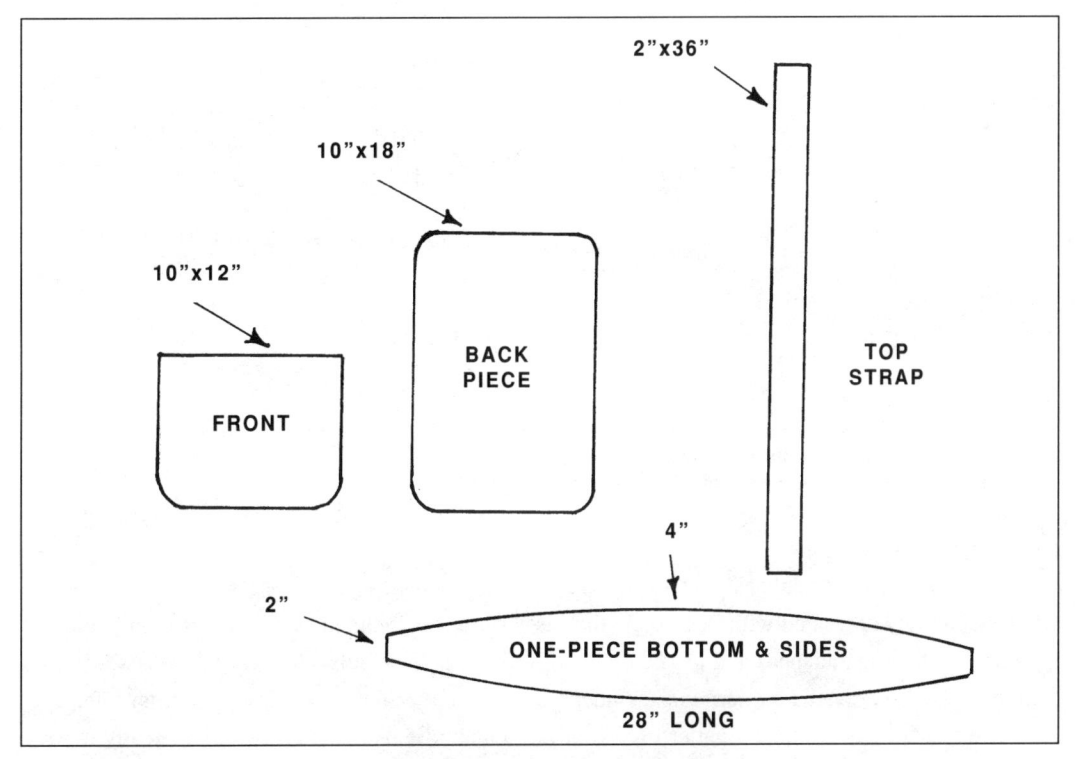

6-25. Pattern for a possibles bag.

The bag consists of a front, a one-piece bottom and sides, a top strap, and a back piece, which also makes the front flap. Use the squared drawing to create a pattern for the pieces, then place the patterns on a piece of fairly soft buckskin or split cowhide. Cut leather pieces to match the patterns (fig. 6-25).

Using a lacing punch, make holes around the edges of the front and the back up to the shoulder strap area. Determine the center of the bottom-side piece and place it in the center at the bottom of the front piece. Hold the pieces together with a clothespin. Beginning at the top edge of the front, punch mating holes in the bottom-side piece. Begin lacing at this point using a running stitch from the outside. Continue around the front, attaching the bottom-side piece by holding the pieces together, punching, and then lacing them in place. When you reach the opposite top corner, tie off the lacing.

Fasten the back in place in the same manner, matching the lacing holes, then lacing with a running stitch from the outside. Place the ends of the shoulder strap on the sides of the pouch extending 1 to 1 1/2 inches below the top. Punch four holes in both sides of the bag and in both ends of the shoulder strap. Then lace the straps to the side pieces in an X or crossing pattern and tie the lace securely.

Cut a slit in the front flap and attach a tie peg with a thong to the front. Fringe could be added to the bag around the bottom and side edges. The edge of the front flap could also be fringed. The bag shown was laced with a contrasting thong that was continued around the front flap for decoration.

Antler, Bone, Horn & Hide

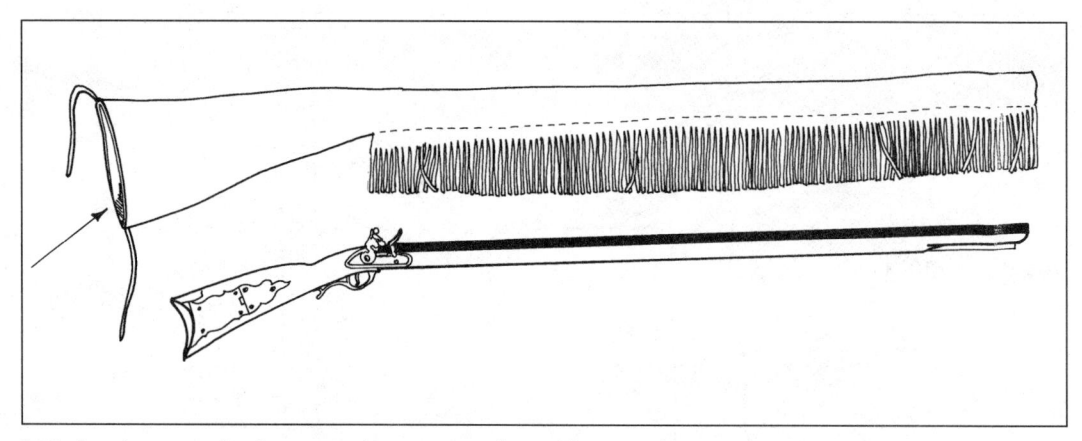

6-26. Another necessity for mountain men was a long-rifle case. The case shown wraps over the stock and ties to produce a fully protective case.

Long Rifle Case

Another very important leather item used by the mountain men was a case for a long rifle (fig. 6-26). Often elaborately decorated with beadwork, the cases were usually hand carried (they usually did not have any carry strap attached) and protected the rifle from the elements when the gun was not in use. The case can also protect a modern buckskinner's rifles from morning dew during overnight camping.

The first step is to make a pattern for your particular rifle. As long rifles differ greatly in lock styles, stock shape, and even length, it's important to have a case that fits your gun properly. The case should be fairly loose, but not baggy. The butt end of the case is made extra long so it can be folded

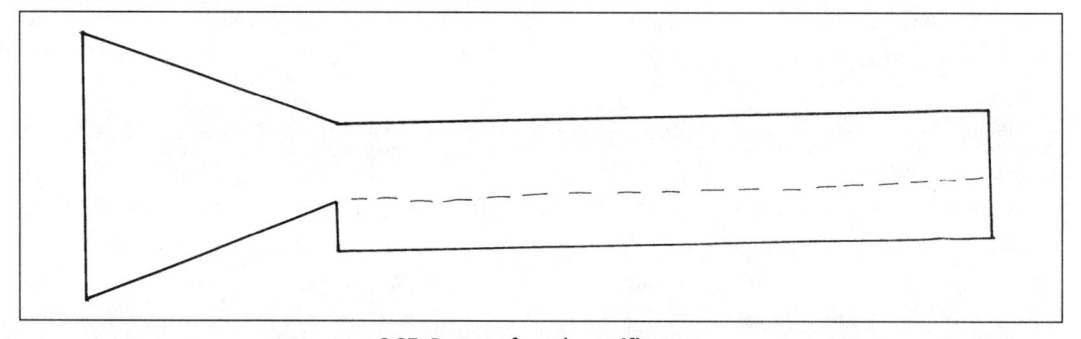

6-27. Pattern for a long rifle case.

over and tied in place. To make a pattern, lay the rifle on a piece of brown paper and mark around the outline. Add an inch all around the barrel down to the lock-breech area. Measure out four inches from the tip of the stock butt and make a straight line from that point up to the existing line at the breech. This makes one half of the pattern. Mark this on a piece of soft buckskin and then flop it over to complete the other half of the pattern. Cut out the leather following the pattern you've created (fig. 6-27).

Mountain men often added fringe to the bottom of these cases. The fringe piece can also act as a seam welt. Cut the fringe piece to size, but do not cut the fringes. Sew the case together wrong side

LEATHER ACCESSORIES

out with the fringe welt in the bottom seam. Then turn the case right side out. Cut the fringe and decorate the case as desired. Punch two holes near the top of the rear edge and run a thong through them and tie it off. To use the case, insert the rifle into the case, fold the rear section over the stock, and tie it off with the thong piece.

Modern Scabbard

Scabbards are used to carry a gun on a horse. They not only protect and transport the gun but make it quickly available when needed (fig. 6-28). The best material for a scabbard is a four- to six-ounce split cowhide. The squared drawing shown is for a standard modern-day scoped rifle. First create a pattern, altering it as needed for your particular gun. Cut a pattern from

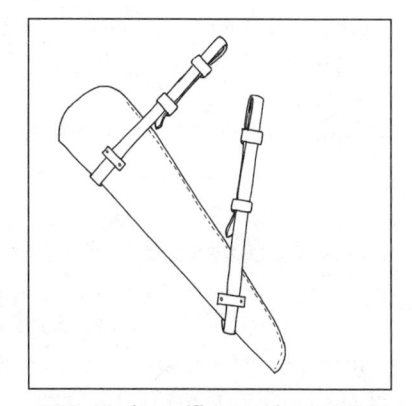

6-28. Modern rifles need protection and a way of transporting as well. You can easily make your own scabbard from heavy leather to protect your favorite rifle.

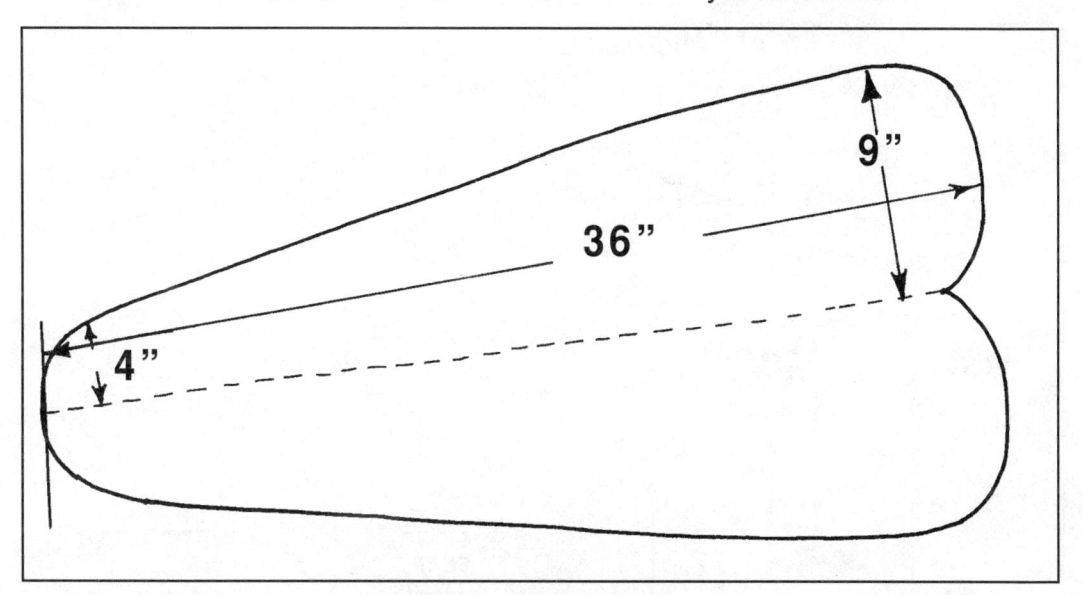

6-29. Pattern for a rifle scabbard

discarded stiff material such as old jeans or canvas and make sure the pattern will suit your particular gun (fig. 6-29). Once you're satisfied with the fit of the scabbard, place the pattern on the leather and cut it to shape using a sharp knife.

To fasten the scabbard to the saddle, cut two straps about one inch in width and twenty-six to twenty-eight inches long.

Moisten the main piece and fold it over. Punch mating holes along the bottom and sides. Cut mating slits in the strap tabs. Stitch the scabbard together using a running stitch with a welt between the seam for extra strength. Install the buckles as per the instructions given for making belts earlier in the

Saddlebags

You can make your own saddlebags to match the scabbard (fig. 6-30). Again, these should be made of four-ounce split cowhide. Enlarge the squared drawing on a piece of heavy kraft or butcher paper (fig. 6-31). Cut out around the pattern, transfer it to the leather and cut out the different pieces. Stitch the pieces together with a running stitch and heavy-duty waxed thread. An automatic awl works best for this type of project.

Stitch the side piece to the front piece of each

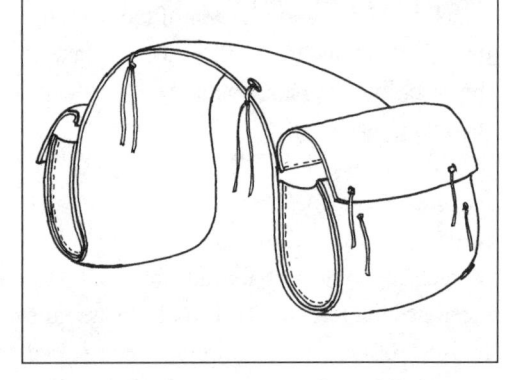

6-30. And you can custom make saddle bags to match the scabbard.

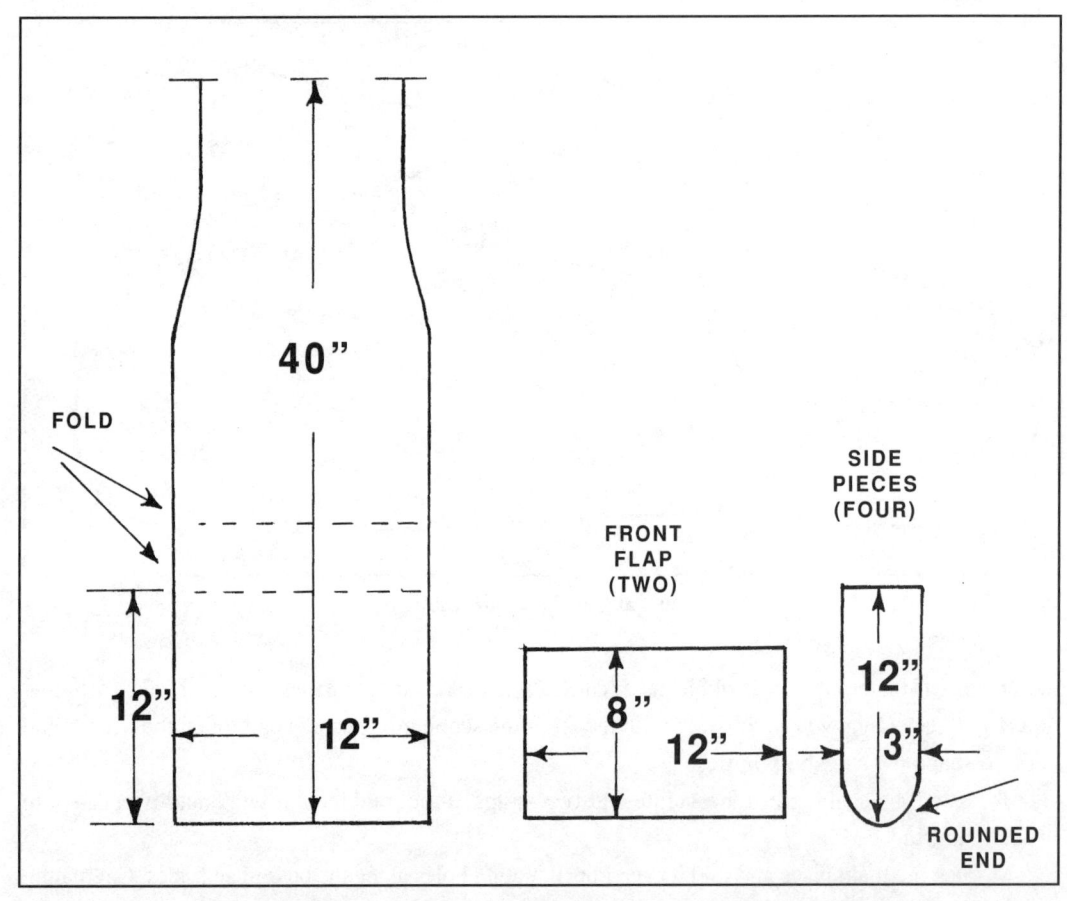

6-31. Pattern for saddle bags. To create a full pattern, fold the leather in half and use the half pattern shown. In the case of not being able to get full, eighty-inch leather, the pattern can be used as is, stitching the two pieces together.

bag first. Place the front-side pieces on each end of the long back piece and stitch these together as well. Finally, stitch the front flaps to the back and install buckles or ties as needed. The saddlebags can also be decorated in many ways including tooling some of the leather.

Quiver and Bow Case

Arrow quivers are also fairly easy to construct and were a necessity for Native Americans (fig. 6-32A). Handmade quivers can also add satisfaction for today's traditional archers.

6-32A. A bow-and-arrow case was important to Native Americans.

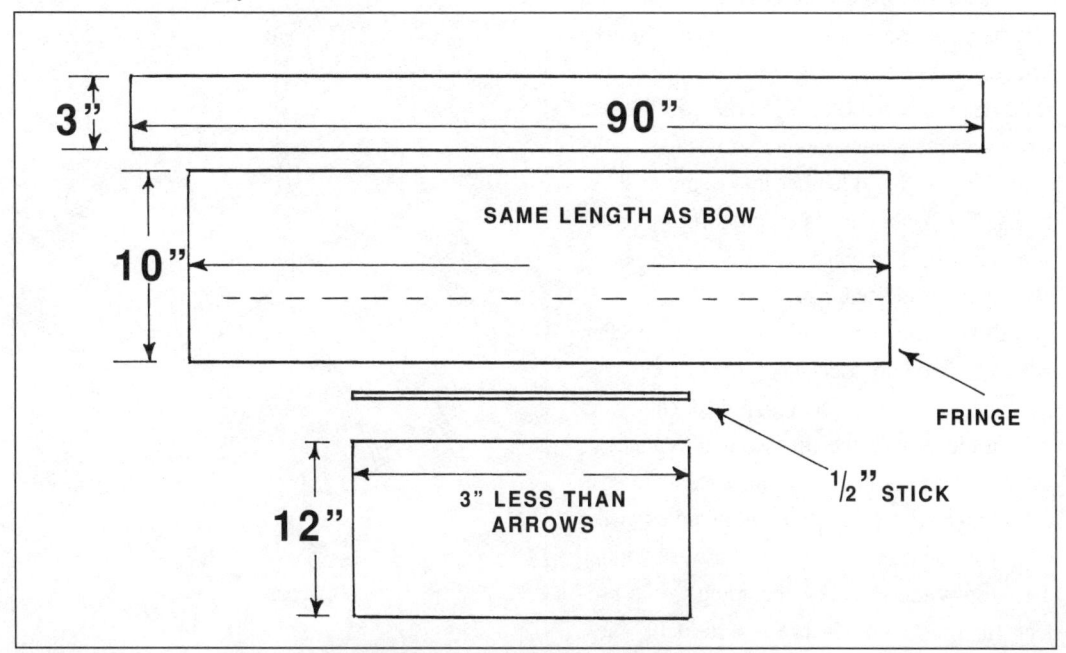

6-32B. Pattern for bow-and-arrow case.

The quiver can be made of buckskin, but for a bit stiffer case, use six-ounce split cowhide. Enlarge the squared drawing for the two pieces of the case onto heavy-duty paper (fig. 6-32B). Cut out the pattern, transfer it to the leather and cut it to shape.

The case side is first sewn using a running stitch and overlapping the edges about one-half inch. Artificial or natural sinew is the best choice. Sew the bottom in place in the same manner. It's not a bad idea to cut the bottom just a bit larger than needed, then trim it to fit the bottom edge of the assembled case. Lastly, cut a shoulder strap and sew it in place. A fringe strip can also be added. Traditionally, these cases were often beaded.

Antler, Bone, Horn & Hide

You can also create a matching bow case. Bow cases were used primarily to protect the bow while not in use and were mostly made of soft buckskin, often decorated with tied-on feathers. The quiver usually has loops on the back so it can be tied to the bow case. Or sometimes the quiver and bow case are assembled separately and then sewn together to create one case. The case shown is sized to fit the unstrung bow at the handle and taper to the tip. The length is slightly longer than the bow so the extra flap can be folded over and tied with a thong around the end.

Make a pattern for your particular bow by measuring its circumference at the largest portion, the handle, and making a tapered pattern. Add one-half inch on each side for the seam. Sew the seam together right side out using a whip stitch. A fringe or welt piece can also be added for decoration. Stitch a tie thong to the top of the case to close it. Attach the quiver to the bow case using a whip stitch.

Braided Projects

Thin leather strips can be braided and used in a variety of horse tack, including hackamore bridles. These strips can also be made into riata (leather rope) or whips. Back in the late fifties I spent many hours with my dad's uncle, watching him braid leather into many of these items. The technique is fascinating but does take some time to learn. The results are, however, equally fascinating.

Begin with long, thin strips of leather. About a three- to four-ounce, grain-side, split cowhide is a good choice. These strips can be cut from a piece of leather in the same manner as described for cutting lacing material, or a strip cutter can be made. The cutter is pulled along the edge of the leather to cut strips of precise widths. The strip width can vary according to the project. The most common size is 3/16 inch.

Several types of braiding styles can be used, including flat and round braiding. Flat braiding is used for belts, shoulder straps for pouches and powder horns, and other flat leather items (fig. 6-33). The easiest flat braid is a three-braid plait. This is done in the same manner used to braid hair. Begin by passing the right outside strand to the left and over the middle. Then pass the left outside strand to the right and over the middle. Continue braiding, working first from the right then the left until the length desired is attained.

A number of other braid patterns can be used, including four-strand, five-strand, and six-strand.

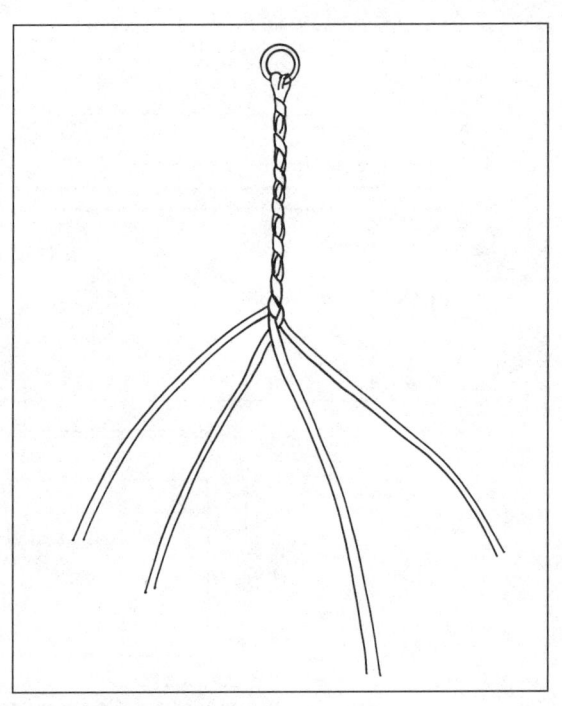

6-33. Thin strips of leather can be braided into numerous useful items. Shown is an easy four-braid pattern.

LEATHER ACCESSORIES

BLIND-BRAIDED BELT

One of the more unusual and fun leather projects is creating a blind-braided belt (fig. 6-34). The same technique can be used for other braided straps as well. Both ends of the belt are closed, or solid. Cut two slits the length desired for the braid, remembering that braiding will shorten the overall length of the belt. Fasten one solid end to a wire or C-clamp on a table or other solid surface. Braid in the same manner as for the three-strand plait described. After three braids, the lower portion of the belt will become twisted. Hold the completed braided portion tightly with one hand while untangling the bottom portion with the other hand. Pass the bottom of the belt up through the tangling loops. Continue braiding and untangling, pushing each braid up snug and tight. The end braids will be somewhat loose. When you can no longer braid, adjust all of the braids to take up the slack at the end of the belt.

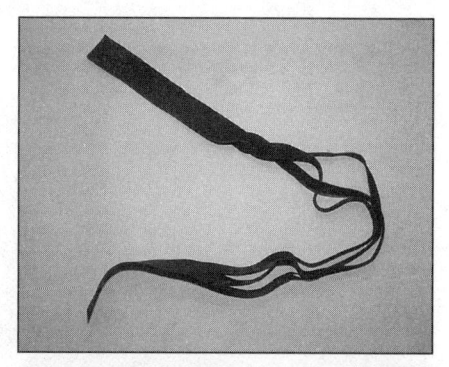

6-34. One of the most interesting projects is a blind-braided belt. The strips are braided in a three-braid. The opposite end is looped through to straighten the tangles after two or three braids. Blind braiding also makes an unusual powder horn strap.

BRAIDED ROPES AND WHIPS

Round braiding is commonly used for ropes, hackamores, and whips. The most common round braid is a four braid. It begins with two long, equal pieces of leather strip. My great-uncle used a piece of sturdy wire fastened to his shed roof as a holder. When the braiding was complete, he simply untwisted the wire. A carabiner used by mountain climbers can be used as well. Thread the two pieces through the loop, and then braid in the pattern shown. It's extremely important to keep the strips pulled tight and snug as you braid. Tie off with a half hitch.

My uncle also made bullwhips. The whips are a bit more complicated, but very satisfying to make. Whips often consist of a wooden handle, a core, a braided interior core extending part way, a braided outer covering, then the cracker. Shown are the basic components for a braided bullwhip (fig. 6-35).

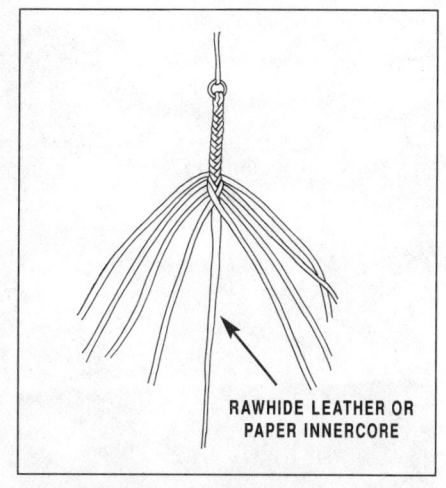

6-35. Bullwhips are also fun to make, but not especially easy. An eight-strand braid is often used.

The inner core often consists of a leather strip with a four-braid covering for a portion of the whip. Then an eight-braid is used to create the outer cover. Shown are the steps in creating an eight-braid.

RAWHIDE PROJECTS

Rawhide is an animal skin that has been fleshed and then air dried but not tanned. Usually, the hair is removed. Rawhide was the do-anything fastener and material of early Native Americans, mountain

6-36. Rawhide, or untanned leather, can also be used for a wide variety of projects. Shown is a cowhide rawhide produced by the author.

LEATHER ACCESSORIES

men, and later cowboys. Rawhide expands when wet, shrinks when dried. This made it an ideal choice for repairing items or holding items together.

Rawhide can be made of any animal skin, although the most common kind these days is cowhide (fig. 6-36). Full-thickness cowhide rawhide is extremely thick, but split hides offer other thicknesses as well. Deer, elk, and moose skins also make excellent rawhide. Small game skins such as beaver and especially woodchuck make good rawhide for small projects.

Lacing

The most common use of rawhide is as a lacing for anything from leather projects to snowshoes. Lacing is created by cutting strips in a circle (fig. 6-37). The rawhide is wetted to soften it, then the strips are cut using a nail and knife driven into a work surface in the method described earlier (page 61). The strips

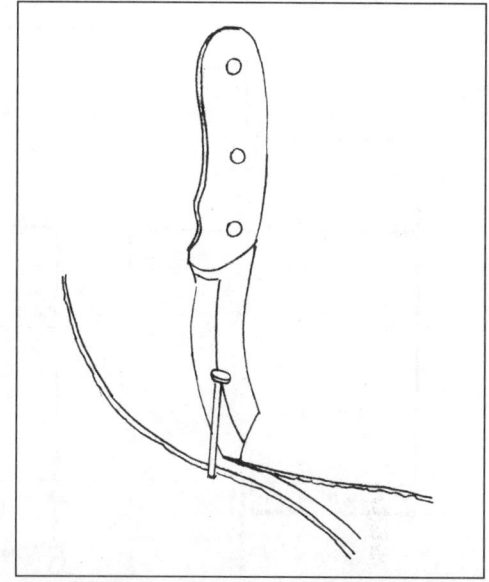

6-37. Rawhide lacing can be used for any number of items. The material is wetted, then strips are cut using a nail and knife driven into a board.

should be stretched before use. To use the laces for boots and other goods, the lacings should be well oiled (preferably with neat's-foot oil), stretched, and oiled again to produce a more supple material.

Parfleche Case

The Native American version of a storage box, parfleche cases were made in a variety of sizes and often brightly painted (fig. 6-38A). The first case shown is a flat case. Lay out the pattern by enlarging the squared drawing (fig. 6-38B). Transfer the pattern to the rawhide and cut it using a very sharp utility knife and a straightedge. You may find it best to wet the rawhide before cutting it, but remember the rawhide will shrink when it dries. Punch the lacing holes in the locations shown.

The top hinge area must be softened to fold easily. This can be done by

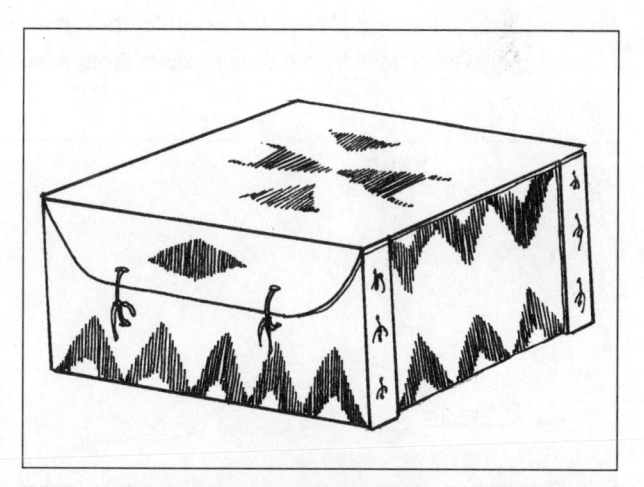

6-38A. Native Americans used rawhide for a number of purposes, including protective cases and boxes.

pounding the area of the fold with a rounded or ball-peen hammer or the end of a round stone. Do this while the rawhide fold line is on a solid surface. Pound until the rawhide loses its translucence

Antler, Bone, Horn & Hide

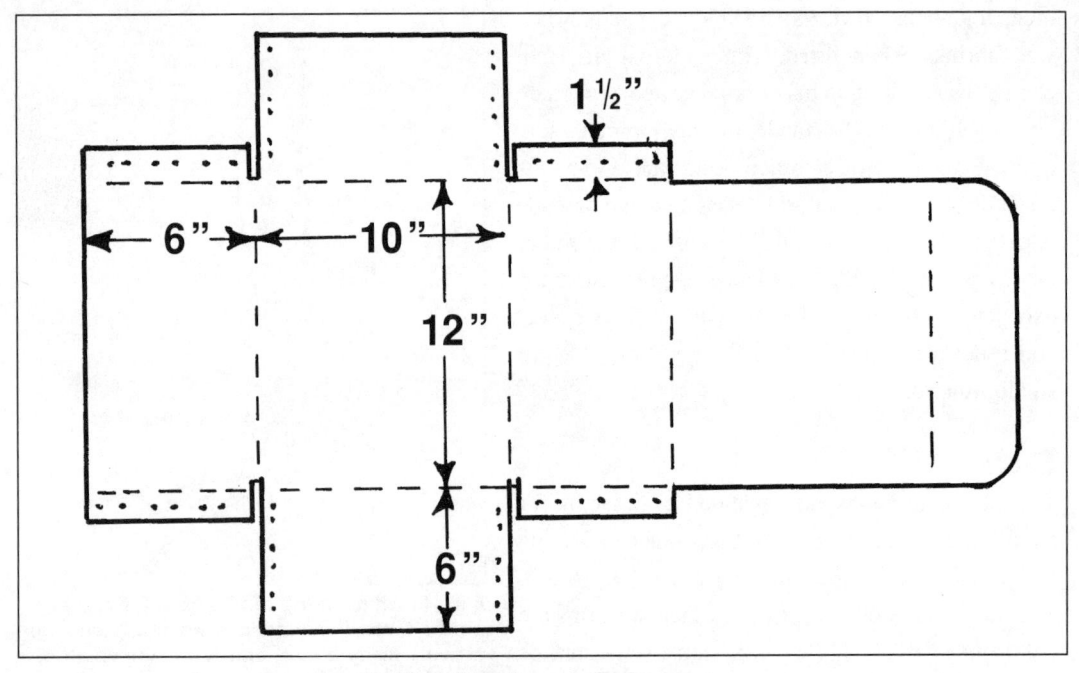

6-38B. Pattern for a parfleche case.

in that area and turns white. Pound the areas of the other seams, but not quite as much. Then fold the rawhide, lace it with rawhide lacing, and weight it down with a brick or rocks to dry.

A square box can be made in the same manner. Enlarge the squared drawing and cut out the pattern. Wet the rawhide thoroughly. Then shape the wet rawhide around the box or wooden block and tie it in place with string. When the rawhide dries, punch holes and lace the edges together. Small boxes can also be created by molding rawhide around wooden blocks.

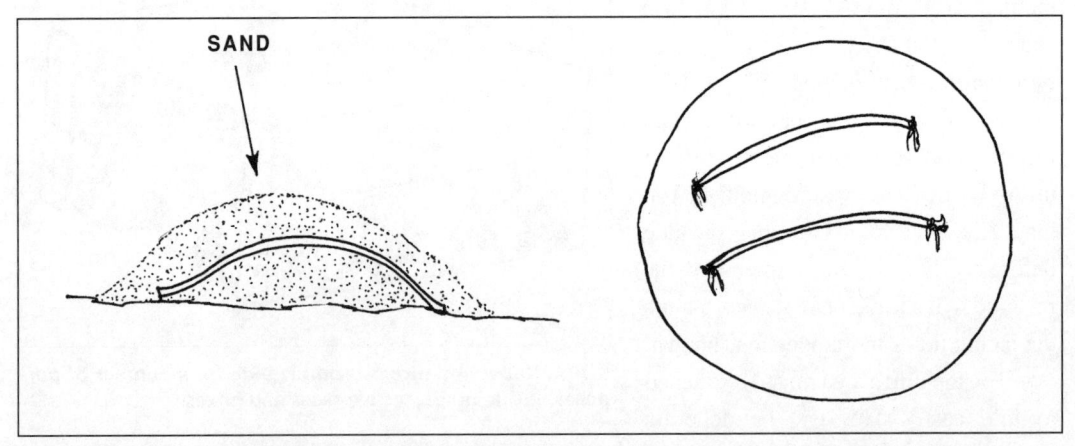

6-39. Rawhide was also used to create war shields and was extremely effective at stopping arrows and spears. The material was wetted and shaped over a mound of sand. Straps were added to the back.

LEATHER ACCESSORIES

WAR SHIELD

For buckskinning and rendezvousing, you might like to make a Native American war shield (fig. 6-40). These shields were typically made from the hump portion of a buffalo hide and were quite good at deflecting arrows and spears. The shield is basically a round circle cut from rawhide. Remember that rawhide shrinks, so cut the circle about a third larger than the finished shield should be. Wet the rawhide and punch holes for the handles. Create a mound of sand, place a piece of cloth or plastic food wrap over the sand and mold the wet rawhide over the sand hump. Cover the rawhide with dry, hot sand (fig. 6-39). The shield will probably not be perfectly round when it dries, but the edges can be pounded out to alleviate some of this problem. Pegging the rawhide to the ground while it dries can help produce a more evenly round surface. Rawhide can also be used for the shoulder strap and hand hold. Hold the straps in place with rawhide lacings.

6-40. These days, ceremonial war shields are more commonly made of soft, tanned leather, laced on a wooden hoop.

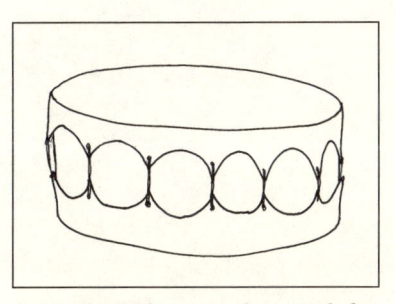

6-41. Rawhide was also used for drum heads. Laced in place on a hollow log or wooden hoop while wet, it shrinks to produce an extremely tight drumhead.

DRUMS

Rawhide was also used to form drums (fig. 6-41). Wet rawhide was formed over hollow logs or wooden hoops, then laced tightly. When the rawhide dried, it provided a tight drumhead.

WATERPROOFING RAWHIDE

The biggest problem with rawhide is that it changes character when wet. Native Americans used a variety of natural resins to varnish the material and protect their rawhide items from further moisture. They also used sizing created from animal hide glue. A good alternative is white shellac. First paint the projects with a good artists acrylic paint, then apply the sizing or shellac. ■

Tools and Materials For Decorating Leather

- Ballpoint pen
- Beads, a variety of sizes and colors
- Box frame
- Clothing dye
- Edge beveler
- Edge creaser
- Graph paper
- Spade modeling tool
- Spoon, old or a piece of rounded, smooth bone
- Sponge
- Stamp–for design and/or an embossing wheel
- Stippling tool
- Swivel knife
- Tracing paper
- Wooden mallet

7
DECORATING LEATHER

Although leather is a very utilitarian material, people through the ages have added a wide variety of decorations to their handmade leather goods. Native Americans have been experts at decorating leather for centuries. They painted, quilled, and beaded their leather garments and accessories in elegant and colorful patterns. Many Native Americans still practice the crafts of their ancestors and produce beautiful beaded and painted patterns.

DESIGNS

Native Americans used a wide variety of designs in their various decorations. Many of the designs were similar across the country, with slight variations. Other designs are associated with specific regions. The Woodland tribes of the Northeast and Southeast created realistic floral patterns, as well as designs with animals and plants. The Plains tribes utilized geometric patterns in many of their designs. The Southwest tribes utilized a wide variety of geometric as well as stylized realistic designs. The Northwest tribes were well known for their designs based on both animal and human forms.

PAINT

Native Americans used paint on many items, including themselves. Often the painted symbols had religious, ceremonial, or even personal meaning for the tribe or the individual. Buffalo hide tepees were excellent examples of colorful painted designs. War shirts and buffalo fur robes were often painted to describe the owner's feats or war victories.

A wide variety of natural materials were used to create various paints, from clay to dyes extracted from plants. These paints can be simulated quite easily with artist's acrylic paints (fig. 7-1). Once dried, the designs will hold their colors, even if the article becomes damp.

7-1. Leather can be decorated in any number of ways. The easiest is with acrylic paints. Anything from Native American designs to realistic painting can be applied to leather.

Antler, Bone, Horn & Hide

Quilling

Porcupine quills provided Native Americans with a very accessible and natural means of decorating a wide variety of items from moccasins to bags and clothing. When the quills are soaked in water, they become flexible. The bendable quills can be dyed different colors and then sewn onto leather in a variety of patterns.

Be very careful removing the quills from a porcupine carcass. Even from a dead animal, a handful of quills can present quite a nasty problem. Even dried, stored quills are sharp and can easily become embedded in your body. Keep the quills safely stored away from children and pets until you're ready to use them (fig. 7-2).

The first step in using quills is to soak them in water to allow them to soften. The quills are then dyed. Natural dyes can be made from plants such as bloodroot, wild strawberries, and sumac, and the root of the buffalo berry can be used to create the traditional red dyes. Black or dark brown is made from walnut hulls or wild grapes. Larkspur produces blue, while yellow comes from the root of the stinging nettle.

However, the easiest method these days is to use clothing dye, which is available in a wide range

7-2. The quills of the North American porcupine provided a most unusual form of decoration for Native Americans.

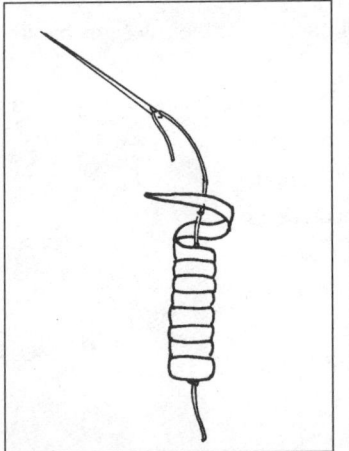

7-3. Quills can be arranged and sewn in place in a number of ways. One of the earliest methods was simply wrapping the softened quill around a single thread.

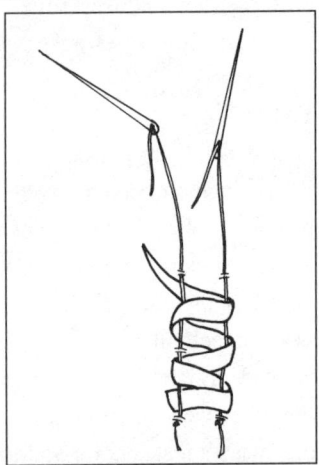

7-4. Two-thread quilling became popular with the Plains tribes and produces a bigger pattern quicker.

of colors in grocery, drug, and discount stores. Do not allow the quills to stay in the hot dye water too long. They can become too soft after only a few minutes.

Quills must be flattened for use. Often Native Americans drew the quills through their teeth after

Decorating Leather

holding them in their mouths to soften. A better method is to use a burnishing tool, such as the back of an old spoon or a piece of rounded, smooth bone, to flatten the soaked quills.

Quills can be arranged and fastened to the leather in a variety of ways. The simplest method is to wrap or fold the quills around a single thread (fig. 7-3). Stitch into the leather, bring the thread out and over the quill, then back into the leather, wrapping the quill around the thread with each stitch. Repeat this step and overlap new quills as needed.

Another method involves twisting the quill between each stitch to create a geometric, "triangular" design. These methods create a one-line design as well as solid designs that are greatly utilized by the Northeastern tribes.

Two-thread quill designs became popular with the Plains tribes (fig. 7-4). This method provides a broader pattern. Two threads are stitched parallel to each other and the quills are wrapped overhand between each stitch. Sometimes the two quills were plaited between the two stitches, alternating and overlapping the threads.

Quills can also be woven on a loom, a common method of the Chipewyan and Cree tribes of Canada. This method produces a very beautiful and consistent pattern that resembles tiny beads.

Beadwork

Native American beadwork provides some of the finest examples of a pure art form applied to clothing and accessories. The earliest beads were made from natural materials, including pieces of sanded and shaped shell and bone, seeds, and nuts (fig. 7-5). Beads made of clay were also used.

As European glass trade beads became available in the late 1600s, they quickly replaced the old materials and were also adapted to some of the quill methods of decorating. A variety of beads in different sizes and colors became available, including large crow beads, smaller pony beads, and, in the early 1700s, seed beads. A wide variety of similar beads are available today for those who wish to decorate clothing and accessories with beadwork.

Larger beads, such as crow beads, can be used individually as decoration or to attach decorative items, such as hair or feathers, to

7-5. The beadwork of the Native Americans is some of the finest practical arts existing. Several different methods were used. *(Courtesy of the Kansas City Museum, Kansas City, MO.)*

Antler, Bone, Horn & Hide

garments. Smaller beads were, and still are, sewn onto leatherwork in several fashions. These methods include traditional spot stitching, lazy stitch, and weaving.

Spot Stitch

Spot stitching consists of stringing beads on a thread, then sewing the beads in place. This type of single-strand sewing allows the stitcher to create curves and naturalistic designs. Spot stitching was very popular with the tribes of the Northeast, Great Lakes, and Northern Plains for producing beadwork with floral and naturalistic designs.

The first step is to create an outline of the design. Then transfer this design to the leather using any of the methods described in the introduction.

Secure the thread to start, then thread on two or any number of beads. Lay out the beads following the design and use another thread to spot stitch over the first thread between the beads (fig. 7-6). String another group of beads in place and spot stitch in the same manner. Repeat until the pattern is achieved.

7-6. Spot-stitch sewing involves sewing individual beads in place. Spot stitching can be used for more naturalistic designs and was extremely popular with the Eastern tribes.

The fewer beads between the stitches, the finer the work. The best work uses only two beads between stitches. Spot stitching can be used to make one or more lines in a pattern or cover an entire surface. Another method of spot stitching was used on moccasins, with each bead sewn on individually. Individually sewn beads tend to withstand the hard use of moccasins a bit better. Again, this technique was primarily used to create small and single-line designs or designs without a filled-in background.

When beads are used on leather, don't allow the threads to go all the way through the leather, but keep them "inside" the thickness of the material. As the stitches are made, tighten the threads and push the beads tightly together to hide the threads and make the beads lie down flat.

Lazy Stitch

Lazy stitch sewing was a common method utilized by many of the Plains tribes, including the Cheyenne, Arapaho, Sioux, and some Crow tribes. The method is very effective for covering large surfaces. Due to the way the stitches are made, the lazy stitch method creates a geometric design.

The first step is to lay out the design or make a sketch of the desired pattern. Graph paper can be used to create the pattern. Then use one of the transfer methods from the introduction to transfer the pattern to the leather. Start the stitch at the bottom of the material, then string beads, normally from five to eight at a time, on the thread and take another stitch (fig. 7-7). Then string the same given number of beads, turn the thread, and lay them down above the first line. Then stitch them in place. Repeat this technique until you reach the top of the pattern. Continue stitching, creating a second row of beads parallel to the first stitching. Work down to the bottom of the material. Work rows of bead-

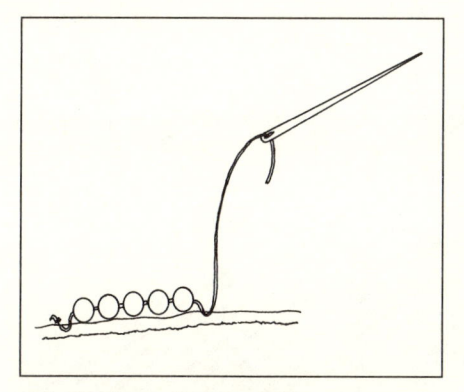

Decorating Leather

ing up and down until the surface is covered. This creates a series of parallel lines and ridges.

Two tactics can make the method easier. The first is to draw parallel lines where the stitches will be. The second is to fasten the leather to a stretcher using thumbtacks or pushpins to help hold the material taut and level for the sewing. Usually, seed beads are used for this technique.

Bead Weaving

Beadwork woven using a loom began with the Northeastern tribes and was also practiced by a few of the Plains tribes. The early looms consisted of a bow with the warp thread strung on it and pieces of wood used as spreaders. A wooden box frame eventually replaced the bow loom and became a method used by both Northeastern and Plains tribes.

7-7. The lazy stitch method was common with the Plains tribes. This method can be used to cover fairly large areas. Due to the method of sewing, it creates geometric patterns.

You can make a box frame very easily from a piece of wood with two warp thread spreader/holders screwed in place on each end. If you need to adjust the length, simply unscrew and move the wooden spreaders closer together or further apart.

This method also creates a more geometric shape, but large beaded areas can be created fairly quickly. Bead weaving is great for narrow beaded items such as headbands or belts. Make a pattern of the design you wish to achieve, but the pattern will be used only as a reference. One design method is to use graph paper and colored pencils. You can then count each square as a bead, giving you a color pattern to follow. It's best to use an odd number of beads. This allows you to have a center bead, creating the typical geometric patterns.

Thread the warp threads in place and pull them fairly tight. Tie off the bead thread to the outside warp and thread the bead needle. String the number of beads needed to fit between each warp thread on the bead thread (fig. 7-8). Position a bead between each two threads, hold the beads in place as

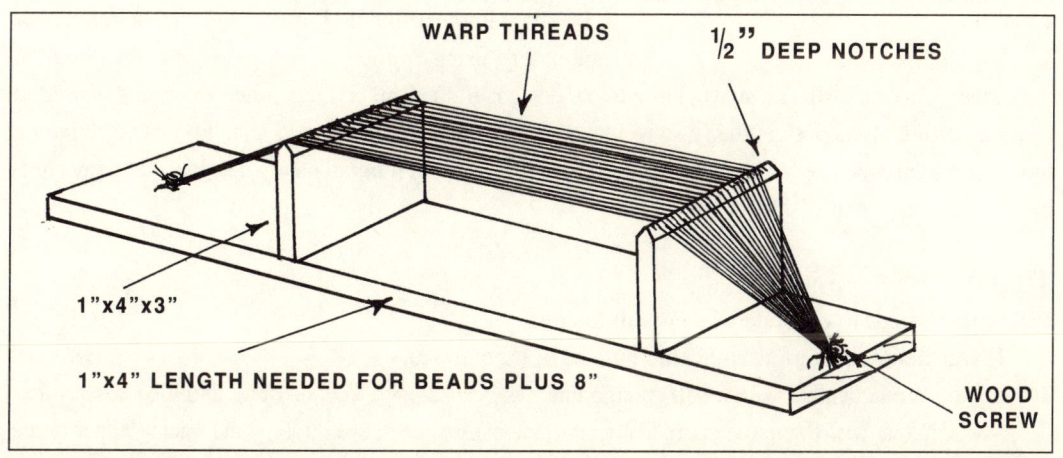

7-8. Bead weaving can be used to create large areas of beading fairly easily and quickly. Commercial bead looms are available or you can build a wooden box frame to hold the warp threads.

you turn the bead thread over the outside warp thread and go back through the beads on the opposite, or under, side. Continue the process until the design is completed. Then weave the bead thread through the last row, over and under several times, and tie it off to the warp threads (fig. 7-9).

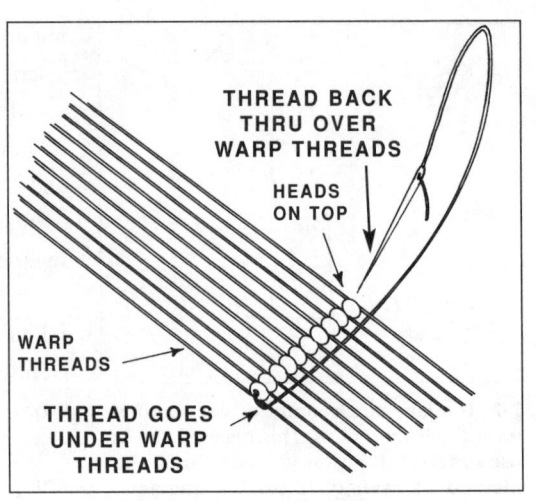

Sew the finished loom beading piece to a cloth backing, then sew the cloth to the leather. As leather tends to expand and contract with moisture conditions, sewing the beading directly to the leather could make the beading sag or break.

Leather Tooling

Another great way of decorating leather is tooling designs into the leather. Tooling became a popular method of decorating leather in the Old West, and is still popular today with Southwestern motifs (fig. 7-10).

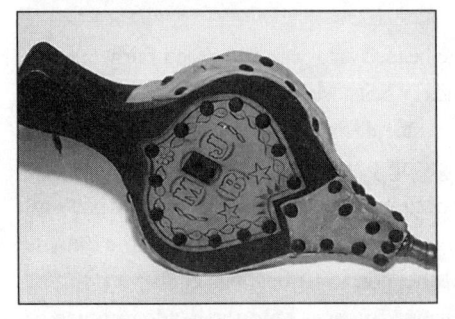

7-9. Bead weaving method

7-10. A popular method of decorating leather is tooling.

Leather can be tooled in several ways: embossing or stamping, carving, or a combination of the two. Leather tooling is normally done on fairly thick leather, usually 2-1/2- to 5-ounce grained cowhides. Leather objects decorated with tooling are normally accessories such as belts, bridles, billfolds, purses, gun cases, and other items that can be assembled from stiffer and thicker leather materials. Heavier, 5-ounce leather is normally used for belts, while purses and billfolds are made of the 2-1/2-ounce weights.

The simplest method of tooling is stamping or embossing, using a variety of stamps to create the design in the leather. Carving utilizes a swivel knife to cut designs in the leather. Quite often, stamping is used to create a portion of the design, then a swivel knife is used to add to the design. Finally, a backgrounding tool or stamp may be used to emboss the background. A large number of stamp designs and many commercial patterns are available.

Tooling

Follow these steps to decorate leather with tooling.
1. Transfer the pattern desired onto a piece of tracing paper.
2. Moisten the leather with a soft sponge that has been dipped in cool water and the excess water wrung out. Make sure the entire leather surface is moistened evenly. Tape the tracing paper to the leather and, using a ballpoint pen, trace the pattern firmly enough to slightly emboss it into the leather. Purchased pattern templates are also available that eliminate the need for tracing paper.

Decorating Leather

3. Make sure the leather hasn't dried out too much. It should not be wet, but dampened and feel somewhat cool to the touch. Use the appropriate stamps as desired to create the pattern. Hold the stamp upright and tap it with a wooden mallet to emboss the leather surface (fig. 7-11). It takes a bit of practice to learn the right amount of striking power to emboss enough to leave a lasting impression, but not enough to cut through the leather grain. A consistent look to the design by keeping the same depth for each impression is also important. Embossing wheels are also available to create a continuous design on the edges of the leather item.

4. Another method is to use a spade or spoon modeling tool to follow the outlines of the design. Hold the tool like a pencil and draw it toward you. It takes quite a bit of pressure to create a good, deep impression. Once the outline has been created, you can stipple the background using a stippling tool or stamp. Make sure the stipples are deep enough to create an impression but do not cut through the grain of the leather. The impressions should all touch each other and the background should look consistent and even.

5. Carving is done with a swivel knife on well-moistened leather. You can immerse the leather in water for fifteen minutes or so, wrap it in a damp cloth, and leave it overnight before carving. If the leather dries out during the carving process, immerse it in water for about twenty seconds. Wipe off the excess water and allow the leather to stand for about five minutes covered with a damp cloth.

   Hold the swivel knife handle with the thumb and third finger, and with the forefinger on the swivel, follow the lines to be cut (fig. 7-12). Tilt the knife slightly away from you as you make the cut, pulling the knife toward you. The cut should be about one-third the thickness of the leather. Further open the cut with the spoon end of the modeling tool. Then emboss and stamp the leather as desired. The carved and embossed portions of leather can also be stained to add emphasis to the design.

6. Finish off all tooled leather projects by first using an edge beveler, then an edge creaser to slick and smooth any cut edges. ∎

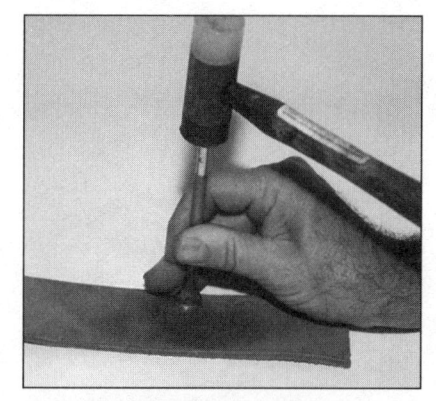

7-11. A pattern is transferred to the leather and stamps are used to create impressions in the leather.

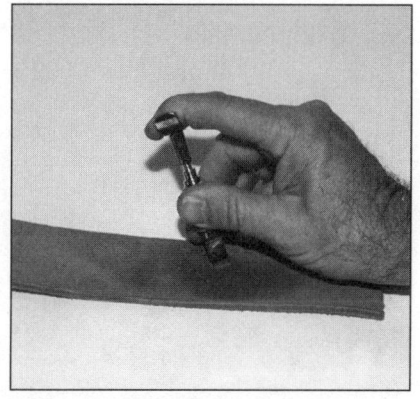

7-12. The patterns may also involve cutting or carving the leather with a swivel knife.

PART THREE

Furs, Feathers, Jewelry, and More

The pelts of many animals have been used as garments and accessories for ages. Many pelts are well known for their warmth as well as their beauty. Using the pelts from animals you have hunted or trapped to create these projects is very satisfying and a method of extending your enjoyment of the outdoors and your hunts.

The beauty and use of feathers as ornamentation is recorded and dates back to early man. Many ceremonies and other aspects of life were created around specific bird feathers. The projects in this section range from making a turkey pen to the more complicated chore of replicating a Native American war bonnet.

Almost anything has been and can be made into jewelry for body adornment. Antler, bone, leather, feather, and other objects are shown in a variety of projects.

TOOLS AND MATERIALS FOR
Fur & Pelt Projects

- Butcher paper
- Cardboard or plywood, large piece
- Cotton material, like flannel
- Darning needle
- Extra material for test-fitting a pattern or lining the project
- Felt
- Goose down, optional for a muff
- Heavy-duty hangers (for wall hangings)
- Heavy-duty waxed thread
- Iron
- Leather
- Leather thong
- Nonskid backing (for rugs)
- Pinking shears
- Pins
- Seam tape, iron-on
- Sewing machine
- Sinew, natural or artificial
- Snaps or ties, for bags
- Utility knife or single-edge razor

8
FURS & PELTS

Furs, or hair-on hides from numerous animals, provided a much-needed commodity to early people—warmth from the cold. Animals from rabbit to buffalo, including raccoons, beaver, coyote, wolf, fox, bobcat, bear, and, of course, the valuable furbearers such as mink and muskrat, have long provided mankind with fur. Many such pelts are still highly prized for clothing and accessories.

ROBES

Hair-on hides of almost any animal can be made into robes. Native American buffalo robes were considered a prize by anyone of the period. Hides from elk and wild or domestic sheep also make great robes. Deer hides can also be made into robes, but the hairs are somewhat brittle and they tend to break off.

8-1. The hair-on skins and hides of a wide variety of animals can be used to make robes.

And, of course, a bearskin makes a great warming robe for the cold. Small game and furbearers' pelts can also be made into robes, although the pelts have become more valuable as garment materials (fig. 8-1).

Making a robe of a big game animal is more a matter of tanning than robe construction. The robes basically consist of a tanned hide. The warriors of many Native American tribes also used the flesh side of the robes to describe their exploits with paints. The real secret in robes is thinning the heavier hides a number of times during the tanning process to achieve a flexible, comfortable, but cold-stopping product.

Small game and furbearer robes, on the other hand, require more effort. Rabbit skins have been a favored robe material in the past because they provide a very soft, flexible, and warm robe that also adds to the decor with the variety of colors and textures in the different skins. With their soft, silky pelts, muskrats also make great robe material. It does take a good number of skins of either to create

Antler, Bone, Horn & Hide

a robe of any size–approximately twenty to thirty skins for a robe forty-eight to sixty inches wide and sixty to seventy-two inches long (fig. 8-2).

A robe will have a more finished look if all skins are first trimmed to approximately the same size and shape. All holes and cuts in the skins should be sewn up. Then, working from the back with a glovers, furriers or whip stitch, sew a row of skins to create the length needed. A leather hand-sewing needle and waxed thread or sinew or an automatic awl will work fine. Make sure the stitches are drawn up tightly

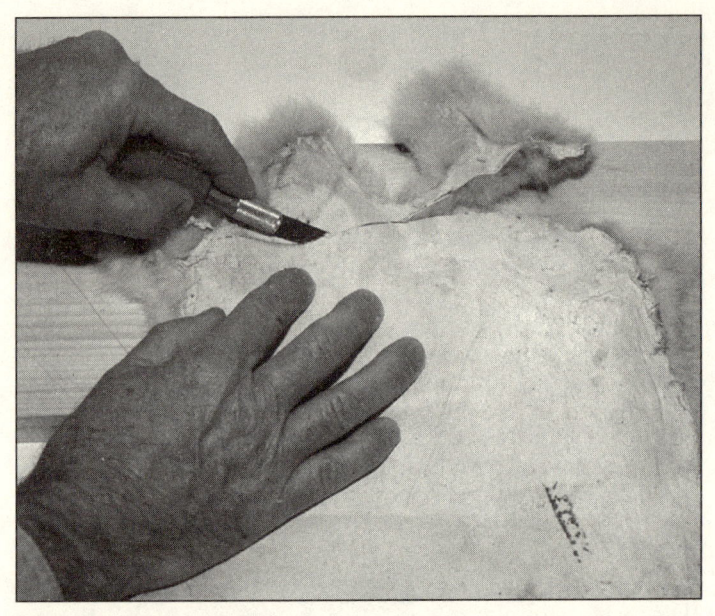

8-2. Even small game skins can be cut evenly, sewn into strips, then the strips sewn into robes.

as a robe takes quite a bit of abuse. The fur should all run one way, for instance all pieces with the tail down, so the fall of the fur is in the same direction. Sew the remaining strips in the same fashion, then sew the strips together. When you're finished, lightly dampen the back of the robe, stretch it out on a smooth flat surface, such as a piece of clean cardboard or a piece of plywood on a sawhorse. Tack the edges of the hides down to stretch the robe and allow it to dry.

Finish off the robe by turning down the raw edges and basting them with a running stitch. Or you may wish to purchase felt, cut the outside edge with pinking shears, and stitch it around the edge of the robe, easing the felt to the robe. Turn the raw edges of the robe under the felt when stitching to finish off the edges of the robe with the pinked edge of the felt. The felt should be about one and one-half times the distance around the robe.

Most robes also have a backing. Cotton sheet material is often used as an inner lining, with a soft-faced cloth such as flannel. The lining can be stitched to the back side of the robe top. A running stitch can be used to sew all the pieces together at one time, or the robe and lining can be sewed wrong side out, leaving a small opening to turn the robe, then using a whip stitch to close the opening.

In most instances a backing is also applied. Cotton sheet material is often used as an inner lining, with a soft-faced cloth such as a flannel used as the lining. A border can then be sewn between the lining and the robe top with a running stitch or the robe and lining can be sewed together wrong side out, leaving a small opening to turn the robe, then use a whip stitch to close the opening. A border can be then be sewn between the lining and the robe top.

Furs & Pelts

8-3. The edges of the rug should be turned down and basted with a running stitch, or add felt to the edge and an inner lining and backing material.

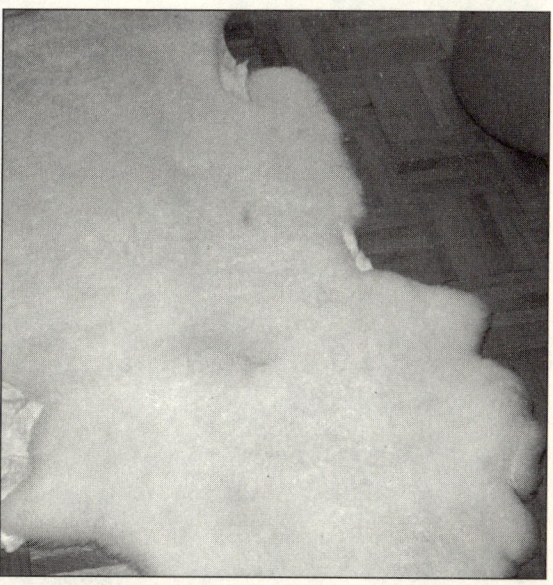

8-4. The hair-on skins and hides can be used to create floor rugs. If used on slick floors, a nonskid backing should be added.

Rugs

Hair-on pelts of bear, buffalo, cowhide, sheep, elk, and other game or exotic animals can also be used for rugs (fig. 8-3). In some instances, nothing more than proper tanning is used for creating these items. Floor rugs, without a head form, are made in the same basic manner as for robes. Usually rugs are left in the shape of the animal, with the tail on but the head off. Prime examples are cowhides or zebra skins. Smaller skins can be sewn together in the same manner as for producing robes. In most instances, a cotton or felt lining is sewn in place, much in the same manner for robes. The felt edge can be "pinked" for a traditional appearance. Large skins need to have the lining stitched to the skin at several places in the center as well. If placed on a shiny floor surface, such as wood or tile, a nonskid backing should be used (fig. 8-4).

Wall Hangings

The beautiful hair-on capes or hides of many animals can also be used as unusual and decorative wall hangings (fig. 8-5). The hides are tanned and treated in the

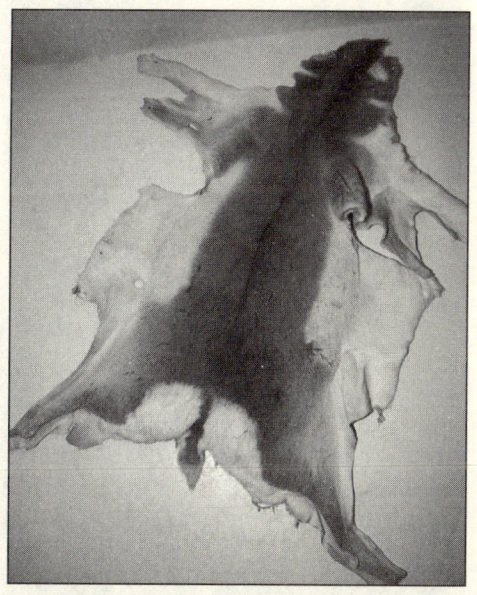

8-5. Tanned capes and skins make beautiful wall hangings.

8-6. Small animal capes and skins have traditionally been made into caps. The simplest involves wrapping a whole skin around the head and stitching the corners.

Caps and Hats

Fur caps and hats have always been popular, probably because they are both warm and comfortable (fig. 8-6). Use a good chrome-tanned hide or tan the skins yourself using Rittel's EZ-100 Tan. These tanning solutions protect against the moisture from weather exposure and sweating. Do not use an alum-tanned hide for a cap or you may end up with a cap that shrinks and expands. The alum can also leach out and cause scalp irritation.

Rabbit Skin Flap Cap

One of the most common fur hats is the army-style with earflaps (fig. 8-7). These consist of two pieces for the crown, two pieces for each earflap, and two pieces for the front and rear flaps or bills. Rabbit skin, muskrat, or other skins with a soft, short nap are good for this cap. Make a pattern of the crown pieces to fit your head using cotton or flannel material (fig. 8-8). This will also be the inner lining for the cap. Use pins to fit the crown pieces properly. You

8-7. A rabbit skin ear-flap cap is fairly easy to make.

want a fairly snug, but not tight, fit. Once you are sure the crown lining fits properly, remove the pins and use it to make a paper pattern of the crown. Then sew the crown lining together, inside out, on a sewing machine or by hand. Sew the lining with one seam from front to back.

Using the pattern created by the lining, cut two fur crown pieces. Position the pattern on the fur and mark around it adding one-half inch all around the top and sides for a seam. Sew the fur pieces together, inside out, using a whip stitch. Make sure the stitches are pulled snug.

Make a pattern for the earflaps and front and back flaps. Cut two of each (eight pieces total). Sew the inside and outside flaps together, wrong side out. Then stitch the flaps to the sides, the front, and the back. Sew a leather thong tie on the top of each flap to tie the flaps up out of the way when not needed. Place the lining inside the cap and sew it to the bottom edge, turning the edges of the lining and fur to the inside while stitching. Finally, stitch the lining to the crown in several places.

TOP-FOUR PIECES REQUIRED

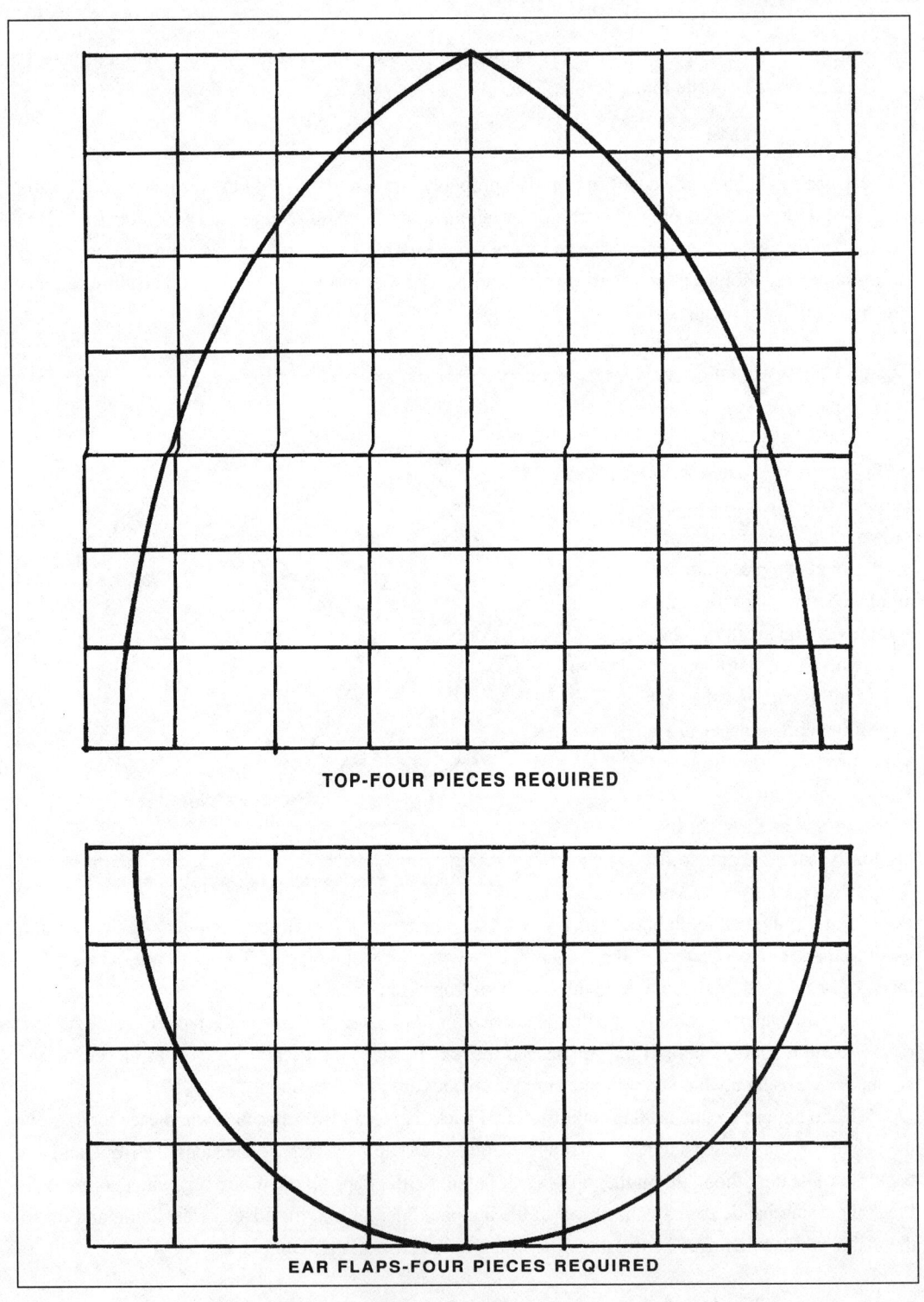

EAR FLAPS-FOUR PIECES REQUIRED

8-8. Pattern for a rabbit skin ear-flap cap on a one-inch grid.

COONSKIN CAP

Daniel Boone and Davy Crockett may have made the coonskin cap famous, but it is still the most popular attire with modern day buckskinners (fig. 8-9). Fox, coyote, and badger are also great skins for this type of cap. Caps can be constructed without the animal's face or with the face added for more decoration. One of the reasons for the popularity of the coonskin cap is that one skin from an extra-large raccoon will make a cap that will fit most.

The first step is to use a cloth tape to measure the circumference of your head

8-9. A coonskin cap was a traditional piece of headgear for settlers.

about an inch above your eyes. A great way of getting a good fit is to create an inner liner first from soft material, pinning or basting it together and trying it on. The squared drawing provides a basic pattern for an average adult (fig. 8-10A). Adjust the size of the pieces to fit as needed. Cut the inner liner pieces from the patterns and dry fit the cap until you're satisfied (figs. 8-10B and 8-10C). Then use these as a basic pattern for the skin pieces. These consist of the four crown pieces and a rear piece including the tail and a top.

Stretch the skin out flat and pin it in place with pushpins to hold it while transferring the pattern. Pin the pattern in place and mark around the pieces with a felt-tip pen. Then cut the pieces to shape using a very sharp knife, hobby knife, or single-edge razor. Cut only through the skin, separating the fur as you make the cut. Cutting through the fur will leave short, cut pieces of fur at each seam or edge.

Join the long side panels together with iron-on seam tape, using a hot iron to adhere the tape. Then sew with a whip stitch using a darning needle or other sturdy needle and a double strand of heavy-duty waxed thread.

Join and sew the two short side panels, one on each side of the rear panel. Then join and sew one end of the long assembled piece to one short side panel. Before completing the entire encircling band, dry fit the hat and adjust it as needed. Remember, it will need to be a little loose to allow for the inner liner. When you're satisfied, join and sew the two pieces together.

Sew the top or crown piece to the circle, wrong side out, using a whip stitch. Make sure all stitches

1"
SQUARES

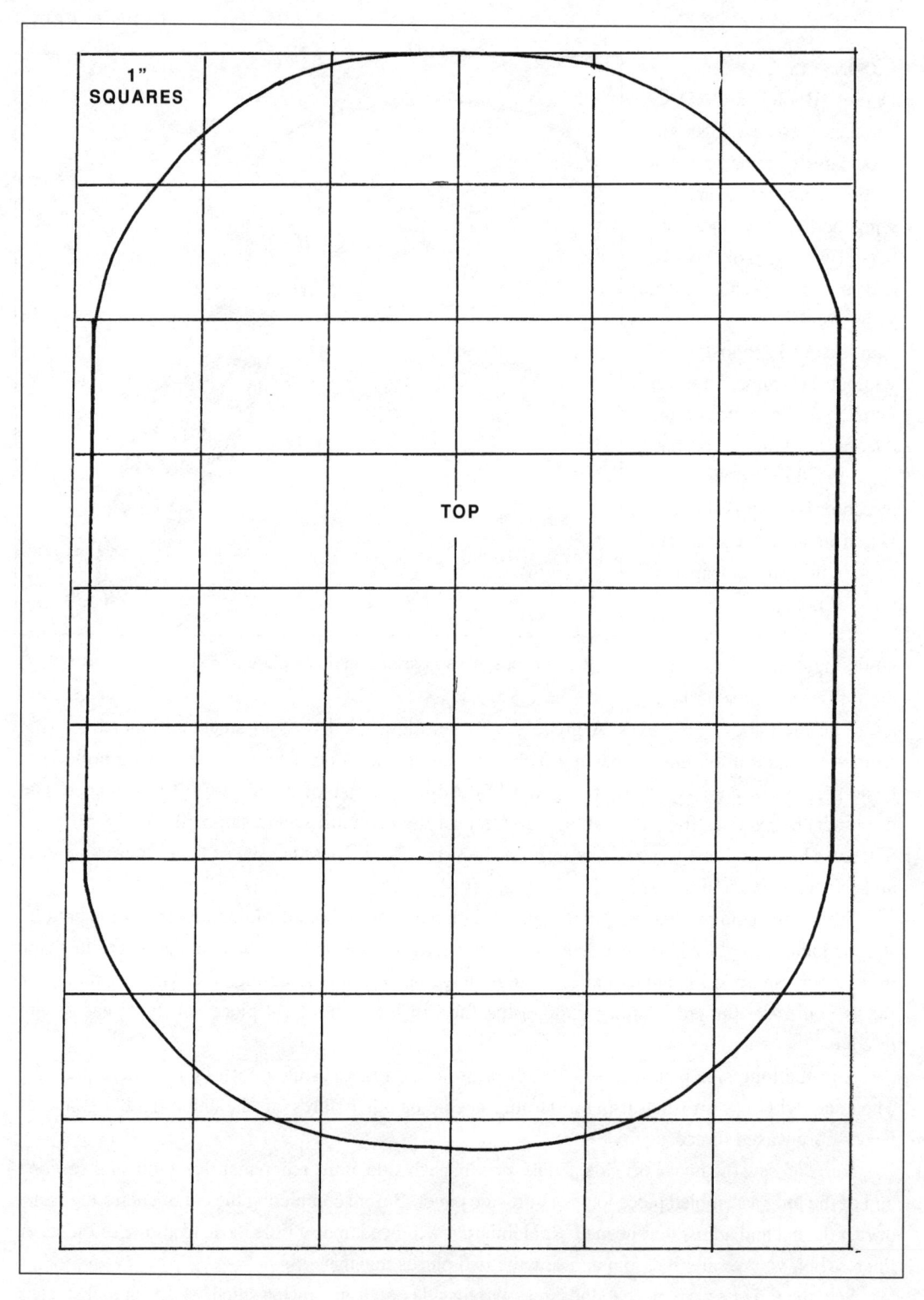

8-10A. Pattern for the top of a coonskin cap.

are pulled nice and snug. Turn the hat right side out and stitch the liner in place, turning the edge of the liner and the edge of the skin under. Stitch the liner in place at the crown and band edge as well. You can also add earflaps to the cap in the same manner as described for the army-style cap. Sew the animal face in front if desired.

MITTENS AND MUFFS

Fur skins have traditionally been used to make muffs and mittens. Rabbit skins are great for both, as are muskrat skins. The skins should be chrome tanned or tanned with one of the modern-day tanning solutions like Rittel's EZ-100 to prevent skin irritation.

MUFFS

Some of the easiest projects to make are muffs (fig. 8-11A). Sheepskin makes great muffs along with the skins of rabbit and muskrat. Very simple muffs can be made by sewing the ends of a strip of fur together with the fur inside and the flesh side out, creating a long tube. A thong neck strap can be sewn to each end.

A more elaborate muff consists of both an inner fur lining and an outer fur covering (fig. 8-11B). These can utilize two different skins if desired, say rabbit for the inside and fox or coyote for the outside. If the skins are not large enough to make the muff, sew several skins together as described in making robes. Stretch the piece out tightly, then cut the pattern desired. The length and diameter of the muff should be adjusted

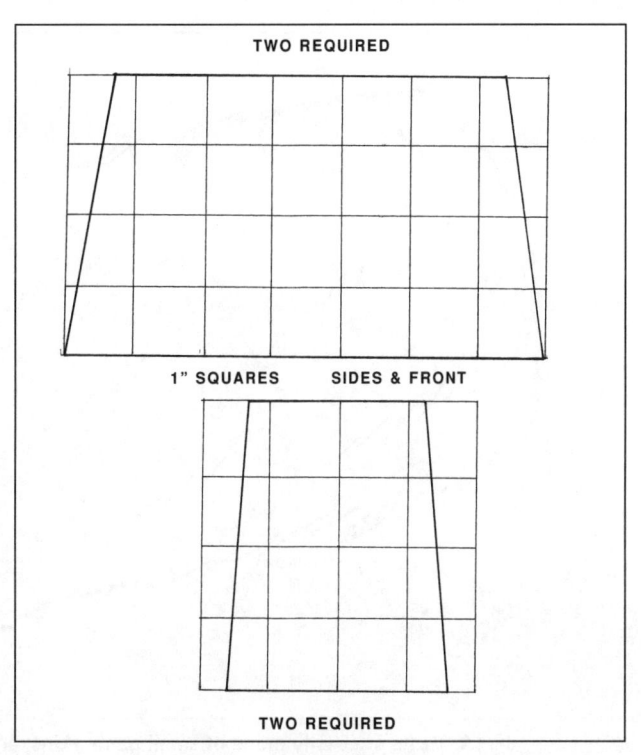

8-10B. Pattern for the sides and front of a coonskin cap.

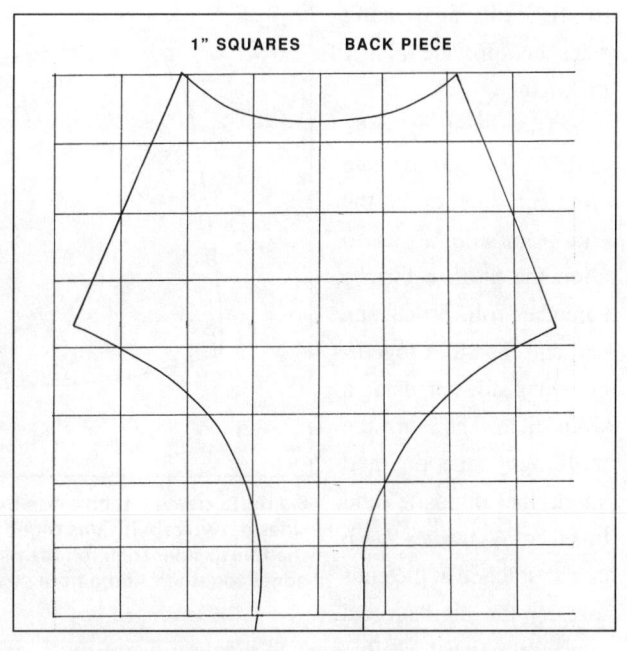

8-10C. Pattern for the back piece of a coonskin cap.

Antler, Bone, Horn & Hide

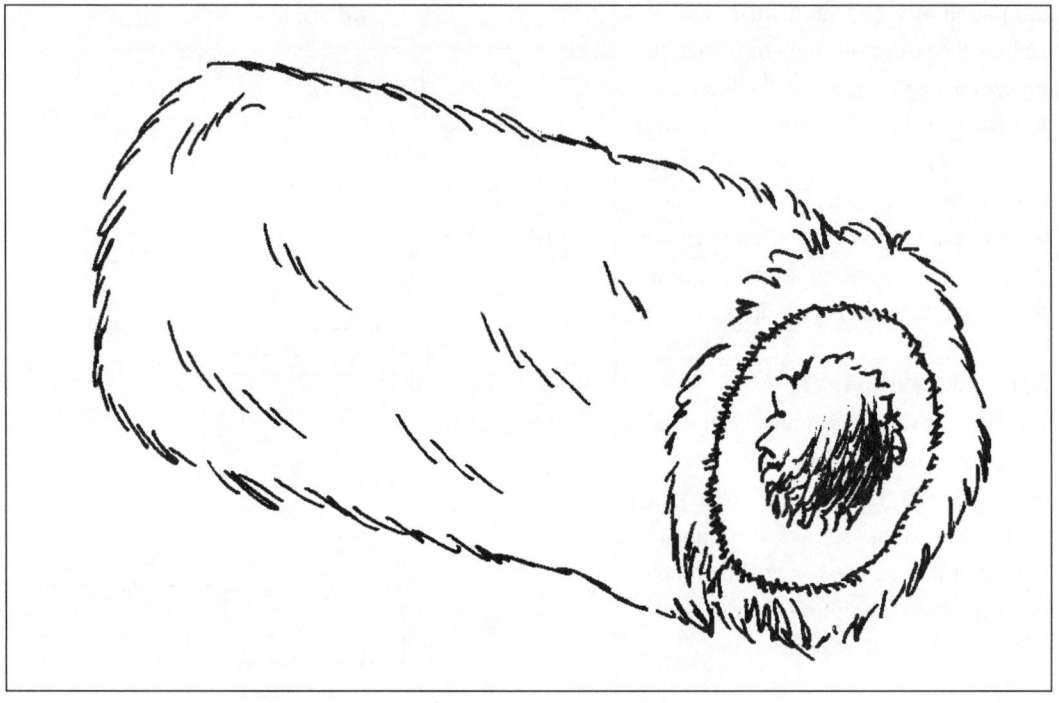

8-11A. Muffs are easily made of small game skins, and rabbit fur is especially warm.

to fit individual hand sizes but provide plenty of length.

After cutting the muff to the approximate size, cut notches in the end seam allowances to allow the muff to form a smoother roll. Stitch one end and the sides together, wrong side out, using a whip stitch. Then turn the muff right side out and stitch the opposite end together. A leather strap can be stitched at the ends to carry the muff around your neck. If you really want to create a warm muff, add goose down between the layers before stitching the inner and outer muffs together.

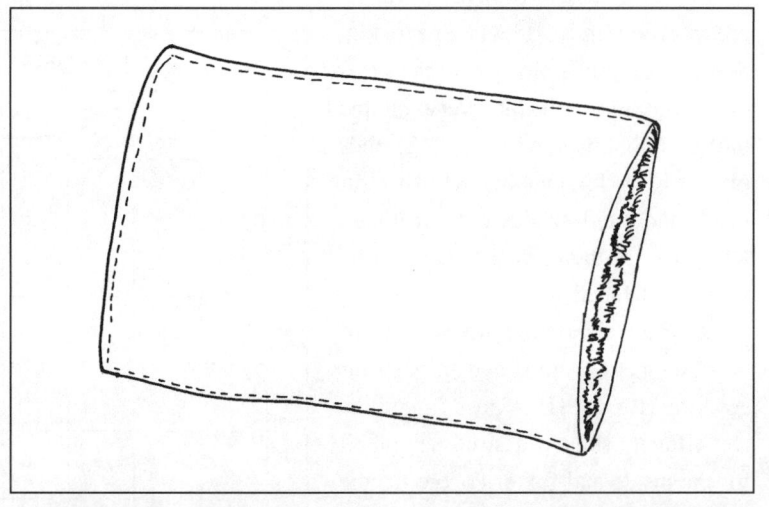

8-11B. To create a rabbit skin muff that is fur inside and out, first sew three sides of two rabbit skins together, turn them right side out, and blind stitch the fourth side. Then roll the piece to create a muff and blind stitch the long edges together. Add a neck strap if desired.

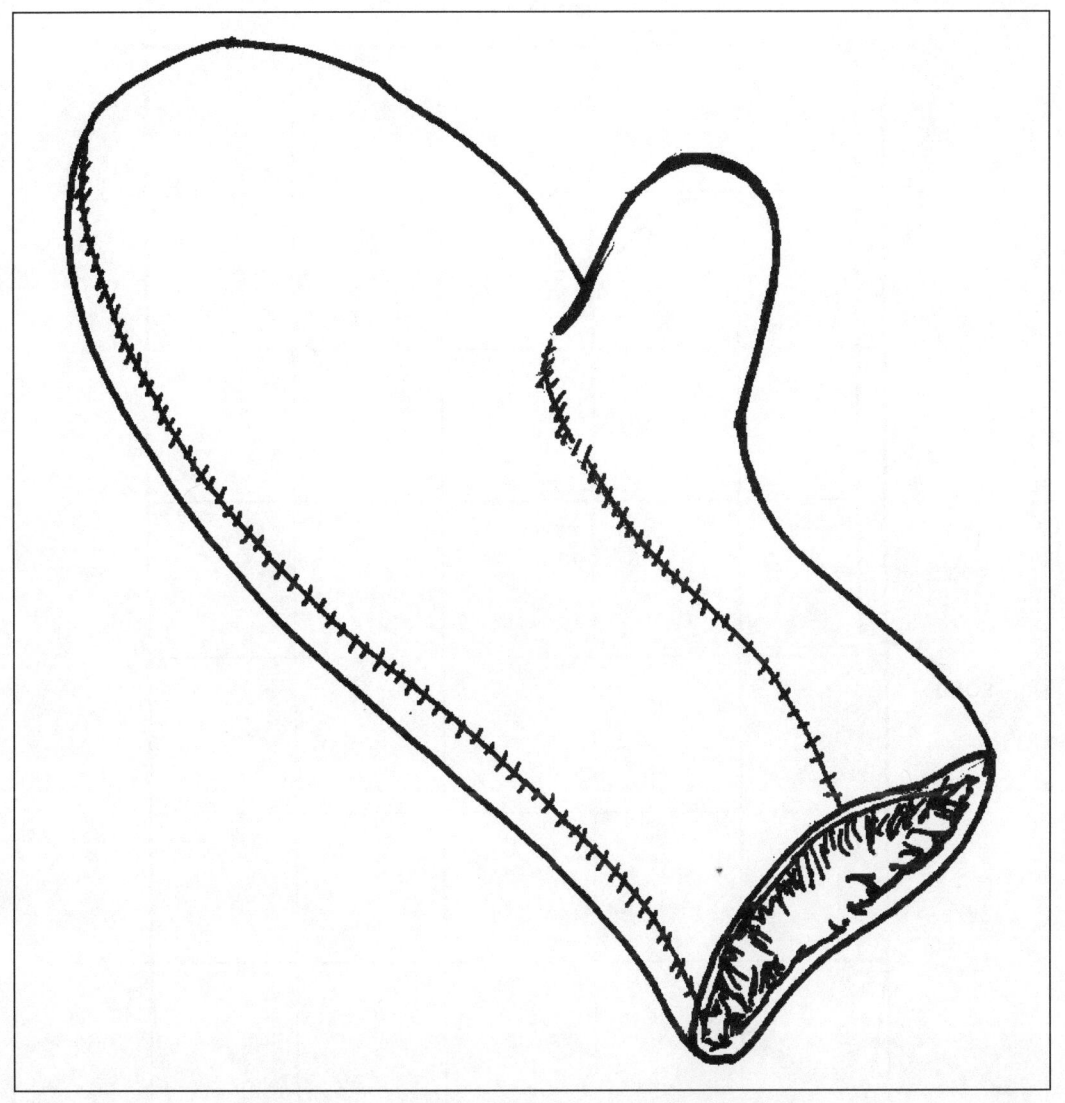

8-12. Fur-in rabbit-skin mittens are also extremely warm.

MITTENS

Fur-in mittens are also extremely warm and comfortable (fig. 8-12). They are just a bit harder to assemble than muffs. Mittens should be made of a very soft skin with short fur, like rabbit or sheared sheepskin, usually with the fur inside for warmth. Mittens are cut long at the wrist to create a cuff. When the cuff is turned down, it shows the fur, but when turned up, the cuff provides further protection between the mitten and the end of the coat sleeve.

The first step is to make a pattern of the hand size by laying the hand on a piece of butcher or other fairly stiff paper. Trace around the hand and add one-half inch for the seams. The squared drawing shows a basic pattern for a medium size mitten (figs. 8-13A, 8-13B, and 8-13C). Adjust this pattern to suit your hand size. Again, it's best to make up a trial pattern using a piece of cotton or canvas. Baste this

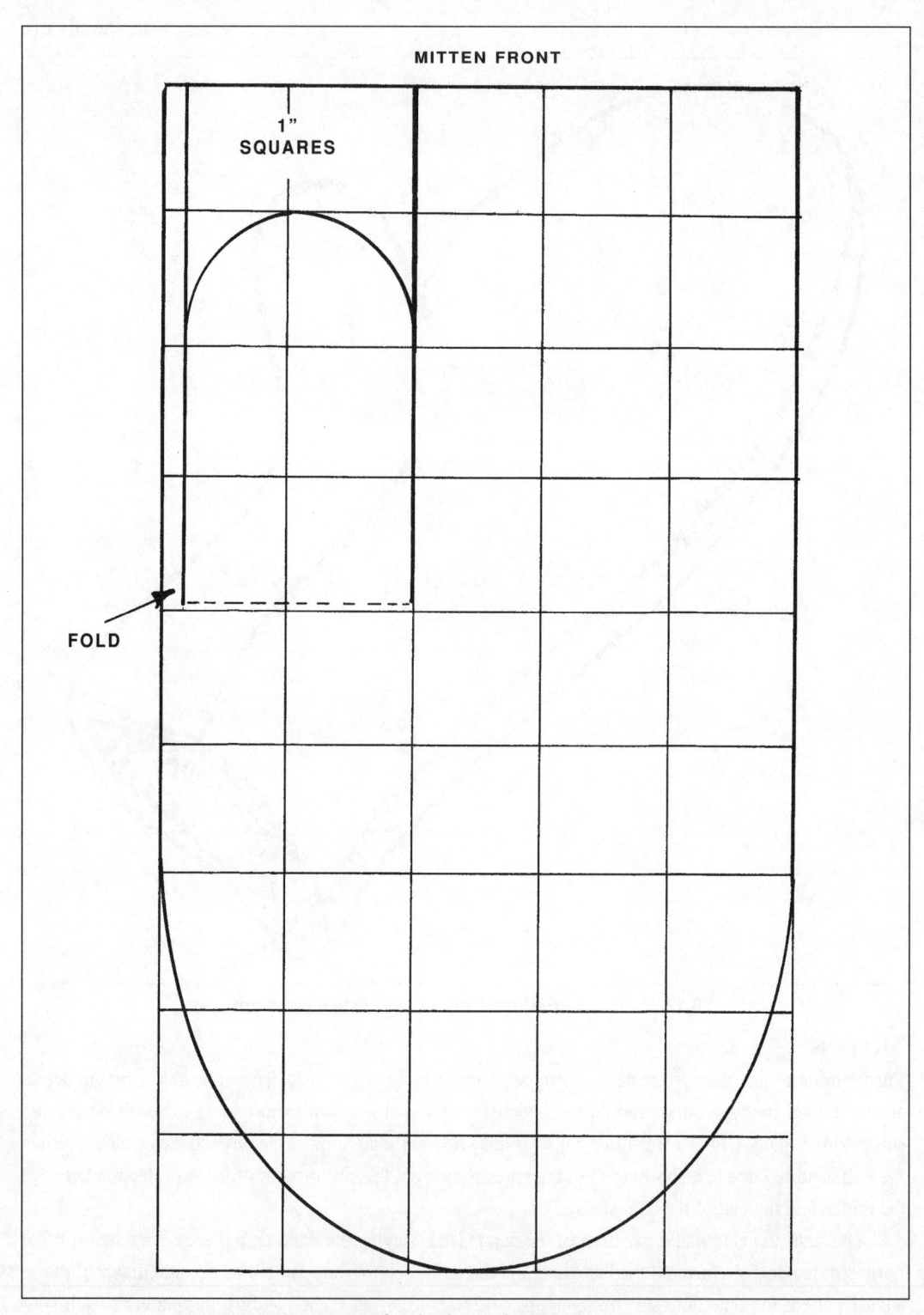

8-13A. Pattern for the front of rabbit skin mittens.

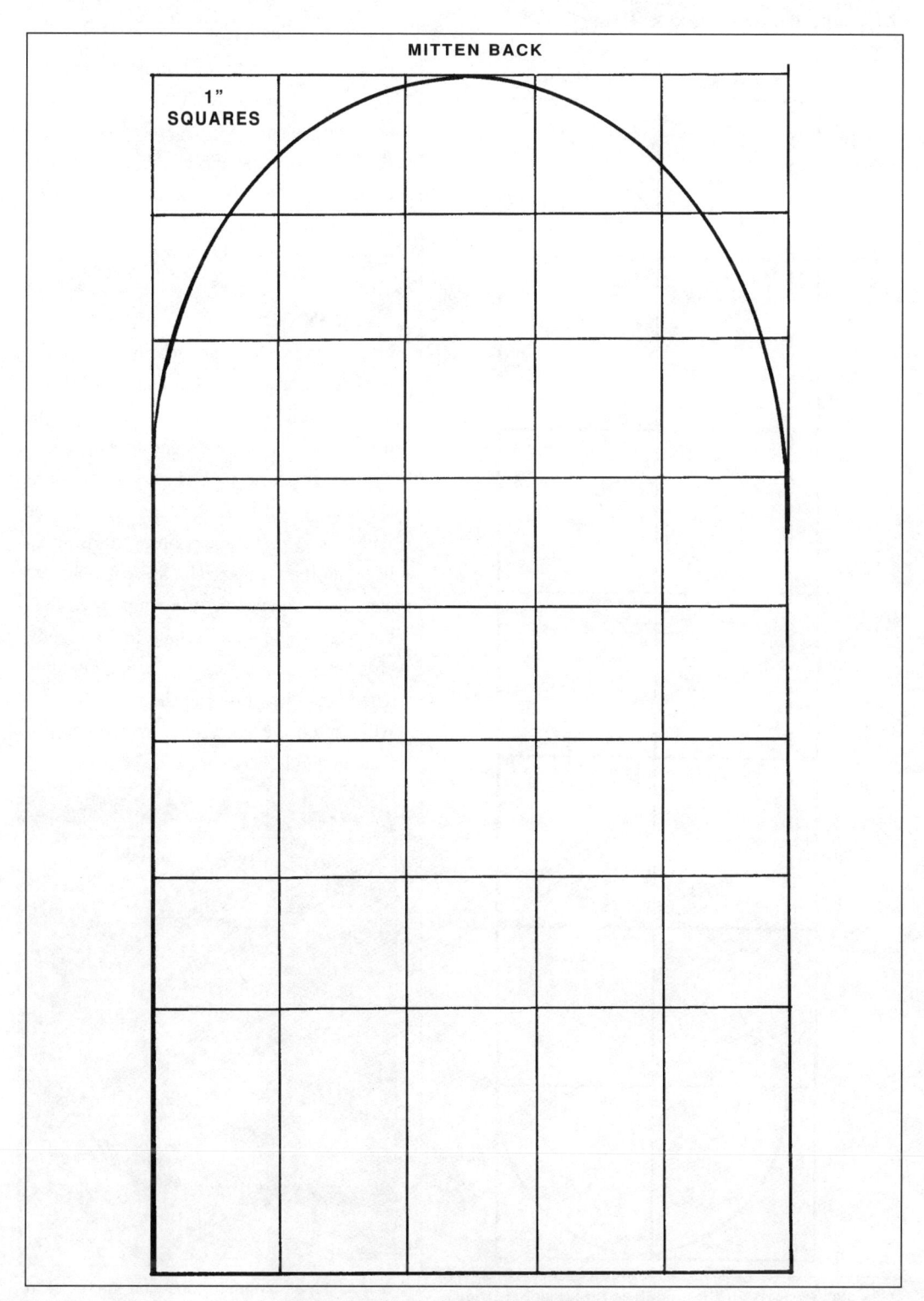

MITTEN BACK

1" SQUARES

8-13B. Pattern for the back of rabbit skin mittens.

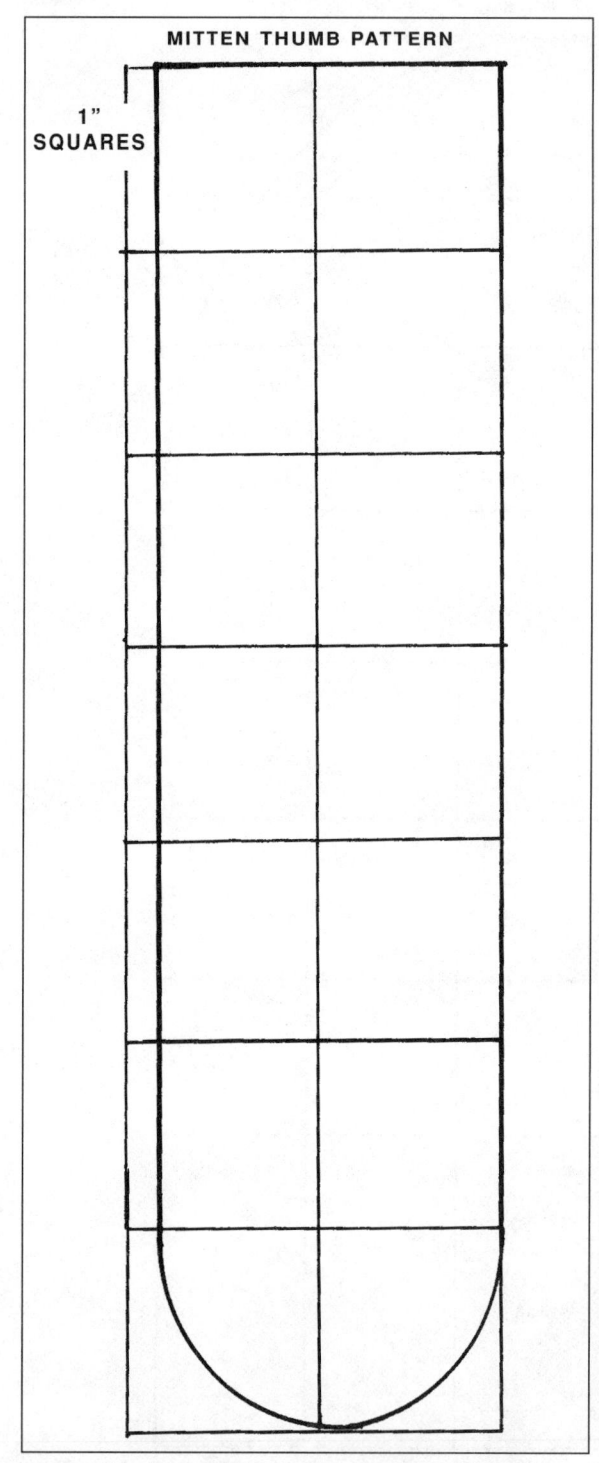

MITTEN THUMB PATTERN

1" SQUARES

8-13C. Pattern for the thumb of rabbit skin mittens.

pattern together to determine proper fit. Then take it apart, stretch the skin flesh side out, and transfer the pattern pieces to the skin. Cut out the pieces, then sew them together wrong side out with a whip stitch. Remember to reverse the pattern to create a mitten for the opposite hand.

Neck Wraps

One of the easiest projects to create is a neck wrap or muffler. Only the softest furs such as mink, muskrat, and otter should be used. Join smaller skins end to end to create the length needed. If very small skins are used, join two long strips to create the width needed. To add a lining, turn under both the lining material and skin edge and sew them together with a whip stitch over the edge. Or sew the fur and lining together wrong side out, leaving a small opening. Then turn the muffler to the right side and whip stitch the opening from the outside. This method conceals all the edges.

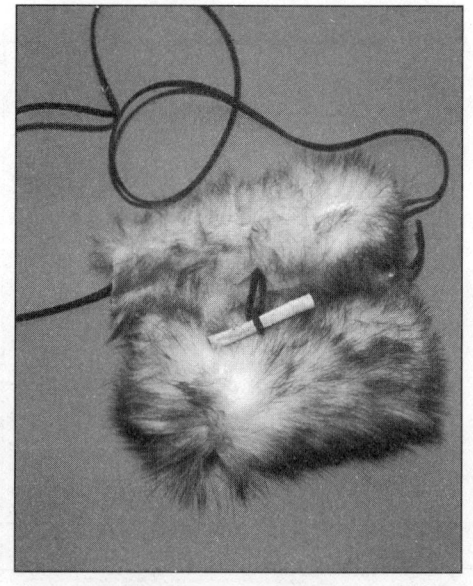

8-14A. Small animal skins can be used to create unusual bags for buckskinners.

Furs & Pelts

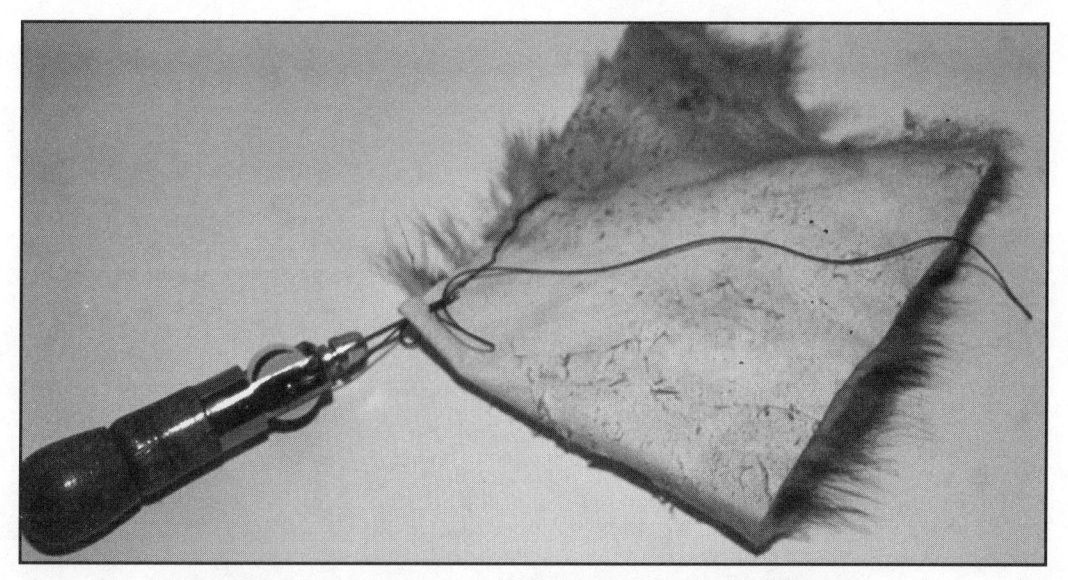

8-14B. An automatic awl is used to stitch this bag wrong side out.

Jackets and Coats

Furs have traditionally been used to create jackets, capes, and coats. The furs of wolf, coyote, fox, raccoon, muskrat, otter, mink, and even rabbit can be used to create beautiful and practical outer garments. Creating fur jackets and coats, however, is a fairly daunting affair unless you have good sewing skills. It can be done by disassembling a favorite old jacket or coat and using it as a pattern. The coat or jacket pattern, however, should have very simple, straight lines and few seams.

When sewing several animal skins together to make any larger fur item, be sure the skins are all sewed in the same direction. The skins for a coat or jacket should all be placed head up for the smoothest-feeling fur.

What many don't realize is the number of pelts needed to make a jacket or coat. Consider that a muskrat skin averages about six by eight inches in size. A short coat requires fifty or more mink or muskrat skins, while a long coat can average over seventy skins. A short coyote coat will require around eight skins, while a full-length coat may require at least a dozen.

Coats and jackets are usually sewn with the seams on the inside. A lining then covers the seams.

Bags

Native Americans used small animals to make any number of bags, leaving the fur on for decoration and also because it was a quicker and simpler method of using the hides (fig. 8-14A). To create these bags simply sew them together, wrong side out, in the size and shape desired. A whip stitch is the most commonly used method of sewing. Natural or artificial sinew can be used for joining the pieces together or an automatic awl can be used. The bags can be closed with flaps and snaps or ties or with drawstrings (fig. 8-14B). ■

TOOLS AND MATERIALS FOR
Feather Projects

- Beads, optional
- Belt-backing material
- Borax
- Cardboard
- Chisel or router
- Cotton cloth or muslin
- Feathers, from turkey, pheasant, or other game bird
- Hook-and-eye or snap closures
- Horsehair
- Ink
- Knife
- Leather
- Leather dye or liquid black shoe polish
- Leather thong
- Metal discs or conchas, optional for headband
- Pushpins
- Rabbit or ermine skin, optional for headband
- Red flannel binding
- Sinew, artificial or real, or yarn
- Stain or varnish, for the board of the turkey fan mount
- Thread, waxed
- Wall hanger
- Wood, softwood or hardwood

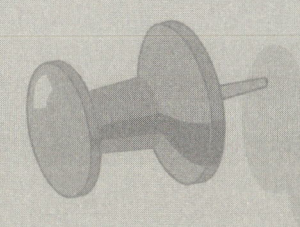

9
FEATHERS

Feathers and the pelts of birds have long been used for a wide variety of decorations and personal adornments. Today, feather decorations, including the skins and feathers from pheasants and other game birds, are still popular. The fan of a wild turkey is a trophy many hunters enjoy. Creating your own feather projects is fun and a great way of utilizing more of your hunting harvest (fig. 9-1).

Native Americans made great use of feathers from eagles, hawks, owls, waterfowl, wild turkeys, and numerous other birds. The feathers of some birds had ceremonial or religious meaning. Some tribes also adorned or cut feathers in specific ways to advertise their exploits. These feathers were often interwoven into the hair or used in headbands or roaches, a decorative headpiece.

HEADGEAR

The simplest form of Native American headgear is a headband. Headbands were often made from a strip of buckskin that was left plain, painted, or beaded. A feather or perhaps two feathers were often stitched to the rear of the headband (fig. 9-2).

Many of the Woodland tribes utilized leather skullcaps decorated with feathers glued in place. Quite often, a single turkey feather was placed in the center of the top. The feather was usually anchored with a wooden or bone pivot placed in the peak of the cap to allow the feather to rotate in the wind.

9-1. Beautiful bird feathers have always been admired and used for a variety of purposes. The feathers by themselves can be added to household decor.

9-2. Feathers were used for a variety of headgear by Native Americans. The simplest was a headband with a single feather.

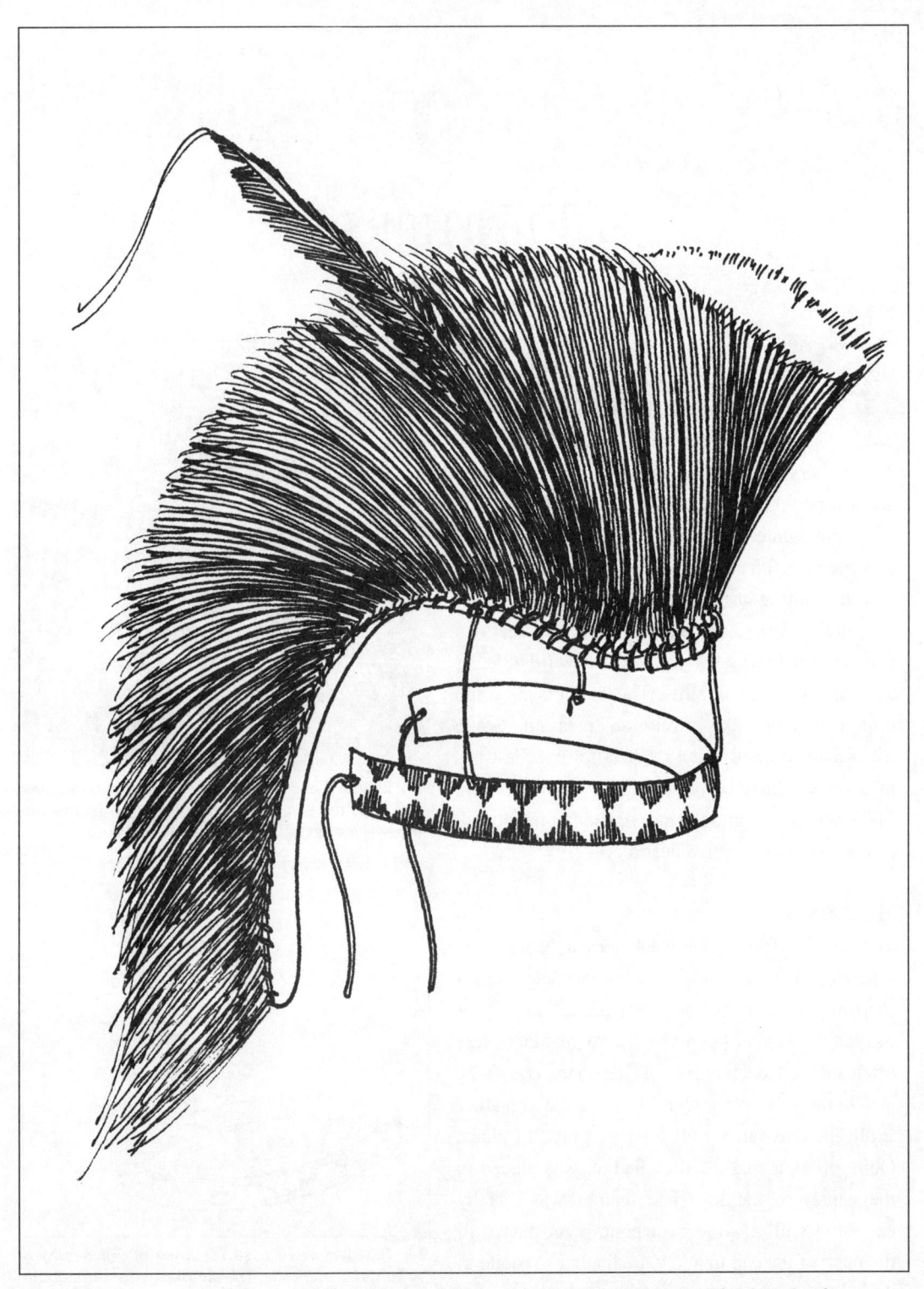

9-3A. Roaches consisted of a rawhide or bone piece used to hold horsehair and feathers in place.

FEATHERS

A quite unusual decorative headpiece of Native Americans was the roach. This consisted of a leather or bone piece shaped to fit the curvature of the head. Holes were punched around the outside and sprigs of horsehair were tied to the holes. The roach was usually attached to a headband to hold it in place (fig. 9-3A). Feathers were also added in the center of the roach.

Traditionally, roaches were made of horsehair, but they can be simulated with binder twine or a similar jute twine. Unwind the twine and straighten it, then cut it into twelve-inch lengths. Place these lengths into bundles about 3/16-inch thick. Fold the bundles in half over a nail, wrap them with thread, then tie the thread ends (fig. 9-3B).

Use a bone, rawhide, or heavy-leather roach to hold the hair pieces. Regardless of which kind of roach is used, stitch the hair pieces or place them in holes in the material so they stand upright. Fasten a large feather or two in the center of the top portion of the roach. Anchor it using a double loop of string, one loop in the roach and one loop tied on the end of the feather. This allows the feather to turn in the breeze. Traditionally, a roach was held on with thongs tied under the chin, fastened to a headband with thongs, or in some cases added to a furlike cap.

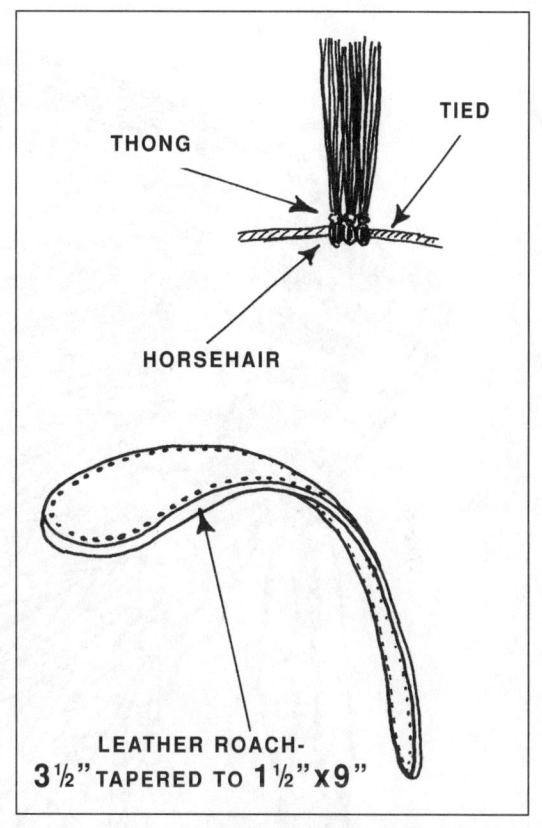

9-3B. Pattern for making a roach.

The most interesting piece of Native American headgear is, of course, the war bonnet. These were worn by the Plains tribes, such as the Sioux and Crow, and were typically made of matching plumes of bald-eagle feathers fastened to a cap (fig. 9-4). Many war bonnets were further adorned with other items, including ermine or rabbit skins and beads. A turkey-feather plume was often fastened in the center of the top rear of the bonnet. Purchased white feathers with the tips dyed black would be a good substitute for eagle feathers and are available at many crafts shops for creating these interesting Native American projects. Domestic turkey feathers can also be dyed and used.

The first step is to create the skullcap of deer hide. Use a piece of muslin or cotton cloth and cut it into four sections to create a pattern that fits the head properly. Pin or baste these pieces together and dry fit the cap to get the right size. Once you have the correct size, take the cap apart, use the muslin as a pattern, and cut and sew a cap of soft buckskin.

The next step is to prepare the feathers. You will need about thirty feathers for a bonnet, about sixty feathers if you plan to make dual tails. If you're not using purchased dyed feathers, dye the tips of white turkey feathers with liquid black shoe polish or fabric dye or leather dye. If the feathers are somewhat

9-4. The war bonnet shown is a Crow design featuring eagle feathers and ermine skins.

FEATHERS

ruffled, hold them over a steaming kettle for a second or two and smooth them with your fingers.

One method of attaching the feathers to the cap is to first glue small loops of leather thong to the feather quills, leaving a small open loop on the end. Wrap a red flannel binding around the quill, inserting a large fluff feather inside the top of the binding and gluing it in place with craft glue. Fluff feathers are made of marabou. The wrap should end on the back of the quill. The ends of the wrap can be tied off with sinew, artificial sinew, or even yarn. Traditionally, these wraps were sometimes beaded. Glue a smaller fluff feather and two strands of horsehair to the tip of the feather (fig. 9-5A). The bottom and top fluffs were traditionally white, but many of the bonnets made today use brightly colored fluff feathers.

Lace the feathers to the cap, starting in the center of the front and working outward (fig. 9-5B). Use the longest, best feathers for the front. Use thong lacing and finish it off with a knot on the inside. Thread a piece of sinew or waxed thread through the quills on the inside and tie it to keep the feathers evenly distributed and held in an upright position.

Make a headband of buckskin and bead it. Then sew it in place to cover the tips of the quills. Side ornaments can consist of strips of rabbit or ermine skin sewed in place. Metal discs or conchas can be added as well.

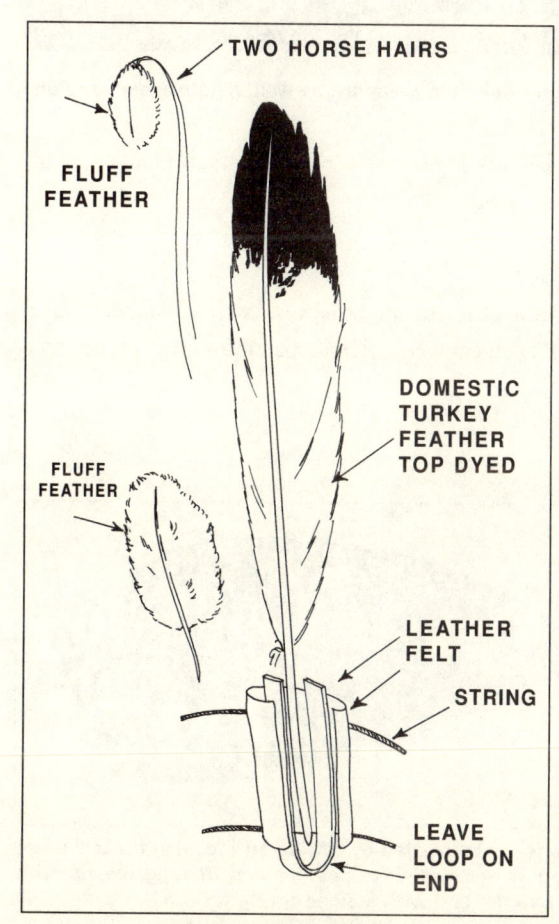

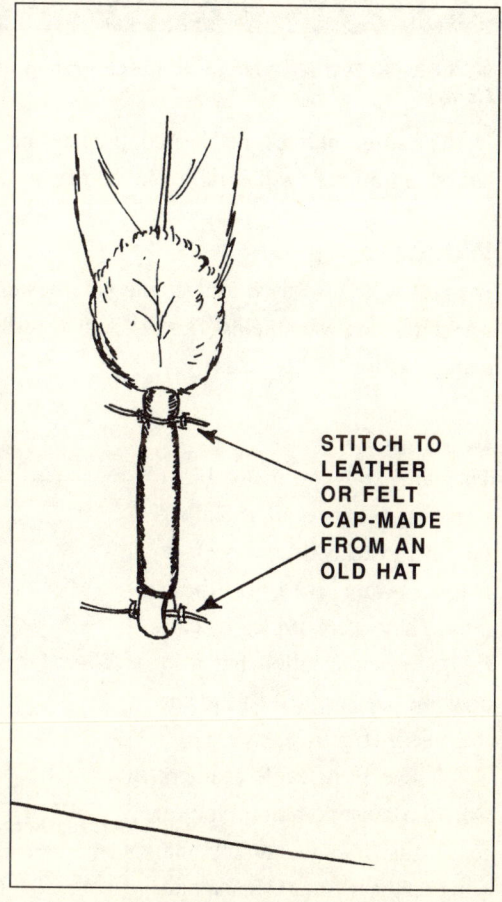

9-5A. War bonnet details.

9-5B. More war bonnet details.

Antler, Bone, Horn & Hide

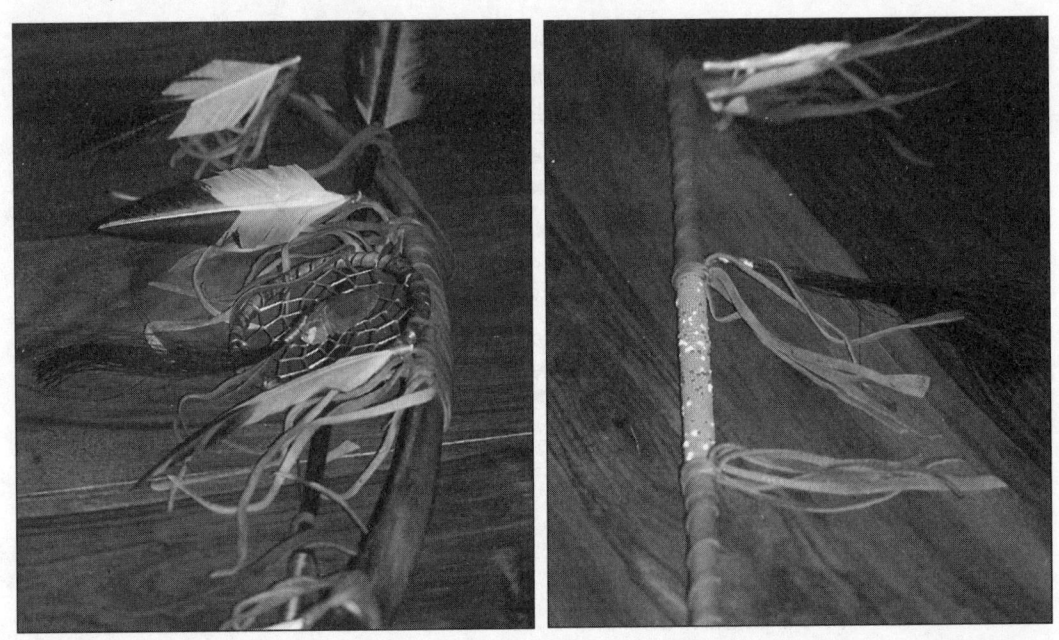

9-6A & 9-6B. Feathers were used for decorating other gear and weapons as well. *(Photos courtesy Peter Fiduccia)*

If trailing plumes are desired, prepare the feathers in the same way and stitch them to a soft buckskin trailer. Sew the trailers to the rear of the bonnet.

War Gear

Feathers were also used to decorate all types of war gear, including lances, coup sticks, war clubs, war shirts, and war shields (figs. 9-6A and 9-6B). Feathers were often prepared for these in the same manner as for the bonnets.

Feather Fans

The wing tips of many birds were often made into feather fans. Almost any decorative bird feathers were used for these fans. They were typically carried as ornamentation but also could be used as face fans to stir the breeze (fig. 9-7).

In the past, eagle feathers were the most common type of feather used. Today, turkey and wing feathers from Canada and

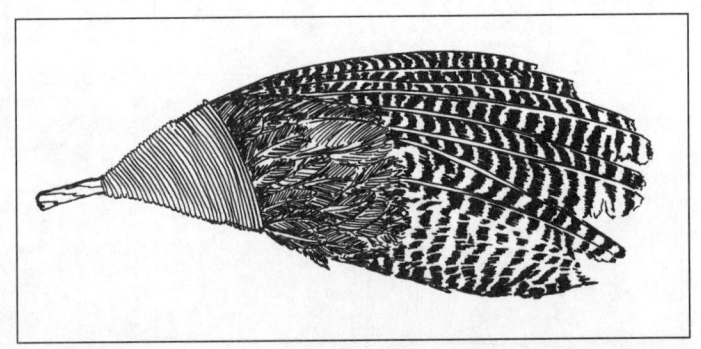

9-7. Feather fans can be created by cutting off the wing tip at the last joint, removing as much meat as possible and treating the tip with borax. Then wrap the end with leather or bright cloth.

snow geese make good fans. These fans can be made by cutting off the bird's wing tip at the last joint, removing as much flesh as possible and rubbing borax into the joint. Wrap the end of the fan with brightly colored lacing that is held in place with craft glue.

WILD TURKEY FANS

The wild turkey is one of America's favorite game birds. Turkey hunters often wish to display the beautiful tail fan of their trophies. They quite often want to display the beard as well, especially if the beard is a long one from an old gobbler (fig. 9-8).

The first step is to remove the beard. Grasp the beard at the base in one hand and, compressing the breast flesh around the beard with the other hand, pull the beard out in one piece. Or the beard can be cut out with a sharp knife and then all the flesh trimmed away. The pulled-out beard has no flesh attached. Dip the beard end in borax and hang it up in a safe place where animals–especially dogs–can't get to it. Allow the beard to cure for about a week, shake out the borax, and dip about one quarter inch of the end in craft glue so these hairs won't separate.

To remove the turkey fan, locate the crease of the "knob" above the vent. Cut the tail fan off at that location. Remove as much flesh as possible, then cover the remaining flesh with borax. Place the tail on a piece of clean cardboard. Fan out the tail, making sure the feathers are evenly spread. Pin the fanned-out feathers in place with pushpins placed just to the side of the upper portion of the quills but not through them. Push the pins in far enough to secure the fan (fig. 9-9).

9-8. Wild turkey fans make great wall decorations and show off your trophy.

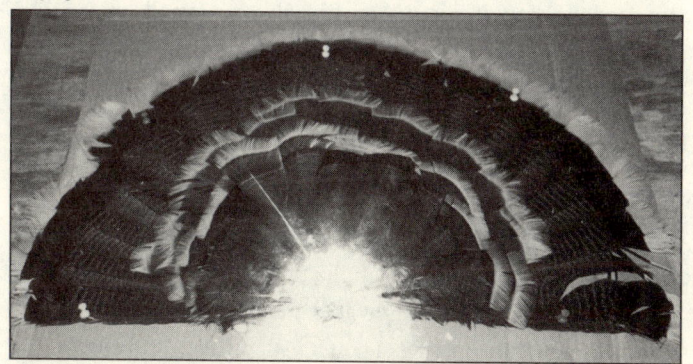

9-9. First cut off the tail at the knob location. Remove as much meat as possible, then treat the entire area with borax. Spread out the fan and pin it in place with push pins to a piece of cardboard.

Place the fan in a protected, safe place. Cats, dogs, and wild animals will definitely get into your trophy if given a chance. In about two weeks, check the fan, wipe or shake off the old borax, and

Antler, Bone, Horn & Hide

apply new. In another week or so, you can display the fan.

Turkey fans can be displayed by simply pinning them to a wall. The best method, however, is to make a display board that can also be used to display the beard and spurs. A number of commercial turkey trophy mounting boards are also available (fig. 9-10).

The board can also be cut from any solid piece of soft- or hardwood (fig. 9-11). Hollow out the back using chisels or a router until there is enough room to fit the tail knob in place. Then bore a hole down through the bottom end for the beard to fit through. Cut a thin piece of board, plywood, or even do-it-yourself aluminum to the shape of the trophy board for the back. Stain and/or varnish the board to produce a nice finish (fig. 9-12).

Place the turkey beard in position, gluing it in place if needed. Place the fan with the tail knob in the back recess and fasten the back board or aluminum piece in place. Fasten a wall hanger in the top center of the back. If you want to add more trophies to the display, cut the turkey's legs off above and below the spurs. Glue the spurs to the front of the trophy board. You can also get small brass plates at trophy shops and have them engraved with the date and location the trophy was taken and its size.

Bird Pelts

Native Americans used full bird pelts for decoration. To preserve bird pelts for use in accessories or even for fly-tying, skin the bird very carefully, then rub the inside of the skin well with borax. Allow it to cure for a week, shake off the borax, and apply fresh borax. Allow the pelt to cure for another week or so, then shake off any excess borax and display as desired (fig. 9-13).

Hatbands

The elegant feathers of many game birds make beautiful hatbands. The feathers can be glued to a leather strip or to a piece of belt-backing material. To make a hatband, measure the circumference of the crown of the hat. Cut the leather or belt-backing material to the length needed, adding about an inch for overlap. The band can be as wide

9-10. A number of commercial trophy mounting kits are available.

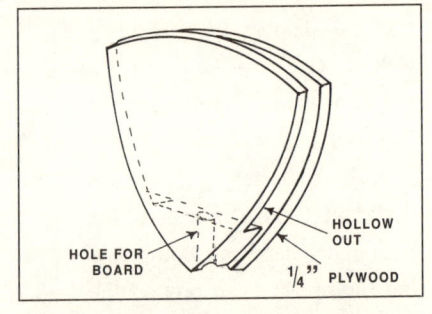

9-11. A hollowed board can also be used to hold the fan to a wooden plaque.

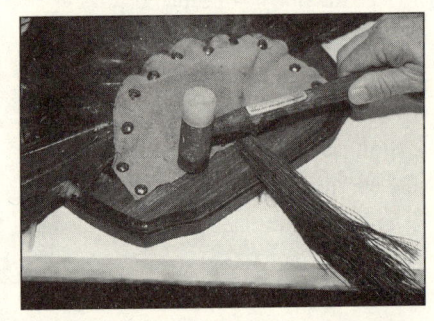

9-12. The fan is attached to a wooden plaque and a piece of leather cut and fastened over the fan end with decorative tacks.

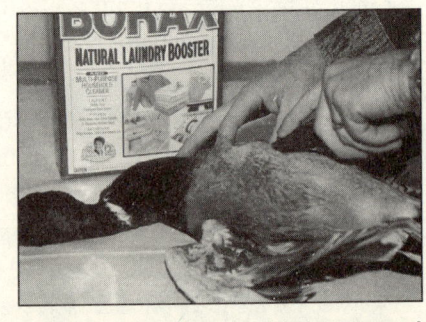

9-13. The pelts of birds can also be preserved with borax and displayed as wall hangings.

or narrow as desired. Arrange the feathers and glue them to the band (with a craft glue such as Tacky Glue) to produce an unusual and beautifully colored hat ornament. Fit the band to the hat and mark the overlap line. Add a hook-and-eye or snap closure to each end of the band to hold it closed. Since feathered bands aren't permanently attached to the hat, several different bands can be made and used on the same hat, to be changed as desired (fig. 9-14).

9-14. Feathers can be glued to belt backing to create beautiful hatbands.

9-15. One fun project is making a quill pen from a turkey feather. Cut the tip as shown.

QUILL PEN

Most of us remember school pictures of the signing of the Declaration of Independence or of Benjamin Franklin with his famous turkey pens. You too can make quill pens quite easily. Using a very sharp knife, cut off the tip of a quill at an angle. Then make about a one-fourth inch slit in the cut end. Dip the pen in ink made from the juice extracted from pokeberries, or any liquid ink, and you're replicating the old-time method of writing (fig. 9-15). ∎

TOOLS AND MATERIALS NEEDED FOR

Jewelry & Miscellaneous Projects

- 1/4-inch dowel
- Alum
- Borax
- Corncob
- Dishwashing detergent
- Epoxy
- Forms for leg or foot decorations
- Glovers needle
- Glue
- Grinder
- Knife
- Mounting board
- Plastic bucket or tub
- Salt
- Shells, turtle and sea
- Slate, small, thin piece
- Taxidermists clay
- Thread, waxed linen
- Wood, thin piece for a striker

10

JEWELRY & MISCELLANEOUS PROJECTS

Like people today, people of the past used a wide variety of items to adorn themselves. These ornaments were, and still are, designed to show wealth, express the person's nature, or simply to look pretty. Antler, bone, leather, feathers, fur, and shells have been used as traditional jewelry for ages (fig. 10-1). Many of the projects and techniques shown here are those of Native Americans. The same methods and materials can also be used today to create beautiful jewelry.

ANTLER, BONE, AND HORN

Native Americans used antler, bone, and horn materials to make many different types of jewelry. Sections of antlers and horns were softened in hot water, then shaped or even bent over a rounded object to create bracelets, earrings, hair ornaments, and other items. Bones and antlers were sanded and shaped into a variety of pendants as well as beads of many different sizes and shapes. These beads were made into necklaces, bracelets, even earrings. Trade beads were eventually added to the jewelry pieces.

TEETH AND CLAWS

A wide variety of teeth and claws were used to create unusual jewelry. One of the most well-known is the bear claw necklace. Real bear claws are hard to come by these days, but artificial claws and porcupine claws are readily available (figs. 10-2, 10-3,

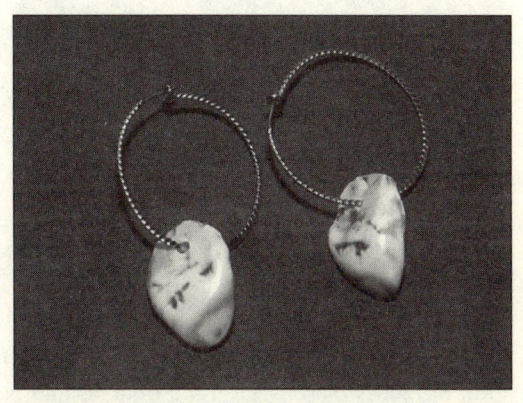

10-1. Bone, antler, feather, leather, horn, teeth, claws, and just about anything else you can imagine have been and can be used to create jewelry, including bracelets, pendants, earrings, necklaces, and hair ornaments. Shown are earrings made from elk teeth.

10-2. Porcupine claws make quite an unusual necklace.

Antler, Bone, Horn & Hide

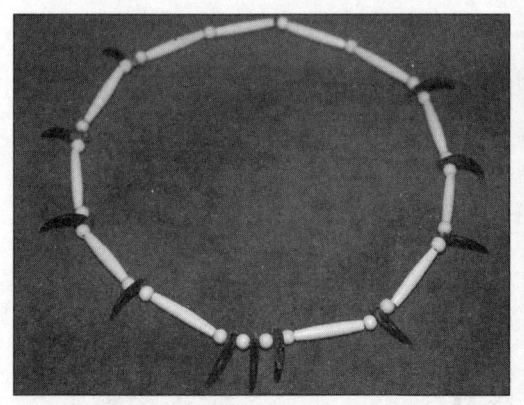

10-3. Turkey spurs can also be used for a necklace and show off your trophies.

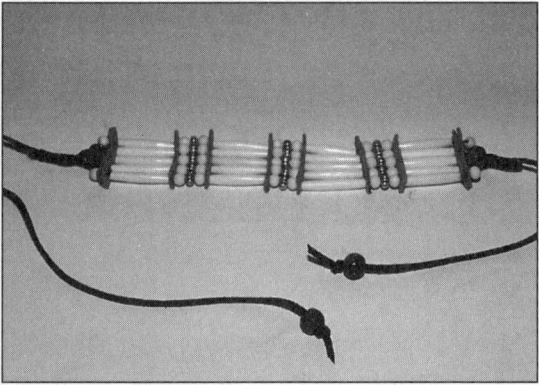

10-4. Combining different claws with beads creates the popular choker necklaces.

and 10-4). Another unusual natural material is elk teeth. These were used as pendants and earrings and still make unusual jewelry, including ring sets.

Shell Jewelry

Some of the most important jewelry materials from earliest times has been shells. Native Americans traded different types of shells from coast to coast. Many of the shell items were actually considered a form of money. For instance, the Iroquois and Northeast Algonquin tribes wampum was made from white and purple beads ground from the quahog or hard-shell clam. The slender cone-shaped tusk or dentalium shells were valued by many tribes. The Plains tribes called them "Iroquois money."

All types of saltwater shells were used as well as freshwater mussels. Even abalone was traded inland. Freshwater mussel and saltwater clamshell beads were some of the most popular, primarily because of their availability (fig. 10-5).

The primitive method of bead making began with removing the rough outer portion of the

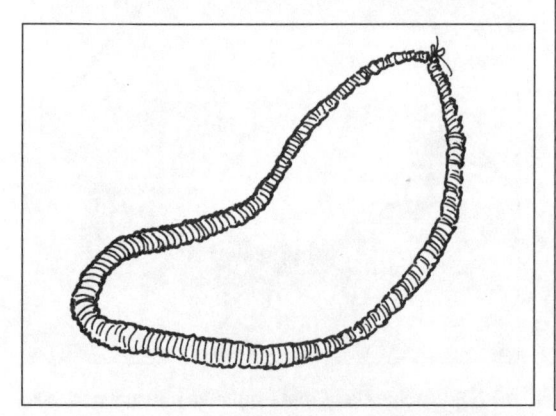

10-5. Shell jewelry was and still is extremely popular.

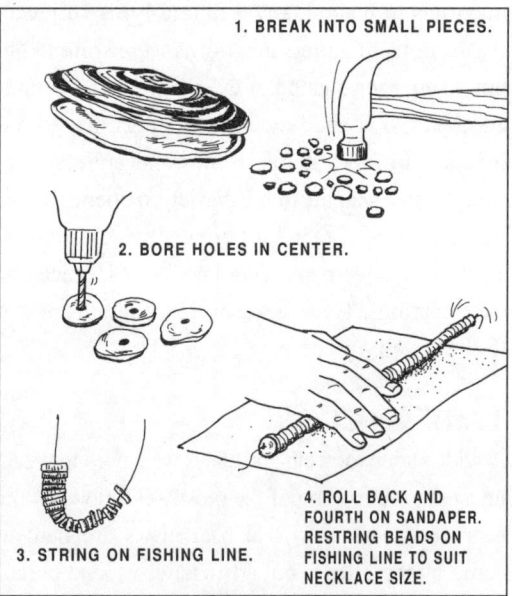

10-6. Details of making shell jewelry.

1. BREAK INTO SMALL PIECES.
2. BORE HOLES IN CENTER.
3. STRING ON FISHING LINE.
4. ROLL BACK AND FOURTH ON SANDAPER. RESTRING BEADS ON FISHING LINE TO SUIT NECKLACE SIZE.

Jewelry & Miscellaneous Projects

shell. Shells were then broken into smaller pieces and these smaller pieces were roughly shaped using pieces of sandstone. A hole was drilled in them. A stone point placed in a wooden shaft and rolled along the leg was the first drill. This was later replaced by the pump drill.

The beads were then strung on sinew and further ground on sandstone. Water was often used to help the abrasive process. These shell beads were strung into necklaces or woven into strips that could be sewn to cloth or leather, applied to baskets, and used for other ornamentation (fig. 10-6).

Many smaller shells were used in their natural shapes. They were strung on necklaces or sewn individually to clothing and other items. Larger shells were carved into pendants, bracelets, and rings. Many were also incised, carved, or inlaid with turquoise or other stones.

OTHER USES FOR SHELLS

Shells were used for other purposes, including dishes and bowls as well as hoes and other implements. Shells were also ground into needles and chisels.

The shells of turtles and terrapins were also utilized. Medium-sized turtle shells were made into dance rattles (fig. 10-7). Larger shells were often painted with symbols and used as an ownership sign (fig. 10-8). To create these the shells were cleaned out, pebbles added, and the shells sewn shut with rawhide. Then, a wooden handle was laced in place with rawhide as well.

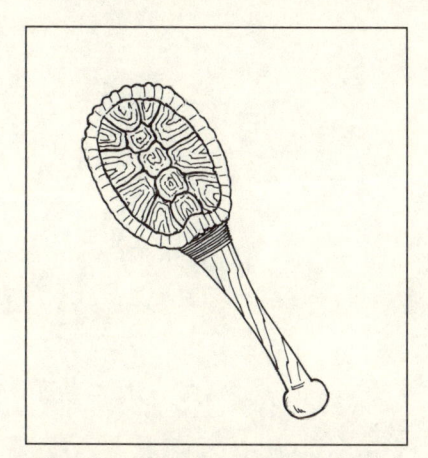

10-7. The shells of turtles and terrapins can also be used for projects such as dance rattles.

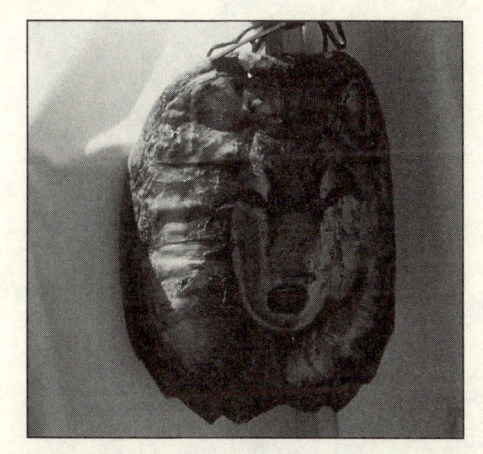

10-8. Large snapping-turtle shells can be painted with designs as household decor or as "totems" for buckskinners.

BOX TURTLE TURKEY CALL

You can use a box turtle shell to make a very good sounding wild turkey call (fig. 10-9). First remove the turtle and clean the shell. Then mix equal parts salt and borax and pour the mixture into the shell. Allow the shell to cure for two to three days, then pour out and replace the preserving materials. In about two weeks, the shell should be well cured. Rinse it in clean water and allow it to dry.

You will need a thin piece of slate, about 3/16 to 1/4 inch thick and of a size that will fit under the top edge of the shell (fig. 10-10). Cut or grind the slate to fit just under the shell and round the ends. Glue the slate in place with epoxy. You will also need a striker. This can be carved from a

Antler, Bone, Horn & Hide

10-9. A box turtle shell call makes a very good wild turkey call.

10-10. The shell is preserved with equal parts borax and salt. A thin piece of slate is cut, shaped and sanded smooth, then glued in place in the shell.

10-11. A wooden striker is scraped across the slate to produce the various turkey calls.

Jewelry & Miscellaneous Projects

single piece of dried wood. The bottom portion should be about 3/16 inch in diameter. Or, you can insert a piece of 1/4-inch dowel into a corncob to use as a striker. In either case, the end of the striker should be well rounded (fig. 10-11). To use, pull the striker end across the slate to make the yelps, putts, and purrs of the wild turkey. Sand the slate to achieve the correct tone. A thick slate produces a deeper but duller sound. A thinner slate produces a higher-pitched and louder sound.

Leg and Foot Ornaments Made from Game

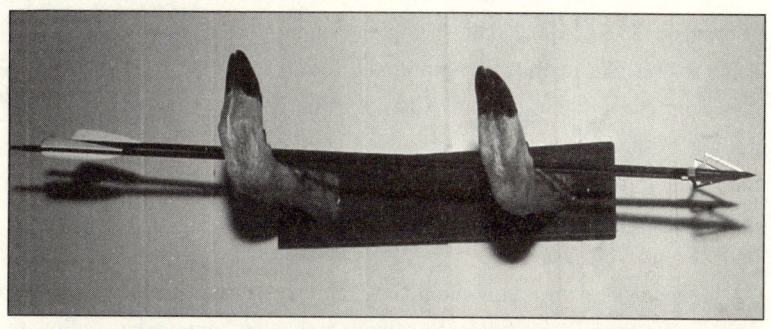

The feet and legs of wild game can be used to create a variety of unusual objects. The feet are normally discarded during butchering but, with a little work, can be used for novel decorative items. The feet of larger animals, such as buffalo, alligator, and bear can be skinned, fleshed, and tanned with an alum and salt tanning mixture or one of the commercial tanning formulas such as Rittel's EZ-100. Taxidermy supply houses have ashtray inserts and other decorative items that can be used with the feet.

The legs of deer are more commonly used. They can be skinned, tanned, and mounted on wooden or plastic forms with a crease at the knee joint. These L-shaped legs can then be mounted to boards to create gun, bow, hat, or clothing racks (fig. 10-12).

The first step is to skin the legs. Cut the skin down the back of the leg to the back of the hoof (fig. 10-13). Peel the hide off the leg until you reach the dewclaws. Then cut through the dewclaw bones, as close to the dewclaw as possible. Continue peeling the skin down to the hooves. Then stick the tip of a sharp pointed knife down into the hooves and cut around them. This takes quite a bit of effort and time. Be patient. If you slip and cut through the skin, you have pretty well ruined it for the project. Once you have severed all the tendons, you can "break" the hoofs off the feet.

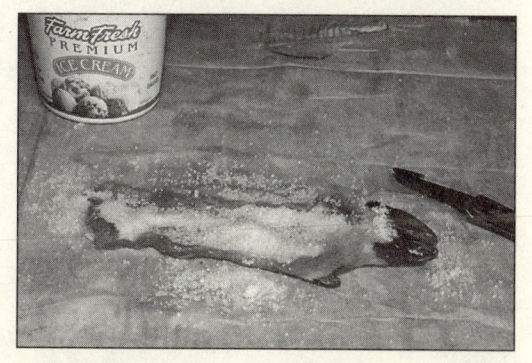

10-12. Unusual items can be made from the legs and feet of game, including gun and clothing racks.

10-13. First skin the legs and tan them.

10-14. Work the salt in the flesh and around the dewclaws and hoofs.

Antler, Bone, Horn & Hide

Once the legs are skinned, spread out the skin and remove all the flesh from it. Then spread salt over the entire surface of the flesh side and work the salt in and around the dewclaws and the hoofs (fig. 10-14). Set the skin aside in a protected, dry place and allow the salt to cure and dry it. This will usually take about a week.

Then place the skins in a pickle bath for about one week. To make the bath, bring one gallon of water to boil. Stir in one quarter pound of borax and one quarter pound of alum. Then stir in 2-1/4 pounds of salt. Stir until all is dissolved, then allow the solution to cool. Pour the cooled solution into a plastic bucket or tub and immerse the skins. Stir the bath several times each day.

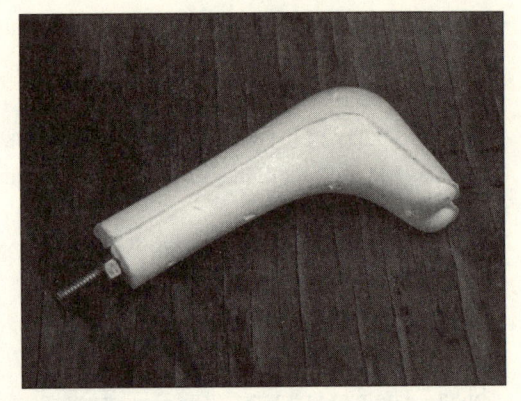

10-15. Commercial forms are available or you can carve forms from soft wood.

Take the skins from the pickle bath and wash them thoroughly in water with a few drops of dishwashing detergent added. Rinse until all the soap is removed and allow the skins to drain. You can cut your own wooden forms or purchase foam plastic forms (fig. 10-15). In either case, a bolt must be in the back of the form to bolt the finished foot to a plaque. Stuff taxidermists clay into the feet to help hold them in place. Place the form inside the skin, adjusting the fit by either sanding off the form or adding more clay to make a full and natural-appearing foot. Sew the skin up starting at the foot, using a glover's needle and waxed linen thread. Leave the top flap open. This allows the skins to dry and cure. The skin will also shrink somewhat.

Let the legs dry for approximately another week, then sand and polish the hooves to a nice glistening finish, using a fine-grit sandpaper and polishing rouge. Cut off the excess skin at the back of the leg. Bore bolt holes in the mounting board and countersink holes in the back for the bolts and nuts. Then mount the legs to the board.

Deer legs can also be mounted on special forms for electrical lamps as well. All the materials needed for these projects are available from taxidermy supply houses.

Snake and Alligator Skins

Both snake and alligator skins can be made into beautiful items. An unusual wall decoration in the Deep South is an alligator wall ornament (fig. 10-16). The hide is tanned and mounted on a board, which is then fastened to the wall. Big gators make very impressive wall decorations. Rittel's Tanning Supplies has instructions and all the materials needed for tanning alligator skins. Some portions of the tanned skins can be used for many other leather projects such as wallets, belts, and hatbands.

10-16. Big alligator hides make great wall decor.

Jewelry & Miscellaneous Projects

10-17. Snakeskins can be tanned and used in a wide variety of items. The author's hat and copperhead snake band is over twenty years old and has seen better days.

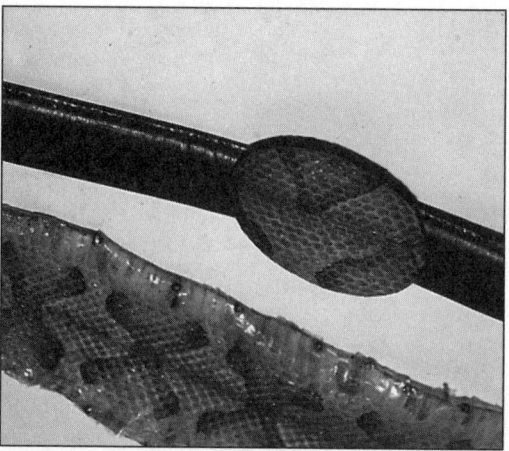

10-18. Newer, more modern snake skin tanning methods can be used today to produce more pliable and longer-lasting skins. Here a skin has been glued to a belt buckle.

The skins of many snakes can also be used for any number of projects. The first step is to skin the snake and tan the skin. Rittel's Snakeskin Tanning Kit contains all the ingredients for descaling and tanning snake skins into durable, fully tanned leather that's soft, plump, and sewable. The markings remain intact and no bleaching is required. This is a great way to make leather suitable for crafts or for garments (fig. 10-17).

Tanned skins make great belt buckles as well as belts and hatbands (fig. 10-18). A belt buckle can be made using a metal "Western style" buckle blank, the kind that is often used for covering with leather. These buckles are available at many leather and craft shops. Cut the skin to fit over the buckle front, allowing one-quarter inch extra all around. Use Duncan's Crafter's Tacky Glue to glue the skin to the buckle. Fold the skin carefully around the back of the buckle and hold the skin in place with a clothespin until the glue dries.

A belt or hatband can be made by glueing the skin around a cloth belt blank. Cloth belt backing is available at craft shops and sewing notions departments by the yard in a variety of widths and in black or white. Again, use Tacky Glue to attach the skin. Hold the skin in place with clothespins until the glue dries (fig. 10-19). For a hatband, cut a belt blank to fit, leaving an overlap at the back for fastening. Glue the reptile skin to the belt backing and stitch or attach small pieces of self-sticking hook-and-loop tape to hold the hatband together at the back.

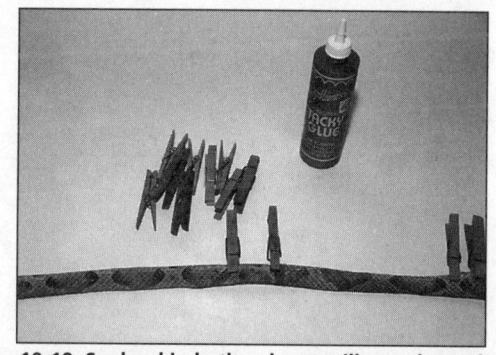

10-19. Snake skin hatbands are still popular and easy to make. Simply glue the skin to a belt backing or a piece of soft leather and stitch the ends together to fit around the hat.

You can also glue shorter lengths of snakeskin to a leather belt blank. Leave the ends of the belt free of the skin, and center the skin at the back of the belt. This not only uses shorter pieces of the reptile skin, but it also makes a longer-lasting belt since the delicate skin isn't rubbed on belt loops. ■

Epilogue

Creating projects of antler, bone, leather, and feathers is fun as well as educational. It teaches us respect for our ancestors and their skill at creating practical and beautiful objects from the simplest materials at hand. Hunters will enjoy using the various materials garnered from their hunts to use in projects. I hope you've found projects in this book to create and enjoy. I had a lot of fun creating the projects shown. Typically, after a book is finished, I continue to think of new ideas. I hope the projects in this book will inspire you to create more as well.

M.B.

DIRECTORY OF RESOURCES

Bass Pro Shops
1935 South Campbell
Springfield, MO 65898
(800)BASS PRO – Toll Free
www.basspro.com

Cabela's
One Cabela Drive
Sidney, NE 69160
(800)237-4444 – Toll Free
www.cabelas.com

Dixie Gun Works
P.O. Box 130
Union City, TN 38281
Toll Free (800)238-6785
(731)885-0700 – T
(731)885-0440 – F
www.dixiegunworks.com

Craftsman – Sears
3333 Beverly Road
Hoffman Estates, IL 60179
(800)290-1245 – Toll Free
(800)390-8792 – F
www.sears.com/craftsman

Crazy Crow Trading Post
P.O. Box 847
1801 Airport Road
Pottsboro, TX 75076
(800)786-6210 – Toll Free
(903)786-2287 – T
(903)786-9059 – F
www.crazycrow.com

Dremel
4915 21st Street
Racine, WI 53406
(800)437-3635 – Toll Free
(262)554-1390 – T
www.dremel.com

Hobby Lobby
5614 Franklin Pike Circle
Brentwood, TN 37027
(615)373-1444 – T
(615)377-6948 – F
www.hobbylobby.com

Lohman – Outland Sports
P.O. Box 220
4500 Doniphan Drive
Neosho, MO 64850
(800)922-9034 – Toll Free
(417)451-4438 – T
(417)451-2576 – F
www.outlandsports.com

McKenzie Taxidermy Supply Company
P.O. Box 480
Granite Quarry, NC 28072
(800)279-7985 – Toll Free
(709)279-7985 – T
www.mckenziesp.com
www.taxidermyonline.com

Michaels
8000 Bent Branch Drive
Irving, TX 75063
(800)642-4235 – Toll Free
www.michaels.com

Rittel's Tanning Supplies
51 Summer Street
Tauton, MA 02780
(508)822-3821 – T
(508)828-3921 – F
www.rittelsupplies.net

Tandy Leather
3847 East Loop 820 South
Ft. Worth, TX 76119
(888)890-1611 – Toll Free
(817)451-5254 – F
www.tandyleather.com

VanDyke's Taxidermy
P.O. Box 278
39771 S.D. Hwy. 34
Woonsocket, SD 57385
(800)843-3320 – Toll Free
(605)796-4425 – T
(605)796-4085 – F
www.vandykestaxidermy.com

Woodcraft Supply
P.O. Box 1686
Parkersburg, WV 26102-1686
(800)225-1153 – Toll Free
(304)422-5412 – T
(304)422-5417 – F

Glossary of Terms

Alum tanned - A method by which a skin or hide is made into leather by using alum, a type of astringent.

Arkansas sharpening stone - A natural stone used as a hone.

Backgrounding tool - A stamping tool for creating background patterns in leather carving.

Baste or tack - To sew an item with loose stiches before it is sewn together tightly in its final form.

Beadwork - Decorative beads sewn on to leather.

Beetles - Special insects that eat away flesh from animal skulls, leaving clean, white skulls.

Billets - Short, thick wooden or bone clubs.

Binder twine - Strong cord that consists of two or more strands twisted into one.

Black powder - Gunpowder used in muzzleloading firearms.

Black powder picks - Thin, stiff pieces of metal or bone used to unclog black powder from its carrying case.

Bone hairpipe - Long, thin bones of game birds and animals. These were later manufactured in the East and used as trade items.

Bone marrow - The fatty tissue that fills the inner portions of bones. The marrow should be removed from any bones to be used as decorative pieces.

Bow loom - An early bead loom that used a bow. It was eventually replaced by a box loom.

Box frame - A loom used to weave beadwork onto a cloth backing that is then sewn onto a finished piece such as a belt or headband.

Brain tanned - A skin tanned using animal brains.

Breastplates - Armor originally designed by Plains Indian warriors and worn to cover the chest. Today, breastplates provide ornamentation for powwows and ceremonies.

Breechcloths or breechclouts - Leather clothing worn around the loin.

Breech- The breech area of a long rifle at the end of the barrel where, except for a muzzleloading rifle, the ammunition is loaded.

Buckskin - The tanned hide of a deer.

Buckskinners - Early trappers. In modern times, people who pursue the arts and lifestyle of the early trappers and mountain men.

Butt end - The end of the antler where it is thickest, where the antler attaches to the skull.

Cape - The hide of an animal such as a deer, elk, or antelope.

Chaps - Leather pants without a rear piece that are worn over regular pants to protect the legs.

Checking - Small cracks.

Choker - A necklace that fits tightly around the neck.

Cold frame - An unheated, boxlike, wooden frame that protects young plants.

Antler, Bone, Horn & Hide

Conchas - Metal disks, often highly decorated, that are attached to clothing for decoration. Conchas are often tied to clothing with leather thongs.

Coup stick - A ceremonial stick used to "touch" an enemy in battle, thereby "counting coup."

Cowhide - Leather made from the hide of a cow.

Crow beads - Beads used by Native Americans living in the upper basins of the Yellowstone and Bighorn Rivers.

Darts - Short folds made with stitches to help shape a piece of clothing.

Dentalium shells or tusks - Shells from marine mollusks, commonly found where oceans once existed in the middle of the United States.

Dewclaws - The "toes" found behind the hoof of a deer or elk.

Dry fit - To assemble all parts of something to test the fit prior to actually stitching or gluing them.

Embossing - A technique for carving or printing a design that is raised above the surface.

Ermine - The soft fur of a weasel commonly found in the northern United States.

European mount - A bleached mounted skull without the lower jaw and with the antlers attached to the skull.

Fan - The tail of a bird (such as a turkey) when spread out to resemble the shape of a fan.

Fleshed - A hidet hat has had the soft muscle tissue scraped off or removed from it.

Flint knapper - A piece of antler used to make stone or flint arrowheads.

Flint scraper - A piece of flint that has been shaped or sharpened to have a sharp edge.

Frog gigs - A spear that is used to spear frogs.

Furrier - One who makes garments from furs.

Glovers stitch - See running stitch.

Graining - The technique of removing the hair from a hide using ancient bone tools.

Hackamore bridle - A leather halter with a headstall that is often used to break horses.

Hairdressers whitener - A chemical used by beauty shops to bleach hair.

Half hitch - A type of knot made by passing one end of a rope around itself and then through the loop just made.

Hammer stone - A large, round rock used as a hammer.

Hide scraper - A tool that is made to scrape the soft tissue off the underside of a hide.

Homespun - Clothing that was made from yarn spun at home.

Horse tack - Equipment used for riding horses such as bridles, saddles, reins.

Humerus - The bone of the arm between the shoulder and the elbow.

Inner lining - A layer on the inside of a piece of clothing that either adds additional insulation or protects the skin from a more abrasive side of the outer material.

Leggings - Protective covering worn below the knee and made from leather.

Long rifle - Any long-barreled muzzleloader.

Medicine bag - A small leather pouch or bag carried by Native Americans.

Mountain men - Early pioneers who lived in the wilderness–an ideal example of self-sufficiency.

Glossary

Muzzleloader - Any firearm that is loaded at the muzzle end of the barrel.

Palmations - An antler that resembles a hand with its fingers spread open.

Parfleche - A case made from rawhide that has had the hair removed.

Patch knife - A knife used to trim the cloth patches used with blackpowder guns.

Pinked - Cloth that has a saw-toothed edge, most often made by a pair of pinking shears.

Pinking shears - Scissors made with blades that cut a saw-toothed edge.

Plait - An alternate term for braid or interweaving.

Putt - A term used to describe one of the sounds that a turkey makes.

Quahog - A large clam from the Eastern United States.

Quill - A bird's large, stiff tail feather.

Radius - The thicker bone in the wing of a turkey.

Rawhide - Hide from an animal (i.e., deer, elk, cow) that has not been tanned.

Rendezvous - A gathering of people interested in the way of life of the early pioneers. Some types of rendezvous include Native American rendezvous, pioneer rendezvous, and mountain men rendezvous.

Riata - An alternate term for a lariat: a rope used for tethering grazing horses.

Roach spreader - An accessory used by Native Americans to hold a person's or a horses hair in a roach (a deocrative headpiece) so that it arches over into a roll.

Robe - A long, loose flowing piece of clothing.

Running stitch - A sewing technique. If two pieces of material are sewn with a running stitch wrong side out (or inside out), the stitching is fairly well hidden on the right side.

Scabbard - A sheath used to hold the blade of a sword; more commonly, a case that holds a gun, especially on a horse.

Scaled-tang knives - A knife with a tang that is the full width of the blade, as opposed to a narrow or rounded tang.

Scalp shirt - See war shirt.

Scapula - The shoulder blade; the flat triangular-shape bone in the back of the shoulder.

Scrimshaw - Detailed drawing or carving on bone or ivory.

Seam allowances - The amount of material added around the edges of a pattern to allow for sewing.

Sewing awl - A small, pointed tool usually used to make holes in leather.

Shaft straighteners - A bone section with a hole in it through which the shaft of arrows were pulled to straighten them.

Sheath - A case for the blade of a knife.

Shed antlers - Antlers that have fallen off an animal such as a deer, elk, caribou, or moose.

Sinew - A tendon.

Smoked - To treat or cure a hide with smoke.

Split - Leather that has been split to provide two or even three pieces of thinner leather. Suede is a common type of split leather.

Spur - The sharp, pointed projection on the back of a turkey's leg.

Antler, Bone, Horn & Hide

Squared drawings - Drawings or outlines of patterns drawn on a paper lined with one-inch squares.

Stag - A mature male European deer.

Stamping - Imprinting a design on a piece of material.

Studs - Small, round metal nailheads used to decorate leather.

Swivel knife - A knife with a curved top to fit your index finger and a swiveling bottom portion.

Tang - The metal end of a knife that fits into the handle.

Tanned - A hide has been made into leather.

Tongue - The flap under the laces or ties of a shoe that resembles a tongue in shape.

Tooling - A technique for making designs on leather with special tools.

Top grain - The grain or hair side of leather.

Totem - An object that symbolizes one's ancestors.

Trade beads - Beads used by Native Americans for buying and selling commodities.

Trade cloth - Cloth used by traders and explorers to trade with Native Americans for furs.

Trailing piece - A piece of leather a foot or so long that hung from the back of leggings or pants and helped wipe out tracks.

Turkey call - A sound made to imitate the cries of a wild turkey.

Turning - A piece of wood that is shaped on a lathe.

Tusk - See dentalium shells.

Ulna - The thinner bone in the wing of a bird, such as a turkey.

Upper - Part of a shoe above the sole, including the vamp.

Vamp - The part of a shoe that covers the instep.

Velvet - The protective covering of antlers during their growth stage.

Vent - The excratory opening in birds such as turkeys.

Wampum - Small beads made of shells aqnd used by Native Americans either for money or for decoration.

War shirt - A garment usually worn only by warriors. It resembled a sleeveless poncho, with the sides either left open or tied with lacings.

Warp thread - The main threads in a piece of weaving; weft threads are woven through the warp beads.

Welt - A piece of leather that is stitched to give reinforcement between the sole and the upper of a shoe; a piece of leather that is stitched between any seams to reinforce the seam.

Whip stitch - A stitch made by whipping lacing or thread over the edge of a seam. A whip stitch is finished off by bringing the lacing or thread back around and through the last stitch on top, encircling it several times and making a knot. The knot is hidden between the material layers.

White stage - Leather that has been tanned but not smoked or dyed.

Yelpers - A turkey call that imitates the "yelp" of a turkey.

Yelps - Sounds made by turkeys that are sharp and short in duration.